Chicken Soup for the Soul®

Tough Times, Tough People

Chicken Soup for the Soul: Tough Times, Tough People
101 Stories about Overcoming the Economic Crisis and Other Challenges
by Jack Canfield, Mark Victor Hansen, Amy Newmark

Published by Chicken Soup for the Soul Publishing, LLC www.chickensoup.com

The publisher gratefully acknowledges the many publishers and individuals who granted Chicken Soup for the Soul permission to reprint the cited material.

Front cover photo courtesy of iStockPhoto.com/peepo. Back cover photo courtesy of iStockPhoto.com/AnaLee. Interior photo courtesy of iStockPhoto.com/aldomurillo.

Cover and Interior Design & Layout by Brian Taylor, Pneuma Books, LLC
For more info on Pneuma Books, visit www.pneumabooks.com

Distributed to the booktrade by Simon & Schuster. SAN: 200-2442

Publisher's Cataloging-in-Publication Data
(Prepared by The Donohue Group)

Chicken soup for the soul : tough times, tough people : 101 stories about overcoming the economic crisis and other challenges / [compiled by] Jack Canfield, Mark Victor Hansen [and] Amy Newmark.

  p. ; cm.

  ISBN: 978-1-935096-35-1

1. Conduct of life--Literary collections. 2. Conduct of life--Anecdotes. 3. Financial crises--United States--Literary collections. 4. Financial crises--United States--Anecdotes. 5. Encouragement--Anecdotes. 6. Faith--Literary collections. I. Canfield, Jack, 1944- II. Hansen, Mark Victor. III. Newmark, Amy. IV. Title: Tough times, tough people

PN6071.C66 C542 2009

810.8/02/06   2009925883

PRINTED IN THE UNITED STATES OF AMERICA
on acid∞free paper

16 15 14 13 12 11 10 09   01 02 03 04 05 06 07 08

Chicken Soup for the Soul®

Tough Times, Tough People

101 Stories about Overcoming
the Economic Crisis and
Other Challenges

Jack Canfield
Mark Victor Hansen
Amy Newmark

Chicken Soup for the Soul Publishing, LLC
Cos Cob, CT

www.chickensoup.com

Contents

❸
~Silver Linings~

❹
~The Power of Positive Thinking~

❺
~Accepting the New Me~

❻

~Fired!~

❼

~With a Little Help from My Friends~

8
~Tough People~

9
~For Richer or Poorer~

10

~Grief and Healing~

11

~Ten Bonus Stories of Faith~

Chicken Soup for the Soul

Introduction

We received an astounding quantity and quality of submissions for this book on tough times and the tough people living through them—thousands of heartwarming, inspiring stories and poems filled with hope, faith, comfort, and humanity. This topic really struck a chord with our contributors and this book is a beautiful expression of their journeys through their personal tough times.

Half the stories in this book are about tough times related to the economy, and the other half cover a wide gamut of challenges, from illness and disability, to family issues and loss, to natural disasters and crime. You will find a common theme—people working together to help each other overcome the challenges described in their stories. Everyone will find some lessons, support, tears, and smiles in these pages.

Many of our writers stressed how happy they are now, despite lower incomes, smaller homes, and simpler lives. Many wrote about the new lives they have come to accept and enjoy after chronic illness, accidents, losing loved ones, or other non-economic challenges. Some were victims of a crime, some watched their houses burn down, and some are living with incurable illnesses or disabilities. Many wrote about finding inner strength, support from family and friends, marriages strengthening in the face of adversity, and rediscovering the joys of their families. They wrote about the silver linings they found in their troubles and the many blessings in their lives. In fact, we had so many fabulous submissions on this theme that we created a companion volume, *Chicken Soup for the Soul: Count Your Blessings*, which will be published in time for Christmas 2009.

We hope you enjoy reading these stories as much as we enjoyed choosing and editing them for you, and we are sure they will provide you with a little extra help and inspiration during these tough times. We've included a bonus chapter with ten extra stories about tough times and faith—a little extra value for you—to say thanks for being part of the Chicken Soup for the Soul community.

~Amy Newmark
Publisher, Chicken Soup for the Soul

Chapter 1

Tough Times, Tough People

Simple Pleasures

Life is really simple, but we insist on making it complicated.

~Confucius

In Praise of the Staycation

He is the happiest, be he king or peasant, who finds peace in his home.
~Johann Wolfgang von Goethe

The airline information was already spread out on the dining room table. The resort brochures were nuzzling it. All was in readiness... almost.

The only missing piece: our consciences.

My husband and I had been looking forward to travel, especially after long years of paying college and graduate school tuitions for our daughters. We'd vowed that in these, our semi-retirement years, we'd step up to the tarmac and fly—literally and figuratively, too. It was, we told ourselves, our turn.

But sitting at that dining room table on an early summer night last year, we also knew that this trip, an indulgence we'd assumed we deserved, was feeling uncomfortable. While our spirits would have embraced a trip to the American West, a region we'd longed to explore, we were uneasy.

Times were bad. And getting worse.

Hard luck was knocking on too many doors, and we heard its echoes.

And like so many others, we were starting to hear other echoes, these more personal: they were the voices of our parents, the stalwarts who had lived through the Great Depression and never forgot it. As the generation just behind them, we learned a bit about saving, not spending, and repairing not replacing.

Sure, we chafed at the messages. Who wants to hear that "goody-goody" stuff about the virtues of going without? Who wants to celebrate the old car, the old clothes, the simple meals, the birthday gifts more practical than fanciful? Not the young.

But suddenly, the experiences and the advice of our late parents were ringing in our ears. And it was suddenly sounding prudent and wise.

So my husband and I took a major step backward, filed the brochures in a folder marked "Future Travel," and rethought our plan. And that's when we took a leap of faith to a far different destination: our home.

We'd do a Staycation.

It was a term — and concept — that had tiptoed into our lives as the economy was beginning its tumble. And while the late-night comedians were already lampooning it, we figured we had little to lose.

Which is how it came to pass that last summer we did not venture more than fifty miles from home, nor did we once spend an overnight away from our own bedroom.

I would love to say that it was the best vacation of our lives, but that would be fudging. Still, I can honestly say that we came to know our town, our region, and yes, ourselves, better in those two weeks than in any other vacation of our lives.

It certainly took some symbolic shifting of gears to set aside any work-related things, from e-mails to paperwork to phone calls, and to establish the clear bottom-line rule that we were simply not available.

Triumph Number 1. On the first several mornings of our staycation, I actually found myself almost sneaking into my home office just to peek at my computer screen for e-mails. But I resisted.

Triumph Number 2. We had determined in advance that we

would try to do something each day—even if it was a trip to the town library to browse in the New Books section.

And even on days when the temperature was climbing, and our air conditioned den beckoned, we still followed our self-imposed mandate to wander, at least briefly.

We discovered the New Jersey Pinelands in our own backyard, a pristine area of lush flora and fauna and deep, dense silences.

We took a day trip to the New Jersey shore as we had in our early married days, carrying our lunch in a shoebox, and finding a beach where the sand was soft between our toes. We splashed in the ocean and drove home in damp bathing suits, singing nonsense songs all the way.

One morning, we had breakfast at the little coffee shop less than a mile from our home that we'd always vowed we'd try. Because it was a day with a breeze and comfortable temperatures, we walked both ways, feeling virtuous even after pancakes with extra syrup.

It was liberating to have none of the tension that distant travel sometimes brings. It was wonderful to rediscover neighbors we seldom had time to linger with as we rushed from car to front door. Now there were splendid, lingering conversations.

In the interest of full disclosure, I must note that by the second week, we were a bit restless. We'd been to several museums, an art gallery, and, on one memorable day that was a belated birthday gift to me, an antiquing expedition.

That was when we went on a movie binge, seeing three films on three successive nights.

In some ways, those fourteen days of our staycation flew by. Sometimes, we did feel a bit weird about lolling around in our own digs. But never enough to regret our decision.

We never did get to a couple of the projects we'd outlined because frankly, they felt too much like work. This was, after all, a vacation.

And when it was all over, we both felt refreshed, renewed, and delighted that while we had barely spent any significant money, we didn't feel the least bit deprived.

Most importantly, we learned that in a long marriage, there are still new discoveries to be made. Who knew that my husband would fall in love with the Pinelands, and that we'd return there several times since our staycation? Who knew that we could go for days without squabbling about the daily irritations that crop up on the domestic landscape when it's "business as usual?"

This I know: somewhere up in heaven, our parents are smiling down on us.

I believe they're rejoicing that at last—at long last—those messages they delivered so earnestly about prudence over indulgence really did take!

~Sally Friedman

Board Game Revival

Games lubricate the body and the mind.
~Benjamin Franklin

'm pretty sure I haven't played *Clue* since I was nine years old. I don't think I ever had as much fun playing it as I did last night. There's a group of us that used to go out to dinner on the weekends, but since most of us are out of work, we stay in and have game night on the weekends. When my neighbor showed up with *Clue* under her arm, I thought it was for the kids. She informed me that *Clue* was her game of choice for the night.

I was a little skeptical that it would keep us entertained, but I was so wrong. We had a great time as we all reverted to our nine-year-old selves. Adam was holding back information and Erica was throwing a fit about it. I was sneaking peeks at others' game cards and my husband was trash-talking all of us. I wasn't aware that you could trash-talk during a game of *Clue*, but he was a master!

We laughed our way through four games, a bag of chips and a bowl of dip before the kids got ornery. Then I remembered an old *Clue* movie we had in the basement and while I popped the popcorn, Erica got the kids settled in the living room, Craig searched for the movie, and Adam hooked up a VCR. We laughed right out loud through the movie. It was funny without being over the top like so many movies are today.

After we'd said good night to everyone, Craig commented on how much fun we had just doing "dumb stuff." I thought about the times we were so grown up and went out to dinner at nice restaurants. Who wants to be a grown up? I want to be a kid again, where my biggest worry is what game to play when my friends come over.

Next week it's our turn to bring the game. I'm sure we have a *Sorry* game somewhere in the house, and they'd all better watch out because I was *Sorry* champion in the fourth grade!

~Christina Dymock

Buried Treasure

If you want to understand today, you have to search yesterday.
~Pearl Buck

'm like a Labrador retriever when it comes to travel, head hanging out the window, tongue lolling with anticipation. When my teenage students ask for overnight trips, I'm usually as psyched as they are. This year, however, some of my students' parents had seen their jobs downsized, and a tighter budget put the brakes on long trips. A local day trip, or "staycation," seemed more realistic, so the kids resigned themselves. "Better than nothing, but nothing new," they said.

On most trips, we're crackling with awareness, searching every tree and roadside building for clues foreshadowing what our destination will be like. This sense of wonder was tough to recreate in our hometown, which my students had already covered by bus and metro, gravitating between malls and movie theatres. Since I'm a history teacher, I considered travel to a different time rather than a different place. Disbelief dissolves in the haze of Old Montreal's gas lamps and in its echoing cobblestone streets.

A vehicle doesn't allow for intimate connection with places, so I sent the students on a walking tour. They had to discover the remnants of at least three cultures that predated 1900. Our point of departure was a triangular slice of land where Montreal's first fort was built in 1642. The kids were shown 17th century manuscripts that designated a plot of land "400 paces" from the fort as the proposed location for the first French Catholic chapel. Each step was now charged with anticipation. The kids "dialogued" with the author of the manuscript, heads swiveling in search of a domed belfry, anxious to see if these directions still "worked."

With free, teacher-made guidebooks in hand, the kids compared today's streets to drawings and photos of the same places as they looked during the last four centuries. The old quarter, they observed, was like "an outdoor museum with no admission fee." They stopped to read snippets of letters at the museums along the way and learned of hardships—fires, floods and epidemics—and more surprising, of hope and faith. They were especially surprised to learn that Marguerite Bourgeoys, who was instrumental in building the chapel, made do with a stable for the city's first classroom. "Sort of makes the recession look like a slow day at the mall," the kids joked.

Most of our walk to the chapel took place along the river that had delivered waves of immigrants to Montreal. "So this is the Old Port where my Irish ancestors landed," remarked Patrick, swinging his gaze back and forth from the guidebook to the port like a pendulum. "They helped build this canal, you know," he motioned to his friends. Patrick had discovered what Barack Obama knew when he followed Lincoln's route to Washington. A pilgrimage connects us to those who came before and makes us participants in their tears and triumphs.

Once we reached the Sailors' Church, the kids climbed the long staircase leading to the belfry and scanned the Saint Lawrence River, as priests who delivered blessings to mariners had done hundreds of years before. They tried to imagine how the sailors felt when they finally spotted land, and they admired the model ships hanging from the ceiling, tokens of gratitude for safe journeys. "So many things could have gone wrong on those boats," the kids reflected.

"Well, that's French and Irish immigrants," they counted off. "We need a third group." We explored stone courtyards now gracing restaurants and condominiums. We traced the eerie outlines of old brick and stone doorways in the cement walls of larger, newer structures built right over the remains. The kids wondered if the new owners appreciated the history holding up their walls.

Finally, we wound up where we had begun, at the point of land where de Maisonneuve had erected a fort. We crossed the street to the raised platform of Place Royal, the spot where the First Nations used to trade fur for European goods. Carved into the pavement is a replica of a treaty negotiated in 1701 between several Aboriginal nations and the French settlers. A peace pipe sits beneath the drawings of animals representing various clans. "There's our third group," commented the kids, "the grandparents of them all."

Beneath the pavement rests the city's first Catholic cemetery, where several natives were buried side by side with French settlers. Nathalie, a native girl adopted by French Canadian parents, stood riveted to the spot long after the others had moved on. "Wow, I used to skateboard over this last summer, and I never knew what it was before," Nathalie gasped. "I never really looked at it."

Back at school we discussed why people feel compelled to visit strange lands for excitement. "Our eyes get lazy," the kids remarked. "It's like a dog that buried a juicy bone but forgot it was in his own backyard. We forget to look deeper." As it turned out, the "staycation" took us much further than expected. More money could have bought a change of scenery, but we had experienced a change of vision.

~Linda Handiak

No Worries

Life, love and laughter — what priceless gifts to give our children.
~Phyllis Dryden

The worst problem with our current economic crisis is the overwhelming sense of worry. It is eating people alive. Worry affects our children, our marriages, our families, our sense of security.

We have chosen to tell our four children, ages thirteen to three, when we do not have enough money, and explain which bills we have to pay with Daddy's paycheck. We let them know, without too much detail, that it is hard to get everything they want right now. They have amazed us. They will even ask what bills we have to pay for a particular week. We expected them to act upset... worried. However, we are learning from their reaction. Sometimes the child teaches the parent.

Now instead of telling me what they want, they say, "Mom, when we will have enough money to get...?"

I pull out change and we count it to see if we can get Frosties at Wendy's. Fast food was something they took for granted, but now it is special.

They are making wish lists and saving birthday and Christmas money for toys or games. They have a blast looking through catalogs.

We spend more time together as a family. We use our TiVo to record programs and movies we can watch together. We make popcorn, turn out the lights, and enjoy our evening. Something that would have cost our family more than sixty dollars now costs about five dollars, and we have the added benefit of hitting "pause" when one of us needs to go to the bathroom!

Boxes are still a huge hit at our house. They turn into airplanes, Star Wars figures, and anything else you can imagine. I'm also amazed that when you hand a child a water hose and a little plastic pool, joy and laughter ensues. Simply turning the hose up into the air, they can pretend it is raining and they can play for hours inventing their own games.

Children's imaginations are endless. Our children have been so conditioned to having constant technology at their fingertips, families have forgotten how to have fun together. Yes, we could choose to worry and stress, but the bottom line is that we have each other.

We live paycheck to paycheck, but somehow we pull through. We have talked to the businesses we owe and made special arrangements. Worry would have us throwing up our hands rather than checking with creditors to work out an arrangement. They really are happy to work with you. They would rather get some money than none at all.

It's all about perspective. Do I miss not having the "extras?" Sure! But I have learned that blessings can be disguised in many ways. Accepting that we cannot control things, such as the economy, help us to let go of the worry. It changes your focus. Things that we used to call "needs" turn out to be "wants."

Our children may not have a college fund, but they will certainly understand how to work and get what they need rather than having their lives served to them on a silver platter. They will go to college. They know what hard work is. They know how to survive. But better than all of that, they will truly understand what it means to have a happy family. And after all, at the end of each day, they will know they are loved, and that doesn't cost a thing!

~Michelle Rocker

Tough Tuna

I refuse to believe that trading recipes is silly.
Tuna Fish casserole is at least as real as corporate stock.
~Barbara Grizzuti Harrison

I t was buried in the back of my recipe box, yellowed with age and slightly tattered. But there it was—my old tuna casserole recipe, a reminder of our early married days. Back then, I'd learned how to stretch a meatloaf ten ways, and yes, how to create casseroles that stretched our tight budget just as ingeniously.

I took that tuna casserole recipe and put it on the kitchen counter. In both real and symbolic ways, it was time....

My husband and I had come of age with Depression-era parents who had counted every penny forever after. We learned thrift in our respective households—mine in the city, his on a farm in the country. The lessons took, and at the beginning of our marriage that background stood us in very good stead.

My husband, a newly-minted lawyer, made even less money than I did as a first-year middle school English teacher. We lived so frugally that even a movie—ninety-nine cents at that time—was a splendid indulgence.

Our major investment was our tiny Cape Cod house, one that cost $12,000 in 1960, and required a $400 down payment that we struggled to put together.

I swapped clothes with my sister so that my students wouldn't see me in the same outfits so often. My husband continued to wear suits that had a suspicious sheen—the symptom of their advanced age.

And life was wonderful.

We both look back on those years as some of our best. Life was deliciously simple. We had no financial advisers because we had such skimpy incomes. We had one car that managed to get us where we both needed to go, if we both stuck to a strict itinerary.

Vacations? A day trip to the New Jersey seashore with lunch packed in a shoe box, and sand in our shoes for weeks after those escapes.

My husband's bachelor apartment sofa, originally purchased at the Salvation Army for $28, was the centerpiece of our living room for those first couple of years. Our parties were with couples in similar circumstances. Spaghetti and meatballs—nobody called it "pasta" back then—was often on the menu, and the wine that went with it was cheap.

And when it was just the two of us, tuna casserole was a mainstay of our weekly diet. Its mix of noodles, tuna, canned mushroom soup, and peas became a celebration when I sprinkled on potato chips as a topping.

The years passed, and providence smiled more kindly on us. We needed a bigger house when three daughters filled the little Cape Cod to bursting. Our next house seemed a palace—the girls even had their own bathroom.

Life got more complicated, and a bit less fun, as we joined the legions of America's consummate consumers. We had things... more things than we needed.

On the day we got a second TV, I remember feeling something akin to guilt. When we got a third, I didn't tell my thrifty parents. The omission was deliberate.

The years flew by, and suddenly, our daughters were gone, off to college campuses and then to lives of their own. America was in its golden years, and so were we.

There were vacations, nicer cars, and dinner parties where

shrimp dishes and exotic Asian foods, not spaghetti and meatballs, were on the menu.

I had the luxury of being a freelance writer—one without any salary or benefits, of course, but ideal for my restless nature.

We thought it would go on and on. We thought our retirement was as safe and secure as the giant, presumably rock-solid companies in which we had invested.

The wake-up call came during several sobering conferences with our financial advisor—and yes, we now had one of those.

The national economy was in a free-fall. Wall Street was having a nervous breakdown. Our savings were depleted.

We had blinked, and a whole generation had slipped away. We found ourselves reliving some aspects of our parents' lives.

While we've been luckier—we're blessed with some degree of economic security as retirees—our outlook is fixed on caution.

When you drive to a store that once was there, and suddenly it's not, that's scary.

When contemporaries who shared Camelot with us are wondering whether their pensions are safe, and whether they can keep their homes, optimism is a scarce commodity.

We may have lost some of our hard-won savings, but we've gained something in the bargain. Perspective.

Friends and neighbors are talking to each other more, and with more openness. We're all in this together, or, as somebody called, we're experiencing "creative commiseration."

We're remembering that living small, not large, can be rewarding.

We recently invited some friends over to play charades and sing old songs with us. It was glorious. We proudly served spaghetti and meatballs.

And I can't wait to make my old tuna casserole.

I suspect that it will taste just as wonderful as it used to.

~Sally Friedman

Good Times in Bad Times

A happy person is not a person in a certain set of circumstances,
but rather a person with a certain set of attitudes.
~Hugh Downs

The economy's failing is what they all say
Don't worry 'bout tomorrow, appreciate today.

Those stocks and 401Ks have shrunk and gone down.
It's my own choice to wear a smile or a frown.

The gas prices shoot sky high, then lower than low.
I have learned to conserve wherever I go.

The cost of heating our home makes me want to weep;
I don double socks, then curl up in deep sleep.

Beans and rice make great protein when meat prices soar.
There is no gas shortage in our home anymore.

Our drink of choice has become good ole H2O.
We have it on the rocks to put on a good show.

We snip out coupons and dream of discounts galore.
We await final sales in our favorite store.

No more nights on the town; we eat more homemade fare,
Which leads to conversing and becoming aware.

Forget box office tickets and the movie debut;
Renting DVDs is cheaper, with no ads to view.

The TV reminds us of things we can't afford.
Turning it off provides its own great reward.

We've rediscovered board games and the fun they bring.
Free books from the library, another new thing.

Getting back to basics has brought us joy and fun.
Could it be this cutting back has merely begun?

There's always someone worse off than we are, they say.
Which reminds us we're blessed in a really big way.

In good times or bad times, we know one thing is true:
Having faith in our God, helps us see our way through.

The economy's failing is what they all say.
Don't worry 'bout tomorrow; delight in today!

~Johnna Stein

What's Really Important?

Who is rich? He who rejoices in his portion.
~The Talmud

Talk about stress overload. "Here, take all of the money I have," I sometimes feel like saying. I have worked for more than forty years, and just when I am thinking about retiring in the next few years, the economy drops into the toilet. That's not fair!

"Lucky" for me, though, I had to have major spinal surgery just before the economy began to get really bad, so I was not totally attuned to the grave nature of the situation around me for a while. I am not an alarmist in the first place, but I am now home every day, watching the stock market drop enormous amounts. And, of course, the television news programs stir the fire even more.

"Let it ride," I keep telling my friends. Things will eventually turn around.

I am one of the lucky ones, however. That is, so far. I have not lost my home and I think I have enough to ride this recession out, even though I may have to work a little longer.

The last time I had to purchase gasoline it was about $4.30 a gallon. Now gasoline is $2.00 a gallon, but I am too disabled at this point to even drive my car. Sometimes I feel like I would like to drive and drive and drive, just so that I can fill my gasoline tank at such a low price. I guess that would not be downsizing nor saving money though, would it? And how can the cost of gasoline be so low when everything else is skyrocketing?

I also refuse to look at my retirement accounts right now, most of which are in stock and bonds. I get updates in the mail and I don't even open the envelopes — and there is no way I am going to go online to check it out. I simply don't want to know. I don't need the money right now and I don't want to see all of those tiny little figures. Ignorance is bliss, and I am loving every minute of my ignorance (or that just may be the pain medication).

I have always been a saver. Even as a child I would not spend my allowance on something I really wanted if I would not have any money left over. I would wait to buy that item until I could purchase it and still have some money left. I think Americans would be a lot better off if they lived by the same standards. We live in a society where we think we have to have the latest "toys" without having the money to purchase them, so we open one credit card account after another and get ourselves into debt.

I don't mean to sound flippant about the economy and the tough times people are going through. The situation is a very serious one, but, perhaps, these rough economic times can teach us all a thing or two about what is really important in life.

The things I have come to love and cherish, and the things which always seem to calm my spirit and soul, are the simple things in life. I would much rather take a peaceful walk at our local nature center than to spend an expensive day being pampered at the spa. A peanut butter and jelly sandwich and a Coke eaten on a picnic bench at our nearby park satisfies me more than dressing up and going out to eat at a fancy and expensive restaurant. And, hey, my car may be seven years old, but it has never given me any problems and it gets me to the same place a brand new Lexus would.

And what makes simple and cost-effective activities much more enjoyable for me is to share them with my family. We love getting together just to share each other's company. We don't have to go to a theme park or even to a movie to have a good time. We love watching DVDs, eating popcorn and joking around. We also love to take long walks in nature with our binoculars and our cameras capturing the beauty of God's creation and taking goofy pictures of ourselves.

I was kidding my fourteen-year-old great-niece the other day, asking her what she was going to get me for Christmas. Her immediate and worried response was that she did not have any money. Amanda is a wonderful poet, so I told her to "just write me a poem entitled, "Aunt LaVerne." Things, gifts, activities don't have to involve money. A simple poem from Amanda's heart will give me warm feelings for the rest of my life, and I hope Amanda learned a lesson from our little encounter as well.

I focus on what I have rather than on what I don't have in life. Houses, jobs, and health will come and go, but the love and enjoyment of family can sustain me through any kind of situation, including a rough economy.

~LaVerne Otis

The Wheels on the Bus

After a day's walk everything has twice its usual value.
~George Macauley Trevelyan

My seven-month-old sat in my lap, blowing bubbles and blinking at the circle of moms and babies surrounding us.

"And that's the way it is for us," Alison said, bouncing her son on her knee. "It's not easy."

I glanced at the clock above their heads and jolted upright. "Oh! I'm sorry, I have to run!" I said, collecting Aidan's blankets and toys and shoving them in the basket beneath his stroller. "The bus is going to be at the curb in ten minutes and I have to make it this time."

As quick as a new mom could, I stuffed Aidan's arms and legs in his snowsuit and hustled out of the classroom, down to the street corner, my scarf flying behind me. It would be close, but because the ice had already melted on the sidewalk, I jogged to the bus stop, sweat already forming beneath my itchy, wool hat.

Slowing down, catching my breath, I wheeled Aidan to the corner and stopped beneath the sign for the 134. Seconds later, the huge white bus wheezed to a halt in front of us, exhaust pluming behind it. The driver kindly helped us aboard and I sat, spent, opposite the back doors, sinking into my seat, admiring my now sleeping baby. I closed my eyes, listening to the rumble of tires beneath us, and dozed on the ride home.

It had been five months since our family had moved and sold

our car. Living in a city as big and vibrant as Boston not only kept us busy, but also kept us watching our wallet. Moving from Fairbanks, Alaska, with a new baby in tow, we knew we needed to cut back on our expenses in order to save for his college fund, our retirement funds, and to be able to eat a good steak dinner once in a while.

We didn't realize that paring down would not only deposit more money in the bank, but also improve our health and the environment. Saving cents quickly started to make sense.

The bus rumbled into the station and moments later, Aidan and I were strolling to our building, about a half-mile walk. The crisp air and early afternoon sun left me feeling energized in the dead of winter.

Without a car, I've had to take the bus each week to the New Moms group across town. The ride, though admittedly inconvenient, has introduced me to my neighborhood and saved us loads on extra car costs — expenses we couldn't rationalize at this time in our lives. Aside from New Mom meetings, my husband, Tim, and I have hoofed it to shops for necessities such as groceries, baby supplies, and household items — something we probably wouldn't have done, especially in February, if we'd had a car.

But, looking up at the bright Boston sky, I resolved to keep at it. I'd already shed my pregnancy weight due to all the walking and I felt good about not polluting the environment with the gas-guzzling SUV we sold in Fairbanks.

That evening, Tim helped me get the baby ready for bed. Aidan lay on the changing table, smiling and cooing at his father as I stood back and watched.

"I'm getting better at this," Tim said, fastening the diaper beneath Aidan's belly. With four quick snaps, he had secured the red cloth diaper. A month ago, he lamented the loss of Velcro, but I couldn't help but admire his deftness with diapers now.

"He looks great," I said. Together, we buttoned up Aidan's pajamas, a fuzzy footed outfit I'd gotten for a dollar on Craigslist. "Do you want to read to him?"

Tim nodded and sat down in my parents' old glider, Aidan in

his lap. "Okay," I heard him say as I left the room. "Would you like to read *The Very Hungry Caterpillar* or *Trucks?*"

Last summer, when Aidan was born, we were overwhelmed with the number of accoutrements that magazines and Internet sites deemed necessary for bringing up baby. The little hats and onesies were cute. So were the baby slings, baby swings, battery-operated gizmos, SUV-sized strollers, and solid wood cribs.

But we couldn't afford all that. We didn't want to get sucked up in the vortex of All Things Baby and have nothing in the bank. "Aidan wouldn't care if he wore hand-me-downs," I said.

"Cloth diapers would save us loads of money, especially if we had another baby," Tim replied.

"If?" I rubbed his arm. "Don't you mean when?"

We researched our options, talked to friends who were scaling back in similar ways, and decided on used cloth diapers.

"It sounds gross," Alison said to me after one New Moms meeting. Her son lay on the ground, his ankles in the air as Alison removed one wet diaper and replaced it with a new, clean one. Pumpkin orange. "But it's not. People take good care of them before they sell." She'd just told me about an online diaper community where people sold their babies' cloth diapers for a fraction of the retail value. "I got a $20 diaper for only eight bucks, shipping included," Alison beamed.

"And that diaper will last you..."

"Months. Maybe even all year."

When I told Tim about it that evening at dinner he nodded. "I've been saying cloth all along."

"And you'll still change him? You'll flick poop in the toilet?"

Tim set down his fork. Maybe my timing wasn't the best. "Sweetie. Get the diapers. I'll flick."

As the ground thawed, flowers bloomed, and Aidan crawled commando-style around the house in his multi-colored diapers, I decided it was time to find some summer clothes. My chunky baby had stretched into a lean, lithe goo-ing machine.

I left one Saturday afternoon with a friend and came home with two stuffed garbage bags. Tim and Aidan sat on the floor surrounded by blocks. "What do you have there?" Tim asked, eyeing my stash suspiciously. The last time I went to a community clothing and toy swap, my net results overtook the living room.

I lay my findings proudly on the carpet. OshKosh overalls, Carter's pajamas, babyGap shorts—all free! "And look at this," I shed the second bag and revealed a Fisher-Price play station that tinkled with music—"London Bridge Is Falling Down"—as I set it up. "Isn't this great?"

Tim pushed a few buttons, the ABC Song starting up, and eventually nodded. "Pretty good." Aidan pulled himself up, wide-eyed at his "new" toy. "And it was all free?"

"Community event," I shrugged, happy with my good fortune. "And we have a place to deliver all our used clothing once Aidan outgrows it!"

Tim smiled. I'd done well. We all had. We lived in a big city and could enjoy it too. We're in better shape today and our carbon footprint is smaller than it was a year ago. At fifteen months old, Aidan is now toddling around in the same cloth diapers I bought last winter.

Resolving to save more money has helped more than hindered our lifestyles. Financial worries exist, but they don't drive us.

Bus 134 does.

And our feet too, of course.

~Mary Jo Marcellus Wyse

A is for Apple,
B is for Brandy

Good apple pies are a considerable part of our domestic happiness.
~Jane Austen

Five years ago, my husband, Ken, and I strolled around the backyard of our new country home and I spied the two apple trees. I immediately pictured the pies Grandma and Mama used to prepare. Sometimes the pair cooked in tandem, staging a mini-bakeoff. They'd vie for our approval, Mama with her expertly fluted lattice-top French apple, and Grandma with her apple rhubarb, crowned with the flakiest crust ever to please a palette.

"Don't you all prefer my apple rhubarb?" Grandma once asked. My older and wiser sister poked me in the back. She knew how I loved rhubarb. Before I could nod assent, she jumped in. "Grandma, it's a dead heat. Your pie is delicious, and Mama's is delectable."

"Even if you're penniless, you always have a treat waiting if you've got an apple tree in your yard," Grandma said, cutting us each a slice.

Patti whispered to me later that we'd always have to say it was a tie if we wanted the kitchen to continue to carry that sweet, spicy cinnamon fragrance.

Though Daddy worked at the creamery and Grandpa took odd jobs wherever he could, the dollars they brought in had to stretch to support a family of four adults and three kids. Fortunately we lived in Scotts Mills, Oregon, where everybody had an apple tree or three. I even plucked wild crabapples on my way to school.

Sometimes I'd wander the aisles of the general store, hungrily eyeing the boxes of Cracker Jack and packets of graham crackers. I knew though that those were treats for special occasions, such as birthdays and holidays. At Christmas, each child could depend on a tangerine, some walnuts, and a small box of chocolate-covered cherries. And at Easter, of course, we'd get baskets with jelly beans, a packet of chewing gum, and a chocolate egg.

But for everyday sweets it was always apple pie or, for variety, a cobbler. Once in a while on sultry late summer Sundays, we'd sit on the porch until twilight. Grandma would haul out her wood bucket ice cream churn, fill it with cream, eggs, and sugar, then cram the top section with ice and salt. I would crank until the creamy smooth vanilla concoction thickened. Then she'd bring out the pies, fresh from the oven. We'd gaze down at our bowls as the ice cream slowly sank through the crust and into filling, and then we'd slowly spoon it all up, our eyes glazed with ecstasy.

On cooler autumn evenings, we lounged on the porch watching the stars emerge. Grandpa would clear his throat and ask Daddy, "About ready for a swig?" Then he'd step inside and emerge a little later with a tray holding steaming cups of particularly aromatic coffee for the two of them, and a pitcher of lemonade for the rest of us. Grandma would follow on his heels, with a tray of apple pie slabs and a platter of sharp cheddar wedges from the wheel Daddy brought home from the creamery.

Now Ken smiled as I gazed at our trees as if they were festooned with ambrosia, the fabled food of the gods, rather than just plain old apples. "You look absolutely enchanted," he said.

"My whole childhood was punctuated with apple pies. I'll bake lots of them now."

I plucked one of the yellow-cheeked red fruits from a branch, and held it to my nose, and sniffed. I sniffed again, and then frowned.

"Oh, no," I sighed. "This is a Red Delicious. Okay for munching, but not the best for pies."

Ken pointed to the other tree. "What about those?"

Bliss... they were Golden Delicious, just about the best pie apples ever.

"That's great. Reds for snacking and applesauce, and Goldens for pies, so we're set."

That evening I hummed a chorus of "Shoo-Fly Pie and Apple Pan Dowdy" as I leafed through my accordion file in search of Grandma's heirloom recipe. It had been decades since I'd baked a pie, and when I finally located the yellowed paper with Grandma's spidery handwriting, I wondered why I had waited so long. As I glanced at the list of ingredients and the instructions, it came back to me.

I never could make a proper crust. Mama said I didn't make it short enough. I understood the secret was in the amount of ice water and the mixture of shortening and butter, but no matter how hard I had tried to follow her instructions, my crusts always resembled patchwork leather. It's a wonder the recipe wasn't blotched with my tears. I'd tried so many times and always failed.

I tucked the recipe back into the file, and decided to forget about the apples. I'd make a pot of applesauce now and then, but otherwise I mostly ignored the trees. They were symbols of my defeat.

But this past autumn, as the economy worsened, I remembered Grandma's words about never lacking for a treat so long as there's an apple tree. I wandered into the backyard with a basket and heaped it with Golden Delicious. Over the years I had collected a series of apple recipes, none involving pie crust, always tucking them away with a promise to try them some day. Why couldn't that someday be today? Waste not, want not.

So I made my first "impossible" apple pie with those sweet cooking apples, and it came out perfect, since it smartly made its own crust. A week or so later I tried an apple crisp, and then apple cheese bread. Besides my usual batches of applesauce, I baked apples and even fried them. I outdid myself with an exotic dish called glazed apple daisy that involved packaged cinnamon rolls and chopped walnuts.

I packed up sacks of the Reds, tucked in a simple recipe for applesauce, and toted them to the local food bank. By October I had stored several sacks of apples in our garage pantry where they would stay fresh through January. I even took a bushel over to a neighbor for his retired race horses.

On Halloween I recalled how Grandma always candied apples, and how grateful I used to be that I didn't wear braces so I could savor the delicious crunch. I coated a dozen and gave them to friends.

Finally, after the first early November snowfall, I climbed the ladder and harvested the few apples that clung near the top of the tree, sampled already by flies. These I tossed over the fence into the pasture for the ravenous deer who foraged each night and who were not picky eaters.

I've mentally awarded myself an A for effort. I might not be as crusty as Grandma or Mama, but I'm just as thrifty. And I suspect that even Grandma would approve of that glazed apple daisy, so long as I threw in a sliver or two of rhubarb and didn't let on that I hadn't made the cinnamon rolls from scratch.

And by baking all our desserts myself, I'd saved enough to buy several very nice bottles of Grandpa's special coffee flavoring.

~Terri Elders

Lessons Learned from a Money Tree

There are rich counsels in the trees.
~Herbert P. Horne

Times were financially tough. That was a disturbing fact as I browsed the gardening section of our local nursery. Since learning that live plants increased the air quality of one's home, I decided to purchase an inexpensive one.

Eyeing the price tags on houseplants, I walked farther down the aisle, pausing beside a row of trunk-braided, leafy trees labeled Pachira aquatica, or "Money Tree."

I liked the tree's appearance, and that its description contained the words "easy care." A low maintenance plant might survive my care, since I'd been told that my gardening skills, or lack thereof, could destroy even plastic plants.

Turning the tag over, I glanced at the first few sentences of a charming little story, learning that the money tree's legend boasted of good fortune. I didn't believe in folklore, but something about the tree's myth hit a tender spot with me.

"We sure could use you," I whispered aloud, thinking of my husband's dwindling income due to economic woes. The past year had been hard enough with the deaths of several loved ones, but then financial challenges arose, compounding our grief. "I need wisdom," I murmured aloud, finding myself praying again for understanding in how to respond to life's trials. Sighing, I made my decision and reached for the healthiest looking tree to purchase.

At home, I positioned the three-foot money tree in a corner beside an upstairs window, and promptly forgot about it. Within several weeks, daily life became more dismal. Friends and family lost jobs, illnesses multiplied, and my husband worked extra hours with less pay.

A cloud of despair hovered over our household.

"Buck needs watering, Mom," my nine-year-old son, Simeon, reminded me. "I can water him before I go outside."

"Buck?" I questioned, learning that he and his sister, Abigail, had named the tree after a dollar bill. "Thanks, honey, but I'll do it," I said, realizing that I hadn't watered the poor thing since purchasing it.

Finding the tree droopy with several crinkled leaves, I was surprised it was not in poorer condition. The tree's care sheet suggested medium sunlight, but with the window blind pulled down, the tree had little to none. Yet, somehow, it had managed to lean towards the small amount of sunlight shining through a slit. "Resourceful little thing," I acknowledged, lifting the shade. "I admire that."

That night, sleep eluded me. Instead of resting, my mind worked overtime with the "what ifs." What if my husband lost his job? What if our health insurance was cancelled? What if I couldn't find a part-time job?

Anxiety weaved itself into our home, subtly at first, but then more aggressively as we allowed fear to dominate our thoughts.

"Mom, I could start watering Buck," my daughter, Abigail, offered one afternoon. "I'll write it on my calendar so I won't forget."

Her gentle reminder that he could use regular care didn't go unnoticed. "Thanks, sweetie, but I'll take care of it."

"Will we be able to go to the movies this Friday?" she asked, her tone doubtful — the result of recent family activities being cancelled.

"Not this Friday, honey," I said, thinking of the electric bill. "Maybe the next, though."

"Okay, Mom," she smiled, breaking my heart with her gentle acceptance of our financial circumstances. "Maybe the next."

I headed upstairs, finding my son beside the money tree. "I was going to water Buck, Mom, but now that you're here, I can help Dad and Abigail wash the car." He handed me the watering can.

"They'll like that," I nodded, taking the jug while considering the tree. My husband had recently placed a bookshelf near the window, blocking part of the sunlight from reaching the plant. Yet, somehow, the money tree had stretched itself towards its need, soaking up the diminutive amount of daylight offered.

Amazed, I peered closer. "Unbelievable. You're actually growing," I whispered, touching a tender shoot. "Buck, you're making the best of a tough environment and a neglectful owner," I told it, sprinkling its soil with water. "I could learn a lesson from you."

Silence ensued as if the tree asked me, "Well, why don't you?"

I didn't have an answer until I heard laughter from outside the window. Moving the curtains, I watched as my husband sprayed our children with the hose. The water drenching Simeon and Abigail seemed to replenish my spirit too. It's so nice to hear sounds of happiness again, I thought, touching the window. So why had I allowed worry to overtake our joy as a family?

Glancing at Buck again, I felt a transformation beginning. Lifting the tree, I carried it downstairs, and positioned it near the front window where it wouldn't be ignored. "If things are going to change, let's start with your care."

I then grabbed a notebook and called my family inside to sit at the dining room table. "I need ideas," I told them, explaining what I'd like to do. "Since attending movie theaters are too expensive right now, what can we do instead?"

"How 'bout a 'family night?'" Abigail suggested. "We could rent movies and make popcorn. That shouldn't cost much."

"Great idea," her father nodded. "We can do it every Friday."

We continued brainstorming, all agreeing that the weekly bowling with friends would now be video games at our house, complete with pizza. As we continued to deliberate, suggest, and vote, our excitement grew and with it, I realized that we were not only making the best of our situation, but we were doing it as a family. I realized this could bring us even closer as I listened to the animated chatter in the room.

And I was right. Several months later, we realized that what we'd sacrificed could not compare to what we had gained. Family nights were now spent snuggled together on our sectional couch while watching a newly released movie. Friends' day with video games turned out to be a much-anticipated hit. And each day, we prayed together and recounted at least one blessing to be thankful for.

The cloud of worry, which had hovered over us months earlier, was now replaced with an enthusiastic resolve to take hold of life and re-shape it for the benefit of all.

Our family had put forth simple steps of practicality, but they were ones that made a significant change in our attitudes.

Retrieving my watering can, I walked over to Buck. His store tag was still propped inside the soil, and I pulled it out. Turning it over, I read the rest of the money tree's legend, learning that when a hard-working farmer had dug up the unusual plant growing in his field, he'd brought it home and learned life lessons from the resilient tree. Soon, the farmer became a wealthy entrepreneur.

I smiled, realizing that my prayer for wisdom had been answered. Touching Buck's leaves, I sighed. Maybe the legend of the money tree wasn't simple folklore after all. Maybe the tree's myth had been built around a universal truth. A truth that where faith, love, and hope abides, the human spirit can prevail in all circumstances.

Sometimes people just need a gentle reminder of that fact — even if that reminder comes from the strangest of sources — like a money tree named Buck.

~Karen Majoris-Garrison

Tough Times, Tough People

Family Ties

Blood's thicker than water, and when one's in trouble
Best to seek out a relative's open arms.

~Author Unknown

The Last Lunch

Me, sexy? I'm just plain ol' beans and rice.
~Pam Grier

Salvation seldom comes when you want it, and generally shows up when you least expect it. Because, given the sense of humor of the Universe, it very often comes at the exact last minute, that edge of reality where the last vestige of hope meets the final fall into despair.

I moved into my grandmother's house the year after Granddaddy died. She needed someone to ease her loneliness; I needed stability from the nomadic life I was living with my mother. When she adopted me I didn't know what it meant. I just knew she promised she'd take care of me from now on.

But I was a hungry six-year-old, and she was a sixty-year-old widow who hadn't worked since World War II. Granddaddy had left her with a little savings and enough insurance to bury him. And in the spring of my seventh year, the savings were running out.

I was, of course, oblivious. I went to school and came home to do homework and play. Supper appeared on the table every night. If Grandmamma wasn't eating as much as I was, I didn't notice.

The problem was that her Social Security survivor benefits didn't cover the expenses of one older woman, let alone that woman and a seven-year-old boy. Much later, I learned of the countless visits to the Social Security offices, the paperwork, the affidavits that she did have a legal minor child.

But there came the day in the summer of 1965 when she called me in to lunch. Meals had been getting simpler and simpler, and what awaited me that day was a little rice and a few pinto beans. There was a single plate on the table.

We said grace: "God is great, God is good...."

She patted my hand and turned away. And she said, in a small voice that I heard very clearly, "I don't know where the next one is coming from."

There was a *Loony Tunes* short on Saturday morning TV in those days. It involved a hobo and his dog sharing a meal. The hobo finds an old tin can containing a single bean. He puts that bean on a plate and, with his knife and fork, carefully slices it like a choice cut of meat. I imitated that hobo every chance I got, because I thought it was neat.

Because it took me a long time to eat a plate of beans one slice at a time, I was still at the table when the mailman came. We heard his footsteps on the porch, and Grandmamma went out through the living room, drying her hands. I heard the screen door close, and there was enough of a pause to slice another bean.

Then I heard her say, "Oh!" And the screen door opened and slammed again, and there was a thump and a great deal of crying.

I rushed into the living room. Grandmamma was on her knees in the middle of the floor, clutching an official government envelope and weeping like a baby. The check had come between the last breath of hope and the realization of disaster.

It didn't make us rich. But we weren't exactly poor, either. Grandmamma had stared starvation in the face. After that, we never worried about being hungry. She always had a meal on the table, and I always ate it. Even if it was rice and beans.

Even now, after all the ups and downs life has thrown me, rice and beans is my favorite comfort food. I associate it not with poverty, but with hope.

~Bill Mullis

Hair Is Overrated

A daughter is a little girl who grows up to be a friend.
~Author Unknown

"One thing I can tell you for certain is that you will lose your hair before your second treatment. And my advice is to buzz your head before it starts to fall out. If you wait until it starts coming out, it will be in your bed, it will be in your food, it will be in your shoes. Look me in the eye. Buzz your head while you still have the power. You take control." These words came straight from the mouth of a veteran chemo nurse, and were spoken directly to the ears of my mother, a sixty-year-old breast cancer patient. So what did we do? We did what all obedient Southern girls do. We got ready to cut some hair.

Mama got out the scissors, the hair-cutting ones, not the paper-cutting ones. Mama is particular about her scissors. Then she got out the clippers that she uses to cut Daddy's hair. Mama is also particular about Daddy. I spread a worn floral sheet on the kitchen floor and pulled Mama's chair in the middle of it. Mama tugged her white T-shirt over her head, exposing one bare droopy breast and one crooked angry scar.

"Are you okay with this? Can you do this?" Mama asked.

"I am and I can but I'm not promising I won't cry."

"No reason to cry. You know I've never liked my hair anyway."

I took a deep breath and started with the scissors. A clip here, a cut there, and short ash-blond hair landed on a bed of faded purple flowers. I worked diligently like an excited cosmetology student. Then I plugged in the clippers and the loud buzz was more than Mama could stand. She insisted on wearing ear plugs while I finished my masterpiece. So there she sat, nude from the waist up, with pink and yellow ear plugs stuffed in her ears. She caught my eye and we giggled. I took a long swipe down the middle of her head. I methodically shaved off hair in perfect rows as if I'd done it a million times before. I told Mama how awesome her head looked but she couldn't hear me. I told her shaving heads was a piece of cake but she couldn't hear me. I told her I was fine and wasn't crying but she couldn't hear me.

And just as quickly as we started it was over. We were done. I ran my hands over the stubble. Mama removed her ear plugs.

Questioning blue eyes stared up at me. "How do I look?"

"You look beautiful, just like my mama. See."

So there we were, side by side as we'd been so many times in so many situations. The mirror reflected two women who were much tougher than they gave themselves credit for. Two strong women. One with hair, one without. One a daughter, one a mother. And both with big wide matching smiles—and not a tear in sight.

~Janet H. Taylor

The Penny Puppy

In every conceivable manner, the family is link to our past, bridge to our future.
~Alex Haley

Years ago, my parents came into possession of a puppy. He is about a foot tall, with pretty brown eyes and a little touch of white on his chin. He requires no care other than a little grooming from time to time. Over the years, he has been bumped and banged about so much that he has little scars everywhere on his body, but he is okay. He is worth his weight in gold. And he has been around as long as I can remember. The only different thing about this puppy is the inch-long narrow opening in the back of his head — for, you see, this little puppy is really a "puppy bank." Just as people have "piggy banks" my parents have a "puppy bank."

He is part of us, part of our growing up, and part of our lives to this day. He doesn't have a name. He is just called "the dog." If my parents, or any of us five siblings, found extra change, we would say it was for "the dog," a statement that was somewhat confusing to those who knew there was no dog in the house. But "the dog" to us was just accepted, and everybody contributed at one time or another, and still does.

When my daughter was ten years old, she came home from school and announced that everyone in her class had "family traditions" and she had none! She was in tears. I assured her we did have traditions, and once they were pointed out to her, she understood more about what we did have as a family. We did not have all our family near us as her friends did. Our families were in Newfoundland; we were in Nova Scotia, but she did have traditions—those of our extended families and those of our nuclear family. I reminded her of the Penny Puppy. She thought that tradition was the best of all, and told her class about it the next day.

A little while ago, when visiting my parents, I emptied my change purse and Dad said, "Going to feed the dog are we?" We had a great chuckle because "feeding the dog" was what it was always called when we added our change to the puppy bank.

I went to my parents' cozy, beautifully decorated bedroom to put the coins into the dog. Sitting on the floor by Father's television stand was the battered little puppy bank. He did not look out of place, because he always has been in their room. Now it is a special thing for a grandchild to go to their room to "feed the dog." One by one they learned the procedure, and one by one they passed it on.

My brother, Dave, had arrived by the time I was through with my deposit.

"What's up?" he asked.

"I was just feeding the dog, and I think I'll take his photo!" I told him.

I took the puppy out to the rhubarb patch, took his photo, and walking back through the house, I ran into Father, who just looked at me and laughed. He never said a word. He knew I was thinking about the puppy and its place in our lives.

This ceramic piece was very important. It had pulled us through when extra money was needed for a special vacation, a new pair of skates, a warmer jacket, or to stop the tears over a fractured bumper we had put on Father's car—again! When money was tight, the dog was opened, all the coins counted and rolled, and everyone would wait with great expectancy for our parents to announce the total. Somehow, it would always be enough to cover the cost of whatever the need happened to be.

"That dog paid for some good family vacations, nice bikes, and pulled us through some tough times, didn't it?" Dave asked.

I had to agree. We constantly fed the dog a penny or two, or a quarter now and then, and the money would build up to a few hundred dollars. It was a splendid tradition to spread a cloth on the table and watch our parents, with the help of one or two of their offspring, start "the sorting of the coins."

These days, my parents are getting older, but they still "feed the dog." Mother can hardly lift him, and she says the dog is gaining weight. Although the comment is expected, it always brings a laugh. They count the money at Christmastime now, and every year it goes where they think the need is the greatest.

Yes, it is a battered ceramic puppy, but in our lives it has been of great importance. Everyone contributed, everyone knew where the puppy was, and everyone gained from it in times of misfortune or need. The little dog never failed us, and we will never fail him. He is part of our family, part of a group of five rascals who grew up around the coasts of Newfoundland, were educated, found jobs, and in due time started their own families. And in so doing, we started our own traditions within our own homes.

I can tell my son and daughter that yes, we do have traditions — those of our family and those of their parents' families. They are all precious. And in starting their own families, they will begin new traditions for themselves. But for us, four girls and one boy, and a mom and dad, we have the tradition of our Penny Puppy, the little dog that pulled us through some rough spots, that we still "feed," and we all still ask at Christmastime, "How much in the dog this year, Dad?" With great anticipation we await his answer, which he takes his time telling us — just for the heck of it.

The Penny Puppy is our special custom. A reminder of how pulling together as a family, working together as a unit, caring and sharing with each other, is so essential. And to think we learned it from a little ceramic dog, and a pair of parents who knew the deprivation of the depression years and the value of a penny. My parents are great-grandparents now, and will continue to teach that lesson to their great-grandchildren.

We will continue to "feed the dog" and pass on the lesson taught to us by a mother and father who knew the meaning of the word "need" and advised us never to "get your needs and your wants mixed up."

~Bonnie Jarvis-Lowe

A Saving Flame

Forgiveness does not change the past, but it does enlarge the future.
~Paul Boese

She hadn't meant to start it. She knew she wasn't supposed to be up in her brother's room, but she certainly didn't set out to start this fire. Still, I was seething with anger. I knew I had to say and do the right things, or my daughter would be scarred for life. I prayed for control and wisdom.

My wife was in tears. "Don! What are we going to do?" she pleaded. "We could lose everything!" All I could do was to keep holding her tight, and wait. I had no answers for her.

"Where is Emily? I asked. "I need to talk to her."

Katie looked up at me. "She's next door, crying her eyes out. I think she's afraid we're going to kill her. She's real upset."

I had arrived home just ahead of the first fire truck that Sunday evening. Katie had met me at the driveway, announcing that our house was on fire. Running to the back door, I saw the lights in the house flicker, then die, just as I reached for the door knob. I felt like I was a guest star in someone else's nightmare. This couldn't really be happening. But the five fire trucks around the house told the sobering truth. This was all too real.

"I am mad enough to kill her," I said. "But I know we have to let her know we won't. We've got to make sure she knows we still love her. I'm going to go find her."

I walked over to the neighbor's yard. Gregg came over and put his arm on my shoulder, asking if there was anything he could do to help. He knew as well as I did that there was nothing he could do except ask.

"Your daughter's pretty shaken," he said. "She's up in Lisa's room looking out the window at your house and sobbing."

"Yeah, I know. She's probably scared to death. I just need to talk to her and tell her it's going to be all right. Would you mind?"

"I'll go get her," he said.

I looked up at the flames coming through the roof of our house—our home. Falling on my knees, I gave it all to God. "Lord, if you will just give me the words to say to Emily, You can forget the house. Thank You for sparing my family from the fire. Please give me the way to spare my daughter from me."

I felt a light tap on my shoulder. "Dad? Are you okay?" I turned and looked at Emily. Her face was caked with dried tears, and wet with new ones. "Daddy, I didn't mean... I'm so sorry!" She began to sob uncontrollably. "Please don't hate me!"

Picking up her nine-year-old body, I embraced her and kissed her and cried. All of my anger was gone. At that moment, the importance of forgiveness was seared into my soul forever.

~Don Verkow

Singing in the Rain

I don't sing because I'm happy; I'm happy because I sing.
~William James

I t had been months since my dad went to work one night and never came home, but we were nowhere near over the divorce. My siblings didn't talk about it. Kelly went out a lot and my brothers, John and Matthew, just sort of wandered around doing what they always did, but in a kind of fog.

My mother cried night after night. Of course it would affect her differently. She had not had a clue Daddy was leaving. The shock of it alone made her cry. She screamed a lot, too, misdirecting her anger at my dad towards us, mostly me. It was one of the hazards of being the oldest child.

Then our house burned down. Neighbors actually stood outside in the street and chatted and laughed as our house burned one January morning. I stood there, shoeless, watching my mother weep and all I could think was, "We are broken."

We moved into the Ramada Inn, where my mother worked, five of us crammed into one tiny room. In no time, we were on each others' nerves. After four months of not having any of our own air to breathe, we were on the verge of just giving up. We were never going to have a home again. Putting one foot in front of the next felt impossible.

One day Mother stood up, looking frenzied. "Let's go for a ride."

Kelly, John, Matt and I looked at one another warily, not sure we had heard right. There were two issues. One, Mother had just been learning to drive out of necessity since Daddy left. Two, she was very bad at it.

"Come on," she urged. "It'll be fun."

This confused us further. We didn't have fun in our family. We fought and cried. Our mother's anger at our father's abandonment had seeped slowly and surely into each of our lives. Fun was something we might have known about once, but which seemed foreign to us now.

Still, we minded our mother and piled into our 1972 blue Ford Torino, a blue so faded as to appear almost white. As the oldest, I sat in the front seat with our mother, while Kelly, John and Matt sat in the back. Mother started the car and backed out of the parking lot. "I thought we'd go look at all the houses we've lived in."

We had lived in quite a few places. Mother drove us by the house where we'd lived when I was just a kindergartener and then down the road a few houses to where we'd lived when I was in first grade. We even hazarded the main drag to see where my parents had lived when I was born, a tiny one-room apartment over a pharmacy that looked about the size of the motel room we inhabited now.

We talked about everything you could imagine — all the things we had to avoid talking about in that motel room. When there were lulls in the talk, we sang. We had always been a singing family, growing up with two parents who loved music. We started by singing "On Top of Old Smokey" the right way and then we sang every strange variation we could think of. We laughed a lot.

After this first foray, going for a ride in my mother's car became a regular thing. Every night we piled into the car and the world changed. We told jokes and sang and looked at houses we wished we had the money to live in. One night we stopped at the grocery and were having so much fun joking and laughing that we were halfway back to the motel before we realized we had forgotten five-year-old Matthew. We laughed hard all the way back to the Kroger store where Matt was waiting patiently outside on the sidewalk.

I loved riding in the car. As spring turned to summer, the breezes blew through the car and cooled us even on the hottest of nights and we were spared the sticky, humid nights of anger in the motel. The singing allowed us to vent emotions we couldn't face back in that cramped space. It was during one of those nightly car rides that my mother taught me how to harmonize.

We sang "You Are My Sunshine" and "K-k-k Katie" and a million other songs. The hope we seemed to have lost in the rest of our life was real again in the car as we sang.

So was laughter. We sang a Lynyrd Skynyrd song, "What's your name, little girl? What's your name?" at the top of our lungs to a tiny girl in another car at a stoplight and fell into hysterics when the occupants of the other cars pointed and laughed at us.

The hymns were my favorite. Mother didn't go to church. God had become a taboo topic since our dad had left. The hymns we sang—"Amazing Grace" and "How Great Thou Art" and "Shall We Gather at the River"—let us connect on a different level than we'd ever been able to in the past and calmed us down at evening's end for the return to the motel. More often than not, Mother and I ended these nights by carrying our sleeping boys, her sons and my brothers, in to bed, exhausted but happy.

One night as we were singing loudly, "In the pines, in the pines, where the sun never shines and you shiver when the cold wind blows..." Mother suddenly slammed on the brakes. "This is it!" she cried.

"This" was a house, and a for-rent sign in the front yard brought me more joy than I could believe.

"Really?" I asked.

My mother jumped out, excited, and ran to peer in the windows of the house. My siblings soon followed, and when I realized we might really have a house again, I got out, too. "This bedroom is mine!"

I realized that night that my mother was just a person, just like the rest of us. She was no better and no worse and she had been through a lot. And her driving had improved dramatically!

We moved into our new house the following weekend. We were very busy and the nights in the car became a thing of the past. The following summer we tried again with the car, but the times had changed and the car was never the same kind of haven for us again.

Better off, we had moved on. New jobs and activities of every kind used up our time now. But we knew that one summer in the blue Torino had saved a vital part of us all. My dad had left, it was true, and we had lost our home, but my mother, whether by accident or design, had found a way to bring us together and keep us that way.

~Marla H. Thurman

Tough Task

All of us have wonders hidden in our breasts,
only needing circumstances to evoke them.
~Charles Dickens

The phone rang at 2:30 that morning and scared me out of my wits.

"Mom, I'm sorry to be calling so late, but I just have to talk to someone about this." It was my son Lee. He had just returned to his apartment after helping at the 9/11 Pentagon disaster.

I asked, "How are you holding up? Have you eaten? How are you feeling?"

He asked, "How is the rest of the family doing? Were there any events in Maryland? How are your patients handling it?"

The tragic story emerged throughout our nightlong conversation. Lee worked across the street from the Pentagon. He heard the explosion and ran over to help.

He went from bystander to rescue worker in one horrible heartbeat. His friends worked in that building and he wanted to help. Lee was not a fireman, military man, or medic. He was there and he was willing to do what needed to be done. Someone gave him directions and a flashlight and sent him to join one of the search teams.

He cried into the phone. "I wanted to help so I could say to one little girl, 'your Daddy will be coming home,' but that didn't happen.

"Mom, there were no bodies... only arms and legs. I wasn't able to save a single one of them. There were no pulses... not one, the whole time." He began sobbing. My heart broke for him. He struggled to continue. "I saw a hand, just a hand, on the floor; it had a wedding ring on it and all I could think of was my Crissy." (Crissy was the girl he wanted to marry.) That said, he wept again. "Mom I never meant to lose my composure—I'm sorry."

"No son, don't be sorry; if you could go through what you just did and not feel anything, you would not be human."

"I'm supposed to be in control of myself. I'm falling apart here," he protested. "Sorry to call so late," he continued in a whisper.

"I'm honored you called to talk to me," I whispered back.

"Since you're a nurse and have watched many people die, I thought you could tell me how to handle it," he said. Then he wanted to know how to regain his composure, so he could go back and continue the search. I told him that the devastation he just saw was not like anything I had ever witnessed.

"You're going to feel overwhelmed because it is an overwhelming situation. There is nothing you can do but rest and go back and do what you know you must do," I said.

He kept repeating, "I have to go back and try to help, but it's hopeless."

With all the love a mother could give, I tried to explain that he had done all he could and that he was only human and he couldn't change fate. I tried to think of comforting Bible verses but none would come to mind. I just kept reassuring him that he had done all he could. He told me that once he rested and regained his composure, he wanted to return to the Pentagon.

"That's why I wanted to talk to you, Mom. How do you do what you do and not break down in front of people?"

"Lee, it doesn't matter if you break down. No one will care about that."

"But," he protested, "I'm supposed to be objective, controlled, and saving lives, not picking up hands and legs!"

"Who said you have to be composed through all this?" I asked. "Is there a rulebook on how you should act in the midst of a terrorist attack? Son, you are reacting like a human. Are you really worried that someone might see you cry?"

"No. It's not that. I just want to handle this and keep my composure and be strong for the families, like you do at work."

Apparently he pictured me as Florence Nightingale attending to war-torn troops. The truth was, in the entire forty years of my nursing career, I had never witnessed the horrors he had seen in the last forty hours! However, I admitted that I had wept with the families when there was nothing more we could do to save someone they loved.

"Hon, we're only human, we feel human emotions."

"Then tell me how to control my thoughts. I have to think clearly," he pressed.

That I could do. "Even when I was crying, I prayed for strength and concentrated on doing my job to the best of my ability, and I continued to do it," I answered. "That's what you have to do, pray and concentrate. Remind yourself that you are there to do a job and do it. Focus on the task and ask yourself what do I need to do next?"

He answered in anger, "I'm supposed to be rescuing somebody but there's no 'body' left to rescue!"

Just then, he let out a gut-wrenching moan and shrieked, "Oh my God!"

I screamed into the phone, "What's happened now?"

"Mom, I just looked down and there are fragments of other people's skin on my arms!" Then he broke into sobs. His heartbreak seeped into my heart and I cried with him.

My mind tried to think of something else to say to comfort or help him. I reminded him repeatedly that even when we can't see it, God is in control. I also reminded him that this life is not the only life we will ever have.

After an entire night of talking, "pray for the strength and do what you have to do to the best of your ability," was the only sound advice I had to offer. After all is said and done that is all we can ever do. Lee went back to finish the gruesome job.

The advice I gave him that night will help him through anything. Lee now knows he can get through any crisis by praying for strength and doing what he can to the best of his ability. That is all I could ask of my son. That was the best advice I had to give.

In the aftermath, I worried that such a horrible experience would scar my son for life. It didn't. In fact, he is a better man for having done such a tough task in a terrible situation. While I wished he had been spared that tragedy, he became a stronger person because of it. He has a deeper appreciation for his life and the people in it. He cherishes each day and he takes nothing for granted.

Lee and I are still miles apart. Yet, we are closer in heart and spirit because of a night spent talking on the phone, sharing tough times.

~Joyce Seabolt

Bank Owned

Where thou art—that is home.
~Emily Dickinson

I've lost my home. The home I bought, cherished, loved.

It now stands vacant. The bare picture windows stare out like hollow eyes. A bank owned sign sticks crudely in the overgrown, yellow lawn. The flowers I planted and watered religiously wilt, hanging low as if weeping.

Indentations in the carpet reveal the outline of furniture, of a life, of a family. Putty and paint cover the holes in the walls where pictures once hung.

Even though the house is empty, images flood my mind of a time when it was filled with life.

On the driveway, we showed our son how to ride a bike. In this house, both kids started school, learned to read and write. We taught our son to tie his shoes, and for several horrific months went through potty-training our daughter.

Since it was our first home, we set right out to decorate, make it our own. My arm still aches from painting my son's bedroom walls a bright blue that needed three coats before it stopped appearing streaky. I remember the plans to paint my daughter's room pastel pink that never came to fruition.

Many injuries and bruises accumulated over the years. There's the time my daughter tried to climb on top of her dresser and it fell over on her. Luckily, she wasn't badly hurt. Or the time my son fell off his bike and scraped his knee.

I remember the excitement about having a master bedroom with our own bathroom and walk-in closet. Many fond memories are associated with the room I shared with my husband. The room we talked in, embraced in, laughed in, loved in.

I'll never forget the time we found a lizard slithering through our hallway. I screamed and jumped up on a chair. My husband caught it and it became the family pet. I wonder now where Ben Casey went after we let him loose in the backyard. I'm sure he misses the excitement and noise back there since now there is only silence.

My heart hurts as we drive away from the house, leaving it in the dust like nothing more than a distant memory.

Behind me my kids' chatter fills the back seat. My husband at my side threads his fingers through mine. It's then that I realize I haven't truly lost my home. My home is not a structure with four walls and a roof. It's not something that can be bought or sold. My home is not the place I live. It's the people I live with. The people right here in this car.

My family is my home.

~Amber Garza

On My Own

In time of test, family is best.
~Burmese Proverb

The doctors had bad news. It wasn't their grim expressions as much as the nurse they had brought with them to talk to me. She was young and obviously new at being present when bad news was delivered to the family. She was scared and I remember feeling bad for her. Afterwards I don't remember anything else about that nurse; I don't remember if she tried to comfort me or not as the doctors told me that my thirty-five-year-old husband had died from the heart attack that brought him into the emergency room that morning. All I could remember was repeating the same question over and over again: How am I going to raise our sons on my own? I couldn't do it; that was the only thing I knew with complete certainty on that day and for many months afterwards. It was Mother's Day 1999 and I had to call my mother-in-law back home in Louisville, Kentucky and tell her that her oldest son had just died.

The next few days were a blur. We were living in Wichita, Kansas, due to a promotion Rick had received with his company. Both of our families were in Louisville, and I waited with my friend Edie for the arrival of my mom and aunt and Rick's parents. Rick's manager had come over to pick up our boys that morning and I had called periodically throughout the day to make sure he was doing okay with them. I wanted to see them but at the same time I was overwhelmed with my emotions, and part of me knew that as soon as I saw them

I would be forced to admit that I was now a single mother and that thought terrified me. Michael was two years old and Nicholas only six months old, and I didn't want to do this on my own.

We brought Rick back to Louisville to be buried and it was decided that the boys and I would move in with my parents temporarily. I needed the help, both financially and emotionally. The bank I was working for had a position in Louisville in their mortgage division, so three weeks after we buried Rick I started my new position. Our temporary living arrangements lasted for five years as I struggled to finish my accounting degree while working full time.

My parents have been a Godsend; they took us in and juggled their roles as parents, grandparents, babysitters, and shoulders to cry on. My Aunt Janet frequently takes vacations with the boys and me, and is one of my best friends. She's always been there to offer her support and serve as a sounding board to me. My other aunts and grandparents have babysat and thrown birthday parties for the boys. My in-laws remained a strong presence in both my sons' lives and mine. My brother, dad, and father-in-law take turns in assuming the dad role when it is Donuts with Dad day at school. My sister-in-law was my saving grace by helping with babysitting for several years and is still always willing to step in if the kids get sick and I can't miss work. Countless friends have also provided their support by taking the kids to sports functions or having them spend the night when they can tell I need a night off.

It does take a village to raise a child. Our journey has definitely been a struggle, but my initial fear of being unable to raise my boys on my own was unfounded. I've not had to raise them on my own; my village and I will continue to raise my sons to be the type of men my husband and I dreamed they would be when we held them in our arms for the first time.

~Holly Sanford

A Child's Gratitude

While we try to teach our children all about life,
our children teach us what life is all about.
~Author Unknown

For four days, I walked around in complete shock. My life had changed in an instant and now I spent most of my hours in a hospital room, worrying about my husband. Little did I know, I would find the gift of gratitude in an unexpected place.

Earlier that day, my husband had pulled out his own respirator. His nurses and other medical personnel in the ICU rushed to his bed, tying restraints on his wrists and stopping him from doing any further damage.

When I came back from lunch and heard what happened, I laughed. The nurse stared at me. "Robbie, he could've really hurt himself."

I laughed more. To me it was the first sign that my husband's spirit was in that body. A body that had flown off a motorcycle, over a guardrail and landed on hard cold ground. A body that had suffered a traumatic brain injury. Four days seemed like four years to me as I watched him, praying that he would come back to me.

Now he was, at least a little. It was just like John to take out his own respirator if he didn't want it.

When I told the case worker that afternoon, she giggled with me. "Well, we like it when patients partner in their own care."

John was still highly sedated and restrained. The few times he woke up it was only for a second. He'd open his eyes and look around, wild-eyed like a crazy person and raise his wrists, obviously trying to get away. Then he'd go back to sleep.

"Mom, when can I see Dad?" My nine-year-old was staying with my brother while John lay in the ICU. I didn't want Noah to see his father with the respirator covering half his face, looking like a strange version of Darth Vader.

But now no respirator covered his face. He still had plenty of tubes and wires and a neck brace, but I decided that my son could handle it. That night, Noah would see John for the first time since the accident.

When some friends brought Noah to the hospital, I pulled him aside and we sat in the waiting room.

"Noah, Dad has lots of tubes and wires in him. He looks swollen, too."

"Okay Mom."

"He will probably sleep the entire time you're there, okay?"

"Okay."

"If he does wake up, it'll just be for a second and he might seem weird."

"Okay."

I breathed deeply and silently prayed. No matter what words I used, seeing his daddy like this was going to shock my boy. I had explained to Noah that John's brain was hurt and we would just have to wait for it to heal. John's accident happened a few days after Noah received a Nintendo DS for Christmas. All Noah could talk about was his new video game system. I was thankful for the distraction. In fact, Noah only asked one question about John.

"How long until he's better, Mom?"

"I don't know, Noah."

It killed me that I couldn't give a definitive answer to our son. He has a black and white, right and wrong personality. The nebulous nature of a brain injury was difficult to explain.

As we entered John's ICU room, he lay peacefully asleep. My

son's face grimaced, but only for a second. He stood still at the foot of his dad's hospital bed.

"Do you want to say hello, Noah? Go up by his head and speak to him."

Noah went around the bed and stood beside John's face.

"Hi Daddy."

John's eyes immediately opened. His crazed look scoured the room, landing on Noah.

"Help!" He cried out in a husky voice, his throat still aflame from pulling out the respirator. "Help!"

Then my husband held up his wrists, tied in restraints, and pulled at them. Again he cried to his son, "Help!"

"John, you're okay, sweetie." I tried to mollify my husband and son at the same time. "Noah, his brain isn't working, you know that, right?"

My son had stepped back when John spoke to him, obviously startled.

John fell back asleep, his body limp once more.

Noah's face began to twist in emotion.

"Noah, do you want to leave now?"

"Yes!" He said and walked to the door.

As we walked down the hall, I tried to give my son perspective.

"It's really good that he opened his eyes when you spoke. He knows your voice, sweetie."

I glanced at my son. Tears were running down his cheeks.

"Noah?"

He stopped and faced a wall, breathing hard.

"Noah, I'm so sorry. You are very brave, you know that?"

A sob escaped him.

"Do you want to talk about it?"

"No!"

I waited for a moment.

"Honey, I need to know what you're feeling. So I am going to guess what your emotion is and I want you to nod yes or no. Are you scared?"

Noah shook his head no, face still to the wall.

"Are you sad?"

Again, he shook his head no.

I thought about making him giggle. Maybe if I joked with him....

"Noah, what are you, happy?"

My boy nodded yes.

It took me back. A realization hit hard.

"Noah, did you think Dad might die?"

He shook his head yes.

"Those are happy tears?"

My son turned his face and looked at me. "Yes," he whimpered.

As I wrapped my arms around my still sobbing boy, I thanked God for the pure heart of a child and I felt shame for not seeing the depth in my son. In the one place I never thought to look, I found real perspective. Within my nine-year-old boy, I saw what was truly important. Fear and pain had caused me to focus on the immediate questions. Would John be the same man I married? Would he be able to work again? Would I have to support my family?

In that hallway outside of the ICU, my son's tears didn't reflect panic about our future income or terror over the outcome of John's brain injury. His tears told a simple story of gratitude. His daddy wasn't going to die.

Noah watched as John experienced what many called a miraculous healing. Two months later, my husband returned to work, his brain healed. Our son walked with us through a very tough time, and it was he who taught us to choose gratitude.

~Robbie Iobst

Little Soldiers

Happiness is a form of courage.
~Holbrook Jackson

stood and ate a bowl of cereal in my kitchen. The almonds tasted delicious! I was so pleased that I had tried the new flavor. As I looked down into the bowl, a hand came from behind me, covered my nose and mouth, and held tight.

"Shut up! Shut up!" a voice whispered. "Don't say anything or I will kill you!" While his words slithered into my ear, I realized, that along with the unswallowed cereal bouncing around in my throat, I couldn't breathe.

"Don't make a sound!" he said. "I will kill you!"

I buckled my knees, hoping somehow I could move his hand so I could breathe. I was right. He couldn't hold my weight. I inhaled, prompting a cough, and spat out my mouthful of cereal into his hand. He was pissed. A fourteen-inch knife appeared in front of my face.

"Don't make me kill you," he snarled.

The next forty-five minutes of my life were unimaginable. This man, who had been released from prison twelve days before, took the crime that had put him into prison—drugs and weapons—one step further. For minutes that felt like hours, this man raped me and sodomized me, over and over again. While it was happening I felt what rape victims, and other trauma survivors, often describe: a feeling of floating above what is happening, an emptiness, a complete lack of emotion or fear, an all-over numbness, a resolution that death would come and it would be okay.

Over the course of that time, I did whatever my rapist asked me to do. I listened and obeyed while quiet tears fell down my face. During the attack my cousin phoned. Since I didn't pick up, his voice came over the answering machine: "Hi, I am ready to meet for dinner. Where are you? Why aren't you home? Call me." Click.

Help! I wanted to scream. I am here!

As I lay under this awful man, I thought about my cousin's voice. I thought about the act of simply leaving a message on an answering machine. It would be different now. Life had changed. As I lay there, eyes clamped shut, my body in shock, I realized I was in a position to actually look at my rapist. He had flipped me over and we were face to face. I forced myself to open my eyes. I had to look: look closely and memorize. When I think back to that, even at my weakest moment, I found strength. I didn't recognize it then as strength, but now I know. After my eyes gave me the information I needed, I closed them again.

Finally he was done. He had been successful. What then? Would he kill me or let me live? He grabbed my shoulder, dragged me into the bathroom, and pushed me to the floor.

"Get on your knees," he said. This was the moment. Would I live or die? I heard him moving, preparing behind me. Taking the wire cord from an electric clock, he bound my hands behind my back. Then he bound my feet. Then he bound my hands and feet together. He took my bathrobe that hung on a hook behind the door and threw it over my face. He left the bathroom.

In darkness I lay quietly and listened. I heard him ransack my apartment. Pulling drawers, rummaging, swearing, slamming, breaking, ripping. After some time, I heard a door close, and suddenly it was quiet. I listened. I listened harder. Nothing. He was gone. And I was alive.

What comes along with many of life's big moments is a separation between "before" and "after." Since my rape, I have always pictured a glass window. The rapist threw a big stone through me, and

I shattered. Shattered into millions and millions of pieces. Looking down at all those pieces—there was no way I would be able to put myself back together again. No way. How could I possibly do it?

The answer was, of course, that I couldn't. I could not do it alone. What I needed was an army of help. And I got it. Little soldiers in the form of doctors and nurses, rape counselors and detectives, ambulance drivers and uniformed cops, and my family and friends, each of these people came together to help. They brought with them whatever it was that they could offer, and they went to work. They supported me, they taught me, they loved me, they held me, they picked up my phone calls, they gave me books to read, they listened, they cried, and they answered my questions. They held the shards of my soul in their hands, and they pieced me back together using their love. I had no power to resist them, to tell them, "Oh, don't worry! I'll be just fine!" Which is what I would have normally done. Each one, especially my selfless family members and my dear brave friends, lovingly put pieces of me back together. Sometimes I myself could put a piece in, other times, not so much. With often tired, bloodied hands from small cuts of glass, these little soldiers marched on.

I am lucky. I was given the gift of life. So many other crime victims are not. I was also given the gift of immediate help. My journey back from being broken started right away, right after the call to 911. From then on, my little soldiers helped me fight back. They carried me until I could walk. They held my hand until I could walk alone. And slowly, slowly, I found that I could run.

Today I realize I am truly blessed. I am married to a wonderful man. I have two beautiful children. As I go about my life, driving my kids to school and wiping up my dirty counter tops, over and over again, I don't have to look far to glance through an unshattered window and see life all around me.

~Jennifer Quasha

The Miracle of the Golden Pothos

Learn wisdom from the ways of a seedling.
A seedling which is never hardened off through stressful situations
will never become a strong productive plant.
~Stephen Sigmund

The year I graduated from high school, I became sick with an extended illness. It was quite a blow, in more ways than one. Not only did I miss prom and graduation, and all the other traditional senior year activities, but my college plans had to be put on hold. I was in bed for months, and cabin fever conspired to drive me almost as crazy as the illness itself. Sometimes, despite my doctor's constant assurances to the contrary, it seemed like I was never going to get well.

I was lucky. My friends and family all rallied around me, keeping the VCR filled with movies and the bedside table loaded with interesting books. My Uncle Carl, affectionately nicknamed "Unc," was a particular bright spot: he filled my mailbox with comics, very bad jokes, and beautiful photos of the wildlife and flowers around his home. But the best thing Unc ever did was to bring me a cutting of a Golden Pothos plant, somewhat haphazardly set into a cracked plastic seedling pot.

"There you go, young lady," he said, setting the pot down amongst the clutter of magazines and prescription pill bottles that covered my bedside table. "You need something green and growing in your room if you want to get well."

I must admit that I was less than impressed. Over the course of my illness, I'd been given many flowers as get-well presents, from the dandelions picked by my young neighbors next door to the cellophane-wrapped grocery store bouquets my classmates brought. In comparison, the little Pothos cutting looked bleak, to put it mildly, sitting alone in its battered pot with only three limp leaves.

"It's very nice," I said doubtfully, and politely searched for an objection that wouldn't hurt my uncle's feelings. "But I'm not sure I can take care of it, Unc. Cut flowers are one thing—nobody expects me to keep them alive for more than a week or so. But plants are different. And it's not like I have a green thumb under the best of circumstances."

"That's why I brought you this," Unc said cheerfully. "The plant I took this cutting from has been living in a dark corner of my office for years. I figured that if it can survive that, it can survive anything. All you have to do is keep it watered, like this."

He took the carafe of water from the bedside table and carefully gave the cutting a good dousing.

"Oh," he added as an afterthought, "and you have to talk to it, keep it from getting lonely. I think this plant looks like a Brian, doesn't he?"

I was skeptical. I was more than skeptical—I thought my beloved Unc had temporarily taken leave of his senses.

I was sure that by the end of the week, if not that very day, I would be left with a collection of dead leaves. But much to my surprise, Brian persisted in staying alive. Somehow, he even managed to grow, sending out tiny shoots that ripened into truly stunning green and yellow leaves.

On bad days, I would just lie with my head on the pillow and watch the sunshine make ever-changing pattern on his leaves. On good days, I'd water the plant and fuss over him, telling him what a good job he was doing, how strong and beautiful he was becoming. And as Brian's vines grew longer, an interesting thing began to happen. I no longer began to feel quite so isolated, quite so angry at being cut off from college and my friends. Instead I began to feel intensely connected to this tiny slip of a plant, bonded in a way I'd never expected. Eventually I realized that you don't have to go college to learn important things. Brian was teaching me more than any university professor ever could.

Those of you who choose to share your lives with houseplants know exactly what I'm talking about. Tending those tiny, fragile shoots of green teaches us so much. We learn about our own power, how our small actions of watering and fertilizing and yes, affectionate speech, can make a difference from day to day to day.

We learn that the human heart can tangle its affections around the most unlikely objects, just like a Pothos twines around its pot. We learn about mystery, and surprise, because even the most inexperienced indoor gardener often has plants turn out in ways she never expected. Most of all, we learn that almost nothing is truly hopeless, that life has a way of recreating itself and thriving even under the most challenging conditions.

As Brian grew bigger and stronger, so did I. By the time he had outgrown his first pot, I was well enough to be out of bed for short periods. The first thing I did when I was able to stand up again was transplant Brian into a newer, lovely ceramic pot. And by the time that pot had grown too small, I was strong enough to leave my sickroom behind for good. I packed up Brian along with my clothes and my books, and we ventured out into the world together.

It's been more than ten years since my uncle brought me that first fragile start. The original Brian has long since gone to the great greenhouse in the sky, but thanks to the miracle of the Golden Pothos's ability to start over from fresh cuttings, one of Brian's descendants has shared every place I've called home.

Today I have a particularly healthy specimen growing on a stand near my computer, where I can look at it whenever I'm writing and the words refuse to come. Its beauty is a constant reminder not to give up, that life may change drastically but always continues.

And when I look, I wonder if my Unc had any idea what he was really doing when he snipped a four-inch section of plant and stuck it in a pot to cheer up his favorite niece.

I imagine that he did.

~Kerrie R. Barney

Chapter 3

Tough Times, Tough People

Silver Linings

Clouds may come, but clouds must go, and they all have a silver lining.
For behind each cloud you know, the sun, or moon, is shining.

~Author Unknown

Endings Are Beginnings

In three words I can sum up everything I've learned about life: it goes on.
~Robert Frost

Seven years ago, I was living in a cushy little bubble... luxury condo on the Upper East Side of Manhattan, a beautiful little boy attending private school, a successful Wall Street husband, nannies, a driver, a housekeeper and all the so-called "comforts." It appeared picture-perfect. It all came to an abrupt halt one morning, when I received a call that my husband, a prominent investment advisor, had been arrested for securities fraud.

Simultaneously, our bank accounts were frozen, our assets were seized and our salacious story of demise was being played out in the media like a soap opera. I remember the terror of standing before the ATM at the bank unable to access even a dollar. I was left with whatever funds could be found in my wallet.

Within days, stories of blackmail and extramarital affairs were revealed in the newspapers. Court-appointed trustees were suddenly marching through our home, taking an inventory of personal items. Realtors were lined up to confiscate and sell our apartment. My life had been flipped over as it went from literally one extreme to another overnight. Suddenly, the perfect picture faded away as if someone was holding a finger on the delete button of my keyboard and in an instant it was gone.

My new reality was filled with lawyers, depositions, court dates, accusations and assumptions as certain friends and business associates faded away. My new life left me bare, raw and exposed. I was forced to take a good look at myself in the mirror.

During the drama, I stood by my husband with the staunch determination of a protective Mama Bear. I believed him and believed that it was my job to support him through this no matter what. Initially I was angry with all the lawyers, judges, clients, employees and even friends who challenged me—I felt under attack and victimized. I ran on adrenaline.

Anxiety and fear permeated the air around us. Fear is a vice grip that will ultimately manifest physically within you. There are no coincidences in life—listen to a headache, a backache, difficulty sleeping, low energy, etc., and ask yourself, "What's really going on here? What am I truly afraid of?" My stress was so traumatic that I entered into premature menopause before my fortieth birthday. All I wanted to do was crawl back into the comfort of my bed, pull the 600-thread count Frette duvet over my head and wake up realizing that this was some bad dream. I had entered a new reality. My grandmother used to tell me, "God never gives you more than you can handle." There were many days I felt as if I was teetering on that brink.

I ended our seven-year marriage, my husband was incarcerated, and I was left to raise our son with no child support. I didn't see the gift in it all when I was forced to move home to live with my parents at forty-one years old and commute by train daily with my kindergartener, one and a half hours each way, so that he could complete his school year and I could work from a friend's office. It was a humbling experience for my ego. Initially it was difficult for me to accept support from friends and family, let alone money. I had much to learn.

When I finally opened myself to receiving, I assumed a new role of victim with great fervor. It was easier for me to blame others for what had happened in my life than to look inward and ask myself what opportunity this was presenting. I had become a victim, and went from one extreme of never wanting to speak about my story to the other extreme of telling anyone who would listen—as if those events defined me. Victims are stuck. Their feet are firmly planted in self-pity, preventing their ability to move forward.

The truth is that we all have an inner voice to help us navigate life's paths. We know when we are honoring this voice and we know how to hide when we don't want to hear it. I always say, you can sweep your troubles under the rug, but eventually you will trip over them. We may not understand why everything is happening to us at any given moment, but we can have a willingness to approach it from another angle.

I had a burning desire within me to forge through this, to not stay bound to this place of utter despair. My paradigm shift did not come easily; they never do. Therapy, energy healing, self-help books, kinesiology, horoscopes, yoga and candles... I was receptive to anything that would facilitate this shift. By calling forth the virtues in each of these, I facilitated healing. I am no longer hiding from my intuition, my heart and my inner voice, forces that I had previously denied or not fully acknowledged. I no longer see myself as a victim.

The purpose of sharing this is not to exploit my drama, but rather to celebrate the gifts that emerge if only you have your eyes open and your heart prepared to receive them. There is an "ah ha" moment when the lights go on. We are never quite familiar with ourselves until we are brought to our knees. Looking back, I realize that I needed to experience the deconstruction in order to prepare for the reconstruction of my life.

Clichés are clichés for a reason. They speak of Universal Truths. "That which doesn't kill you makes you stronger." Amen. But first you must choose; choose to explore what brought you to the crossroads; choose to take a step back with the willingness to look at things differently; choose to recognize the gifts around you. Once I opened my eyes, these gifts were everywhere, in all forms, in all sizes. My happiness was not found in the bricks and mortar of a luxury apartment that I had previously placed so much emphasis upon. I have chosen to see what I have gained, not what I have lost. Although my bank account may be small, my life is abundant.

And now... seven years later, I find myself in a crazy little farm house nestled into the mountains of a small town with the happiness that my previous life did not hold. Stories always have a beginning, a middle, and an ending... but I am only in the midst of my life. All endings give way to new beginnings. I know that had I not gone through all that I did, I could not have arrived at this moment — so I am profoundly grateful for the ride. I am now in the relationship I have waited my life to find. My little boy is thriving. There is a peace within our family and home that transcends any financial reward. I am still working on my personal financial recovery. Don't get me wrong, I miss my money, but I am no longer a passenger in the back-seat of my car. I am the driver, my eyes are open and I am account-able for my actions. It is a wonderful journey.

~Kristen Eberhard

Seeing the Rainbows

The only way to see a rainbow is to look through the rain.
~Author Unknown

When my husband's deployment orders ended in 2007, our small family found itself without a job for the very first time—and with a very new baby.

We put out resumés and my husband applied to every possible place he could think of, regardless of locale. He took a job across the state—more than four hours away—and we began making preparations.

We cleaned our home in record time and virtually lived out of suitcases as the "For Sale" signs were pounded into our lawn. We tried to leave no trace of living in our home because we knew that at any moment we could be asked to leave for showings. We said goodbye to our friends and family, and prepared for more heartache and distance. We were leaving our entire family behind.

Then something magical happened—our prayers were answered, and in the nick of time! We had another job offer! And it was local. We wouldn't have to move after all! Everything seemed perfect, like it was all falling into place.

With great enthusiasm, we uprooted the real estate signs and began planning our life again. This new job paid much less than the previous job, but we had enough in savings to last until the raise he'd been promised came. Things were going to be just fine!

Until they weren't, of course.

Within months, our savings were depleted and things had changed in the company. The money we'd been holding out for was no longer something we could count on. With a slow job market, we began to prepare as things began to get worse. My husband and I pored over our finances and marked off anything we could live without, including our home phone and television service.

Despite the cuts, finances were still extremely tight. So, we borrowed some tools and planted a small garden in our backyard. We planted the vegetables we knew we would no longer be able to afford at a supermarket. We began looking to trade our services for other goods or services we might need.

Meal planning and coupon cutting took up more and more of my time as I calculated meals that could feed our family for less than $1.50 per serving and compared prices between the two local grocery stores. Gas became precious and was only used as a means of getting to and from work. Entertainment had to be creative because we could no longer afford to pay someone else to entertain us.

Everything seemed to be spiraling downhill quickly—and then our insurance stopped. I researched natural alternatives, things I could grow in our garden or find in nature, to alleviate our smaller medical troubles. It felt as if Murphy's Law had swooped down on us and everything that could go wrong was going wrong.

We continued sending our prayers up, hoping for a break somewhere along the way, hoping we'd find a way to pay the electricity before they came to cut it off again.

As the days passed, nothing seemed to change. We were barely getting by. But as my hands dug into the rich soil, uncovering the rooted vegetables as they peeked through, I knew there was something different. I watched as my daughter, who had just learned to walk, tottered down the rows of our family garden and stooped over a bucket to fill it with lettuce leaves, and I smiled. Indeed, nothing on the outside had changed. But it was because God was changing us on the inside first.

What at first seemed like a tragedy for our family turned out to be what forced us to change for the better.

Sure, we no longer had television service, but instead we cuddled together by the campfire in the backyard or we chased bubbles on the patio. We could no longer afford to go out to eat with our friends or to the movies, but now we spent our time hiking together and exploring the local parks. We were no longer cooking quick frozen meals. Instead, we were eating carefully prepared, healthy meals with fresh vegetables from a garden. A garden that taught two adults who thought they knew it all and a little girl who found even the worms and ants exciting.

We had prayed for change, and change is what we got. It just took us a little more time to recognize the blessings bestowed upon us. We just needed a little more faith to see the rainbows through all the rain.

~Ashley Sanders

Bitter Sweet

When it is dark enough, you can see the stars.
~Ralph Waldo Emerson

"I'm not saying you are going to die within the year, but I am saying you may not live to see your children grow up." I am in a chair listening. I am thinking about my four young children. My surgeon is talking. We are discussing my prognosis and my pending surgery. My fortieth year is spinning into a mid-life crisis where everything is hitting the fan. Cheerful by nature, I find I am not my perky self.

When I see my first ever mammogram, the sprays of white stars with two dense clusters, tumors that look like a couple of suns against a black night sky, I am intrigued that cancer can look so pretty. I can see the concern on the faces of the people who have to give me the news and their angst that I have come alone. I have come for the test knowing I probably have breast cancer. My local doctor was convinced—my husband, still hopeful, was not.

Whatever the diagnosis, I wanted to be able to deal with cancer privately, matter-of-factly. But like every human, I have many roles: wife, mother, sister, daughter, friend, neighbor. So my drama became public domain—a genuine blessing to have so many souls who care but a real burden to shoulder their fears for me.

Leaving my surgeon's office, I hope retail therapy will cheer me. I wander a store and consider buying shoes. "They may as well be cheap since who knows how long I'll get to wear them!" The thought makes me laugh at myself. I think about the old man who jokes about not buying green bananas anymore. I rarely allow myself the indulgence of patheticness.

I call my husband. He is stoic. We will get through this.

I think about my children. I remember I gave birth to three of my four kids without intervention — no drugs, happy gas, or epidural — my body having it out with nature, my sweet supportive husband there, the midwife to guide. I took hours of labor one moment at a time. Somehow this comforts me. I know I can be tough. My words to cling to: "This too will pass..." and my favorite quote by an inspired religious leader: "We are asked to drink of the bitter cup, but not become bitter ourselves."

I determine to live without regret. Leaving my young family motherless is the source of my greatest fear and the source of my greatest inspiration to survive. They are my anchor.

During my chemo treatments, my five-year-old tells me a child in her class said, "One day your mom will fall over and never get back up again." Odd how many people also told me sad stories. I am truly grateful to the wise generous souls who choose to share survivor stories. Those are the helpful ones. Not that I am averse to reality, but hope is a necessary reality for healing.

I tell my five-year-old that if anything should happen to me, she has plenty of people to love and watch over her. I realize she got the point when she says, "Yeah, you could die but that's okay, I'd be alright...."

This was the same child to whom I gave a pair of scissors a couple of months earlier and told to have fun cutting my hair. I had long hair — I had it cut short before it fell out so the change would not be so dramatic. I figured I might as well go even shorter, so I wore a surprisingly cosmopolitan do, given by a five-year-old, for a week. With short hair falling out, I then shaved it all off. There is something liberating about taking the tiger by the tail, before the tiger pounces.

Cancer made me pause and think about the legacy I would leave my children. I created a children's book for them. One I wished someone had given to me. A friend suggested I publish it. I felt shy about it — a cancer survivor writing another cancer book. But I did publish it and I am grateful that through it I have been able to help others. Who would have thought cancer would open this avenue to me? I had always wanted to write children's books. I am embracing the silver lining.

These days, so grateful to be in remission, when I visit my oncologist for checkups, I pass the chemo room. My heart aches for the people in those chairs. I remember being there, feeling like I was being immersed in a pool of bleach.

I think back to the elderly gentleman I overheard kindly but firmly decline more chemotherapy, the nurse pleading with him to try another regime. I think of him because later he turned to me and asked sincerely how I was doing, and I felt his compassion, his sincere hope for the best for me. We shared a bitter cup but he offered me sweetness. His grace was amazing.

Thinking about him reminds me of what tough times can do for our souls.

~Linda McCowan

Downshifting

*Joy is what happens when we allow ourselves to recognize
how good things really are.*
~Marianne Williamson

A Harvard professor calls it "downshifting,"
That noble or necessary slashing,
Of the luxuries, the soft and velvety excesses,
Those swollen, insatiable appetites of the "me generation."
But the pork bellies are all shrunken and emaciated now.
The debt outweighs what we earn and,
Only one of my three small children has any college savings.
So I downshift.
I drive past Starbucks,
And settle for the memories of expensive meals,
Seasoned so perfectly I swooned in that moment,
When the spoon met my tongue.
I blow a mournful kiss to those gentle waiters,
Who smiled and asked,
"May I take your coat?"
"Would you like something to drink?"
"Is there anything else I can get you?"
I shimmy into last year's bathing suit,
(It's a little tight after twelve months of obliging waiters.)
And take the smoke filled el train instead of driving downtown.
At home, the thermostat holds firm at sixty-five degrees,

Even when the temperature outside plunges below zero.
Inside the cheaper grocery store, I choose generic beans and,
Half a pound of ground beef to make a chili.
We'll eat the leftovers tomorrow and maybe even the next day.
The adults in our family don't exchange Christmas gifts this year.
We're all grown up now.
And maybe the kids don't need so many after-school activities.
Because,
I hear bursts of laughter upstairs as they reenact scenes,
From the musical Annie.
I'm standing in a stripe of sunlight and,
Folding the last of the laundry.
I pause and press a sweet scented towel to my chest.
They are singing, "It's The Hard-Knock Life"
Followed by the peal of giggles.
It dawns on me then,
Drama class costs $355 per child.
And oh my, the joy of no carpool!
Also —
When I take the el train, I get to read,
Whole chapters of library books,
Uninterrupted!
And while I am visiting the bright side,
My freezing cold floors have prompted the discovery of,
Blissful fuzzy slippers and, after ten years, the warmth of,
My husband's body again,
Necessary now,
Even under our down blanket.
And the truth is,
I still look fine in that bathing suit.
And the stress that once lived between my shoulder blades and
Rode the backside of my neck,
Has faded, along with some of our credit card debt.
The Harvard professor says,
"Downshifters are happier."

They clear out the clutter,
Reject the brand labels—the fancy and the fine.
Focusing on the things that matter,
Like family and stretches of time instead of moments.
Finding the particles and pearls of pleasure,
Of breathing in and out, standing in the sunlight,
Listening to "It's The Hard-Knock Life"
But no longer living it.

~Juliet C. Bond, LCSW

26

Disabled but Not Destroyed

You may not realize it when it happens,
but a kick in the teeth may be the best thing in the world for you.
~Walt Disney

On the outside, I seemed great. I was an attractive, youthful-looking mom with a smiling demeanor, and well liked. I had been divorced for five years and many envied my apparent ability to keep it all together—coaching my children's sports teams, volunteering in the community, working full time, and managing to have a bit of a dating life too. But on the inside, I was literally falling apart and living my life in constant pain.

Because I had long since mastered the art of hiding the hurt, no one knew how serious my condition was. I was in denial about it too. But MRIs, CT scans, X-rays, and nerve conduction studies revealed that my spine, already damaged from scoliosis and two major surgeries, was in far worse shape than I'd imagined. Many ailments, including spinal arthritis and multiple bulging and herniated discs, produced severe upper and lower back pain from which I could find no relief. Pinched nerves caused pain to travel down my legs and arms as well.

On the job, I could neither sit nor stand for long periods and I had a modified workstation so I could do both, constantly changing positions to keep the pain tolerable.

Sleeping through the night did not refresh me. Pain greeted me with its ugly face each morning and sometimes made me cry out in my sleep—I know this because my own cries would rouse me from slumber.

After second and third opinions, I was told there was no surgical cure for a spine as badly degenerated as mine. One disc herniation, maybe two or three, could be surgically helped, but not the multiple conditions I had.

My doctor ordered plenty of bed rest to relieve the toll on my spine, told me to minimize stress in my life, prescribed swimming and physical therapy at least three times a week, and was very emphatic that pain management must become a way of life for me. He recommended books on living with chronic pain and encouraged me to join support groups. He prescribed anti-inflammatory drugs and strong opiate-based painkillers, and advised me to stop working full time and focus on my health. He predicted my conditions would, in fact, worsen with time.

I collapsed in tears as I sat in his office. How could I follow his orders? How could I minimize stress and somehow squeeze three appointments per week into an already packed schedule? Join a support group? How could I stop working full time? There was no way! If I don't work, my children won't have food or shelter. He pointed out, even before I burst into tears, that unrelenting, intractable chronic pain produces clinical depression.

I was a mess and could no longer deny or minimize my conditions. For the next few months, I tried to work swimming therapy into my schedule by going during my lunch break. This proved extremely stressful as I was away from the office longer than the allotted time and would rush back to work in a frenzy, hoping I wasn't missed.

The medications provided a little relief, but they made me drowsy and I had a near fatal reaction to one. I changed medications and was determined to continue living a happy lifestyle, taking care of my children, and going to work every day with a smile on my face despite the constant pain.

Then one day my boss called me into the Human Resources Department. My job had been eliminated as part of a major Reduction In Force. I would still be an employee for the next two weeks, but I was not permitted to enter the building anymore and was promptly escorted to the parking lot without the chance to say goodbye to anyone.

The timing could not have been worse. I was not in any physical condition to begin going on interviews and looking for another job. I had been barely managing this one! Stress multiplied as I worried about my loss of benefits. What would I do about medical insurance for my children? How would I provide for them? I curled up into a ball for a very dark day or two, fearing my ex-husband would try to take my daughters away. Two years earlier, I let my son go live with his dad and new stepbrothers.

I had already lost the marital home and was living in a way-too-small condo. I had lost my health, my job, and I feared losing my daughters too. My lawyers had lost a fight for increased child support and I owed over $10,000, now with no way to pay it. Even love had eluded me as I had not had a significant relationship since my divorce five years earlier.

For a brief period, I lost my smile and wondered what else I could possibly lose? I took inspiration from the Biblical character Job who had lost everything, and remembered that he made it through without losing faith. I had always trusted that my life was in God's hands and I called out of the darkness to God for help and strength. I did not know in what form that help would come, but I knew He heard me.

Because I was still an employee, I was entitled to all the company benefits, including disability, and my doctors quickly submitted the paperwork. After all, they had advised me months back to stop working.

I applied for government disability benefits and went before an administrative law judge and an impartial medical expert. One look at my extensive medical records and test reports, and my application was accepted. I had contributed to a private disability plan while working, which helped bridge part of the gap between my government benefits and the salary I had last earned. I discovered that my company disability package also included extended medical and dental benefits for me and my dependents. This was all good.

I began physical therapy several times a week and re-joined a gym to strengthen my abdominal and back muscles. Gradually, the severity of my pain began to diminish as my body got more conditioned and my core muscles became stronger. I was grateful that I was able to greet my children with fresh-baked cookies or homemade soup when they got home from school.

I started a small business that I could operate from my laptop while I rested in bed. Although it doesn't produce much profit, it keeps my mind active. I began writing an upbeat humor and inspiration column for a local newspaper. I took art classes and found that producing artwork for class projects became a form of therapy, providing a distraction from constant pain.

The quality of my life as well as the quality of our family life greatly improved. My children remained in my custody and flourished, making me proud every day. I continued to live frugally, but was able to buy computers, cell phones, party dresses for my daughters, and even take modest vacations.

Over the years the pain became more and more manageable, even though my condition continues to worsen as predicted. I no longer minimize or deny my health situation—instead, I address it.

I am still a busy single mom with a full agenda, but my life is more stress-free than it was before I was laid off. And because I lost my job, I was able to make my health the priority that it should be.

When I first lost my job, I thought it was the worst thing that could happen, but it turned out to be one of the best things that ever happened to me and my family. Being laid off was only a little story within the bigger story of my life. And my life now, although hard, is a very good thing.

~Monica Giglio

RV Summer

A truly happy person is one who can enjoy the scenery while on a detour.
~Author Unknown

I n 1985, when we were living in Tennessee with our three teenage children, the oldest about to become a high school senior, my husband was let go from his job. As a family who was already living paycheck to paycheck, we were blind-sided by the event.

My husband, Don, searched for a new job, but there was very little available in his field of plastics. I remember being very homesick for my siblings back in Pennsylvania and Delaware, and wishing I were closer to them to benefit from their support at this difficult time. My parents had passed away by this time, but my husband's mother still lived in Delaware and offered her help if we needed it.

There were lengthy discussions regarding our options and whether or not the children would acquiesce to moving away from friends and schoolmates if he took a job in another state. We put our house on the market with the idea of returning to family in Delaware. After the house sold, we took some of the money and purchased a large recreational vehicle to take to his mother's home. We knew that we could live in the RV parked in her backyard, if necessary, while my husband found a new job in that area.

Suddenly, the job loss turned into a new adventure for our eighteen-year-old son, Steve, our fifteen-year-old son, Donnie, and thirteen-and-a-half-year-old daughter, Julie. What a fun summer it was as we stopped at various parks along the way, where they could swim and enjoy nature as they never had before!

Things changed, however, when we arrived in Delaware. Steve had begun a relationship with a girl in Tennessee that year, and he seemed so sad most of the time. The three children seemed restless and unhappy. I know they missed the south and their friends and familiar surroundings, and so did my husband and I. Reuniting with my siblings and sharing enjoyable times with them was great, but there was an emptiness inside me that only my beloved South could fill. We all wanted to go back.

When Steve's closest high school friend in Tennessee offered to let him stay with his family and finish his last year of high school there, we allowed him to return. That was when I knew I could not be away from him, living in another state. I was so sad after he was "missing" from our family.

We stayed long enough for Don to check out some job opportunities, and exhaust the options in Delaware. Then we decided in a "family meeting" that we would head back to Tennessee in our RV. The first goal was for Don and me to find jobs—no matter how much of an income reduction we had to accept—get an apartment for a while and save our money, and sell the RV in hopes of getting a house again one day.

We were happy again and hopeful. And we realized we had to enjoy that RV while we owned it. We made trips to the Atlantic Ocean and let the children see it for their very first time! I will never forget the image of Donnie in the water, jumping the waves hour after hour. It was so hard to get him out of that water because he was in absolute ecstasy! He truly loved the ocean. Julie enjoyed just sitting on the beach, soaking up the sun and sounds of the surf. The ocean was my very favorite place to be, and I was so pleased my children could finally experience that in their lives!

We traveled south and stayed at RV parks in Virginia and North Carolina. The beautiful Smoky Mountains soothed our anxieties about the future, and I gathered grapevine at one woodsy park and made wreaths. Our children swam in campsite pools, hiked the woods, built fires at night, and absolutely loved every minute of our vagabond existence that summer. We watched hang gliders dive from a mountainside at one campground, but were all too chicken to try it!

I know if it were not for the RV summer we enjoyed, the whole "out of work" ordeal would have been much more traumatic for the children. The difficulties of feeling unsettled and uprooted were appeased by the perpetual "vacation" atmosphere in the RV.

Needless to say, the story has a happy ending! We lived in an apartment in Tennessee for approximately a year with our two younger children. Because the apartment had just two bedrooms, our older son stayed in the home of his closest high school buddy just a few blocks away, and they graduated from high school together. We were blessed to have such generous and helpful friends during an unsettling time. The RV eventually sold, and the money from the RV was our down payment for a house the following summer.

It was truly a blessing that we were able to again reside in our beloved state of Tennessee, with many wonderful memories of our RV summer!

~Beverly F. Walker

Humor + Faith = Recovery

We are all in the gutter, but some of us are looking at the stars.
~Oscar Wilde

By the time Hurricane Ike came ashore, 2008 already had been a difficult year for my family.

In May, at age fifty, my mother suffered a severe case of mononucleosis, an ailment most people experience by their late teens. Like many ailments, "mono," as the virus is usually called, is worsened with age, leaving Mom to use a month of sick leave in an effort to recover. Little did we know, then, how the term "recovery" would take many different forms prior to the year's end.

In June, a week after Father's Day, my dad passed away at the age of sixty-one. Dad's death, while somewhat expected given the multitude of his ailments, was still a surprise. After all, are we ever really ready to say goodbye? Granted death is not an easy process for anyone to accept, but my father's passing was especially difficult for me.

On a balmy Sunday afternoon, I had been talking with my father about a baseball game and our plans for the future. Three hours later, Dad was gone, the victim of a massive heart attack. It was a reality check for me, recognizing how precious and brief our stay on this earth can be.

Over the years, thanks in part to my own life's adversity and the obstacles I had to overcome as a premature infant, I thought I understood the meaning of faith and the strong will to survive. It took Hurricane Ike, the third blow in an already trying year, for me to fully appreciate the beauty of our individual strength and a human's motivation to recover.

Mom had a two-week vacation at the end of the summer. The vacation was something Mom pre-planned in February, and she made it quite clear the break was going to be devoted to "small household repair and reorganization."

During those weeks, spanning the end of August and beginning of September, Mom and I spent quality time together, straightening, cleaning, and re-beautifying the inside of our home.

Near the end of her vacation, with all of our "goals" met, we marveled over our accomplishments: the sweet smell of fresh lavender paint in our home's front hallway; the varied aromas from burning candles purchased during a respite in our cleaning mission; and the restored neatness of our upstairs, thanks to plastic storage bins and shelving units.

While we celebrated this small success, we kept an eye on the Gulf of Mexico. Hurricane Ike was forming and preparing to change our lives and the landscape of our region forever.

Ike formed off the coast of Africa on September 1st, which was Labor Day. While we in Southeast Texas enjoyed our holiday and our final barbecues of the summer, we were oblivious to the fact that Ike would cause months and likely years of "labor" for the residents of our region.

By September 7th, the "eyes of Texas" were watching Hurricane Ike more closely and making the typical mad dash for last-minute hurricane supplies. Two days later, as Ike continued his path across the Atlantic and into the Gulf of Mexico, both gasoline and ice were in high demand and short supply.

On September 10th, Mom's vacation ended and she returned to her role as a nurse at the University of Texas Medical Branch (UTMB) in Galveston. By the time Mom left for work, we were becoming more nervous at our home in Texas City, fifteen miles inland from the Gulf of Mexico's coastline.

While Mom worked, I carried the swimming pool furniture and other possible "hurricane debris" to the garage and noted the eeriness in the air. The sky was so dark that it was nearly black—there were no visible stars—and the air was unnaturally calm. Though the storm was still a little more than two days from landfall, it had become quite clear that tough times were brewing offshore.

In the early hours of September 11th, Mom and I met with our neighbors. Some were planning to ride out the storm in their homes, while others were making final preparations to evacuate. Our community was not planning to issue mandatory evacuations. The decision to stay or leave would be ours alone. At first, we decided to stay.

But that afternoon, Ike made a turn to the east, meaning that the Houston/Galveston area would, at best, be on the more dangerous side of the storm, with the possible storm surge reaching twenty-four feet or higher. Mom and I packed some of our most prized belongings in the van and headed toward the East Texas town of Lufkin.

Hurricane Ike made landfall on Galveston Island in the early morning hours of Saturday, September 13th.

As Ike pushed farther inland, we lost power in Lufkin, and for the next day we worried about the condition of our home. On Sunday, our next door neighbor told us via cell phone that our house had survived well—the windows were intact, and other than a few downed tree limbs, we were okay. Our hopes could not have been higher, but they'd soon be crushed.

A few hours after the good news, we received a phone call from neighbors who reported that our brick chimney had broken, pushed through our roof, and was sitting in our living room, leaving an eighteen by twenty-four foot hole in the roof between our two skylights.

We would not be allowed to return home until September 17th. When we arrived home, our neighbors flocked to our sides to assist us. We opened the front door to find a six-foot tall debris pile in what was once our living room, a blocked stairway, broken banister, and damaged wood paneling.

I ducked under the fallen steel roof beams, walked across pine needles and insulation to the stairs, and then carefully climbed upstairs to the view I'd always loved. I looked toward the skylights and the gaping hole in the roof which showed a beautiful blue sky and fluffy white clouds.

Without hesitation, I exclaimed, "Wow! A third skylight!"

My neighbors could not believe I was making jokes instead of crying, but laughter is always good medicine.

It was with that joke that I knew, given time, everything would be okay. Humor, when added to faith, can equal our individual recovery from any difficult situation.

Hurricane Ike taught me so.

~Jill Eisnaugle

Old-Fashioned Ways

Chop your own wood, and it will warm you twice.

~Henry Ford

We named it the year that wasn't — wasn't good, that is. The dog died. We buried him in the backyard and cried like babies instead of acting like the stalwart adults we knew we should be. Then the central air conditioning and heating unit went out. The repairman said it couldn't be fixed; it would have to be replaced. A quick overview of our savings showed us that we had barely enough to purchase a new one. Then my husband lost his job. When education budgets get cut, those with the highest salaries usually go first. It doesn't matter that you are two years from retirement.

We were stunned. Although I also worked, my job alone would not pay our bills. Should we use the little bit of savings that we had to replace the heating unit or hang onto the money, in case we needed those funds for car payments and all-important "incidentals" like groceries? I decided that I liked eating, and my husband concurred. So what would we do about staying warm during the approaching winter months?

Our house is what my grandmother would have called "old-fashioned." We have wooden floors, high ceilings, and a main hall that separates one side of the house from the other. A wood-burning stove sits in a spot central to that hall. I am sure that at one time, the previous owners of the house must have used the stove to heat the entire 2,600 square feet. But could we?

We called a chimney professional to inspect the stove. Having it pronounced "safe to use" launched us into trial-and-error mode. There are no gas starters in old-fashioned stoves. We had to learn to build a fire the Boy Scout way—twigs, paper, and kindling in a sort of teepee, and then a log perched on top so that the air could circulate beneath it as it heated up. After several attempts, we had our first roaring fire. The next step was to get more firewood. We reasoned that we could buy cords of firewood. But if we could cut our own, we would save even more money. After checking with a local policeman, we learned that we could cut up fallen trees along the roads near our house. That required a chainsaw, but my husband's birthday wasn't too far away; so we asked family and friends for gift cards to the hardware store to purchase the saw.

Getting the family involved evoked a lot of curiosity and several e-mail exchanges. They were a little amused at first, imagining my husband in his Paul Bunyan role. But then when we saved $100 on our monthly power bill, they all took deep breaths and started thinking of other old-fashioned ways that we could save money.

My daughter suggested that we go through the closet and check the care instruction tags on many of the items that I routinely sent to the cleaners. Some of them said "can be hand washed," so we made a list: red blouse, brown skirt, blue knit top, etc. At the top, I wrote, "Wash by Hand." Some of our sweaters were even washable! At the end of one month, I checked our budget. We had cut our dry cleaning bill in half.

A friend suggested that we have a fall garden. We found a spot on the screened-in porch that was somewhat protected from the wind and used two large flower pots to plant a few veggies. I'll admit that it did take a bit of attention, covering them when the nights' temperatures dipped; but it was worth it.

A neighbor gave us two cats. They took care of any unwelcome visitors in, under, and around the house, and we were able to cancel exterminating services. That saved us another small chunk each month. And though we knew we were spoiling them a little when we occasionally gave them table scraps, we felt better about not wasting any leftover food.

We also decided that since there are just two of us, we didn't need to use the dishwasher, opting instead to wash dishes by hand. To save money, I was cooking more at home, with fewer drive-through stops at local fast food restaurants. That, together with our home-grown vegetables, provided the means to eat healthier as well as to cut the budget in yet another way.

All my husband's wood chopping was death on the socks he wore with his Paul Bunyan boots. I surprised myself when I offered to darn them instead of rushing right out to buy him new ones. I wasn't exactly sure how to do it. But I remembered my grandmother putting something inside the sock to make it stretch out, then sewing thread crisscross over the hole until she closed it. And yes, mending by the fire does create a rather nice picture for the memory section of the brain. So does reading to each other, snuggled by the fire. The year that "wasn't" was becoming the year that "was."

It is almost springtime. In years past, I would have headed to the garden center to purchase plants for the flower beds. But this year, my husband and I rode down the roads where he had cut wood in the dead of winter. There — among those same fallen trees — were volunteer wild flowers peeking out to test the warmth of the sun. Having traded his saw for a shovel, my husband dug up flowers to transplant into my flower beds. They've never looked lovelier.

My husband was offered a job at a local college. We are elated. But we are not going to abandon our "new" old-fashioned ways. We did go through some of our savings, so retirement had to be put off a few years. The change in our lifestyle will help us accumulate extra dollars each month that can go back into that fund. We'll start a spring vegetable garden and continue washing dishes by hand. And we'll chop, split, and haul wood to prepare for the winter. But the best part of it all is that we are healthier. In fact, we both lost five pounds. We didn't go to the spa or join a health club. We just worked hard. And we slimmed down and toughened up—you guessed it—the old-fashioned way.

~Elaine Ernst Schneider

30

Better than a Tent

Other things may change us, but we start and end with the family.
~Anthony Brandt

Rain dripped from our noses as we attempted to make sense of the three-room-castle that was to be our new home. Unmarked tent poles and the onset of the night sky fed our irritation, and the only words between my husband and I were heated ones. Our toddlers' muffled screams called to us from the back of our soon-to-be-repossessed SUV. They had been strapped in car seats for nearly nine hours, yet I could do nothing.

With a new diving job in Baltimore the following morning, Tim had desperately wanted to call it a night at a cheap hotel, yet I refused. One night of comfort equaled three nights in the woods, which were already paid. Wasting that money was just not an option.

The few hundred dollars we carried were the result of a yard sale held at our old home near Pittsburgh. Everything acquired in our four years of marriage slipped away for pennies. Our confused girls watched their toys and beds being carried off by strangers. One tightfisted woman asked for two pieces of girls' clothing for twenty-five cents, instead of fifty. Tim laughed, yet agreed. Had she only known that we were essentially homeless, maybe she would have been ashamed. We left our newly bought home, never to see it again, with enough money for the first two weeks of camping, a few tanks of gas and a cooler full of bread, peanut butter and hot dogs.

After a long, wet hour and a snub from the park host, we looked at the structure before us and sighed. Despite the leftover rods, it was shelter. Eager to eradicate memories of the day, we opened the zippers and peered inside. What we found were three inches of water covering the entire floor.

Eventually, the girls were brought into the soggy tent; delighted to be free from their seats. We, on the other hand, were anything but happy as we realized just how bad things had become. Our entire life together had been compressed into two baskets of clothes, a cooler of food, a few stuffed animals and a safety box with important paperwork. Our beautiful beds had turned into a queen-size air mattress for us and a twin-size one for the girls. After filling them with our exhausted breath, we finally nestled under the blankets and accepted our new home.

Every day during our six weeks of unorthodox living, the girls and I searched empty campsites for abandoned firewood. They saw it as a game; I saw it as saving money. Ridiculously small logs cost a dollar apiece, all of which were unusable anyway due to constant rain. When we were fortunate enough to have fire, we feasted on hot dogs and potatoes. On rainy nights, without the flames to feed and entertain us, we could only chew mindlessly on peanut butter and jelly. Even still, some days were worse. Although an inexpensive commodity, bread was often scarce, as we had an ongoing battle with the squirrels. Even after putting everything into the tent, the determined creatures dug a hole under the flooring directly to the bread. They came in large numbers during our afternoon naps, and mocked us with their scratchy voices as they carried off the peanut butter.

The thunderstorms were the worst aspect of our living arrangement. Unable to sleep, we listened to the terrifying cracks of lightning hitting just beyond our fabric walls. Numerous times we were forced to evacuate at midnight. Whether or not we would have a place to return was uncertain.

Despite our flimsy walls, we had what mattered the most—our family. After a six-month separation and consequential financial ruin, my husband and I remained together. Our home was foreclosed and Tim lost his job. He grew thin, too stressed and financially strapped to eat right. Our older daughter became physically ill from depression and began therapy, all while attorneys demanded money. With a new job in Baltimore, we saw our chance to begin again, with nothing but our love and terrible credit.

As weeks passed, we desperately tried to think of a plan. We couldn't camp during winter, yet we couldn't afford rent prices averaging twice our old mortgage. The only thing we could come up with was a much modified version of our dream, and so, we went to the bank. To our surprise, our credit scores had yet to reflect the foreclosure and we were approved for a small loan. After seeing an ad in the paper, we set up an appointment to see a possible new home.

The final morning in our tent was the most dreadful storm yet. At four A.M., we threw our soaked belongings into the car, a smaller vehicle given to us by Tim's father after the SUV was repossessed. After a long drive, complete with our daughter's car sickness, we arrived at the marina smelling like vomit and looking like wet, homeless cats.

The sight of the twenty-seven-foot 1983 Tiara was incredible. Even a small boat was so much more appealing than a fabric enclosure. More importantly, we had always wanted to live aboard, although we imagined it a bit differently. Regardless, it was what we had wanted, and to say that we were excited would have been an understatement.

The cabin space had a forward bed that doubled as a couch and the aft cabin was plenty big enough for two small children to sleep and play. Despite a few minor plumbing leaks and the ridiculous expressions of the owners when we stated that we were going to live aboard, we wanted it. Their opinions didn't matter, as they knew nothing of what we had endured to get there.

Without our separation, Tim and I would never have reconnected. Losing everything forced us to see what really mattered. Because of a lost job, we were forced to move where we couldn't afford an apartment. Every seemingly bad turn brought us closer to a lifestyle that we would never give up for one on land. We are happier and more connected in our small space, even with the laughs that go along with an old boat. Our girls' smiles prove it. Sitting in our marina on the South River, with friendly faces all around, we finally feel at home. Although we have yet to officially change the name of our boat, the choice is obvious. It is "Better than a Tent."

~Deanna Lowery

Tough Times, Tough People

The Power of Positive Thinking

Once you replace negative thoughts with positive ones, you'll start having positive results.

~Willie Nelson

31

Going For Broke

Though no one can go back and make a brand new start,
anyone can start from now and make a brand new ending.
~Author Unknown

I push again, hard, and the door to the courthouse grunts open. Inside, the security man brusquely asks for ID. He peers at my driver's license, narrowing his eyes.

Room 173 is just around the corner. A sign outside the door warns, "No waiting in the hall while court is in session."

I open the door and lights flicker on in the empty room. The only décor is a white sign on the wall with blaring red letters, "The FBI prosecutes bankruptcy crimes." I lower my head, feeling like a child who has trespassed, and sit in one of the rows of freestanding metal chairs. My breathing is shallow.

The door opens and I look up, hoping to see my attorney, Erlene. It's a young couple, the man with a round face, close-cropped black hair, and soft frightened eyes and the woman with glossy ash-blond hair, looped into an awkward bun, looking determined and strong. We flash quick smiles, the woman and I, then look away.

I never thought I would be sitting in such a room. I pay my bills on time and rarely spend beyond my means. I do not have credit card debt. Yet this long ago loan from a bad business decision has hovered over the last decade of my life, growing so large that finally bankruptcy became my only sensible option.

The door opens and Erlene enters, smiling and radiating calm.

The woman with her has spiky brown hair, sharp features, thick make-up, and the hint of a dimple in her lower cheek. Erlene introduces me to Kathy, her other client today.

The bankruptcy court trustee enters, trailed by his assistant. The trustee is an attorney with an expertise in bankruptcy law. Both settle their laptops and briefcases on the long wooden table at the front of the room.

The trustee summons the couple. I clench my hands, my fingernails digging into my palms.

She was injured in a hit and run accident, she tells the trustee.

"Were you able to get the license plate of the person who hit you?" the trustee asks.

"No sir." She sits up straighter. "We had medical bills. Then we had a baby and things went downhill from there." Her voice breaks.

I bite my lip, thinking of this hardworking man and woman, felled by a careless driver and an unfair health care system. More than half of the almost million people who file personal bankruptcy each year have overwhelming medical bills. I think of all the people across the country who are in the same kind of meeting room, going through the same process.

Kathy is next. She gives the trustee the sassy smile of a woman who is used to flirting her way out of situations. Her business partner and lover stole money, her money, from their mutual account, she says.

"Have you tried to find him?"

"Oh yes sir, I have tried," Kathy says, her voice sharpening.

"He done her wrong," echoes through my head. My throat tightens. Then it is my turn.

I hand the trustee my ID, swear to tell the truth, and I answer the initial questions.

"So, how did this debt occur?" the trustee asks.

I tell him, briefly, my own "done me wrong" story: an SBA business loan with a partner. When we closed the business, my partner signed a contract promising to pay my part of the loan ($7,500) in exchange for inventory. He never paid and later went bankrupt. The interest and penalties accrued. Years later, I received a letter from the Justice Department. I still remember sitting down, my legs weak, my hands shaking, trying to understand the words—"You owe one hundred thousand dollars. Do not send cash."

When the trustee is finished questioning me, Erlene, Kathy and I leave the room.

Erlene explains that creditors have sixty days to object to the discharge of my debts. If no objections are filed, the court will issue the official discharge on April 1st, April Fool's Day.

When I leave the building, an icy wind hits me and I feel the tears rising up. After twelve years of struggling with this debt, getting legal advice, trying to settle, then hoping to wait it out, learning there was no statute of limitations, searching for the right attorney, then planning for bankruptcy, I am almost free of this burden. My knees buckle and I stand still for the moment, letting the wind brace me.

"It's over," I whisper and then say it out loud. I feel both heavy and light. My freedom has not yet sunk in.

The young couple walks by, their arms hooked together.

She looks back at me and I see the redness rimming her eyes. Even though our lives are probably quite different, I am reminded of how alike we are, how alike we all are. Sometimes our lives unfold easily and we feel strong and successful. Other times, something or someone crashes into us and knocks us off balance. And then, there's simply nothing else to do but stand back up, ask for help, and start again.

~Deborah Shouse

Laughs, Prayers, and Every Bloomin' Thing

Mirth is God's medicine. Everybody ought to bathe in it.
~Henry Ward Beecher

When my husband Bill was diagnosed with a blood cancer, mantle cell lymphoma (MCL), we braved our steepest mountain yet. We had both dealt successfully with tough health issues in the past. We scaled them, learned to live with them, and kept a joyful attitude in spite of them. Could we rally and pull through again? We knew we faced a daunting test of our resourcefulness.

On a late-May day in 2005, we returned home from the oncology appointment reeling from the grim news. A warm, gentle breeze reigned under cloudless soft-blue skies. For gardeners, the day had been perfect for planting. For us, the day produced an onslaught of information about non-Hodgkin's Lymphoma, tests needed to stage the disease, and options for treatment and clinical trials.

Although dazed and devastated, we held onto hope. The long Memorial Day weekend loomed ahead, taxing our patience about the wait for additional tests and results.

After we phoned family and friends, Bill said, "You know, I'm going to do what I'd normally do... plant flowers!"

Bill, the gardener in our household, bought dozens of annuals—petunias, marigolds, vincas—in bright hues. Over the next week, in between appointments, scans, blood draws, and a bone marrow biopsy, Bill pulled on his gardening clothes, put on his hat and gloves, and went outside to plant flowers and tend to the beds.

"I'm planting my victory garden," he told neighbors who stopped to eye his progress. The flowers became beacons of hope, a collage of beauty destined to grow and bloom no matter what our inner states. Bill's blooms of beauty brightened the neighborhood and brightened our daily life, now pared to essential tasks with our energies directed toward Bill's medical treatment and healing.

Over our twenty-five years of marriage, I sometimes called Bill "the smile man." Humor—making others laugh—had been his lifelong trademark. Now, facing cancer and intensive treatment regimens, humor became vital for its healing capacity. After we chose a treatment plan, Bill mused, "I wish we could think of a funny slogan to wear on a badge for my first chemo session."

We bandied about several slogan ideas, then picked our favorite.

On the first day of chemotherapy, we sported badges with our slogan: "Go to Hell, Mantle Cell!" The resulting chuckles in the doctor's office and the treatment center gave Bill a laughing start for treatment, which lasted through the summer and into the fall, culminating with a stem-cell transplant. Bill often told the story about his motto, punctuated with his hearty laughter. We posted our badges in prominent places. Every time I sat at the wheel of my car, I saw it: "Go to Hell, Mantle Cell!" This phrase focused us on the desired outcome. It prompted a prayer for strength and courage to carry on.

Our personal prayers were joined by those of others: family, friends, church and work colleagues, even prayer chains of people we didn't know. Prayers also arose from a surprising source.

One afternoon when we returned home from Bill's chemotherapy, we observed our two cats, a tuxedo named Gilligan, and Tiffy, white with swirling patches of gray and brown, sprawled on a multicolored rag rug on our living room floor. Their fur shimmered from the sunlight spilling in the window. Their heads, with eyes shut, tilted toward the rug. Each cat had one front paw stretched to touch the other's paw. We turned to each other and smiled.

One of us said — we don't remember who — "They look like they are praying." From then on, through the long haul of treatment, we called them the "Purrs and Prayers Team."

Christening our cats the Purrs and Prayers Team distracted us from the rigors of fighting cancer, and centered us on what heals. Drawing strength from people, pets, interests and activities in our everyday environment boosted our spirits and alerted us to not over-look readily available possibilities for comfort and inspiration.

After Bill achieved remission, and qualified for a stem-cell trans-plant, he entered the University of Iowa Hospitals and Clinics in December for the several-week procedure that would last through the holidays. A worrisome time, due to the rigorous procedure and the potential for infection, Bill's Type I (insulin-dependent) diabetes posed yet another risk factor.

We forged ahead, determined to set up a haven for healing. We decorated his room with cheerful holiday decor. We tacked photos of his beloved flower garden, as well as our pets, friends, and family, on the mammoth bulletin board. After Bill's stem cells were harvested, before they were transplanted, he endured a week of daily intensive chemotherapy. After the transplant, we waited for blood counts to rise. Waiting became our job, a rugged test for demonstrating patience and an optimistic outlook.

Even though the extensive transplant regime wore him down, Bill rallied every day to crack a smile and to stimulate laughter by telling jokes and stories. He had help from the "Cuddly Carolers" to provide entertainment for staff and visitors. The three stuffed cats sang "Jolly Old Saint Nicholas" in harmony while turning their head to the music's tempo. Humor gave Bill a positive way to contribute to a healing environment dedicated to the care and treatment of seri-ously ill people.

Every day during the transplant process we heard from friends and family. Visits. Phone calls. Mail. On days when Bill wasn't up to reading, I read the letters, cards, jokes, and stories to him. We felt surrounded by a cloak of prayers and blessings.

Many strategies helped us embrace a healing attitude. We learned that natural strengths, like Bill's gardening and humor, were life-affirming measures. Reframing our sunning cats as the Purrs and Prayers Team reminded us that we could invent healing possibilities. Feeling support from family and friends, and basking in their kindness, buoyed our spirits and cemented our belief in the capacity of community, caring, and compassion to create the critical elements for healing.

Later, after Bill recovered, we wondered how we mustered the tenacity and pluck required to conquer our toughest time ever. How had we weathered the rough terrain? Could we sum up our formula for facing tough times?

The answer came when others asked, "What helped you cope?"

We smiled, then said, "Laughs, prayers, and every bloomin' thing!"

~Ronda Armstrong

Escaping
Domestic Violence

Fear and courage are brothers.
~Proverb

No one was there to respond to my pleas for help. How could this be happening to me? I held my hands over my face to block his blows, but angry fists found their target, leaving bruises on my arms and shoulders, as well as under one of my eyes. My husband straddled my waist, pinning me to the couch as he unleashed his temper in a violent rage.

"I'll teach you to tell me I'm lazy," Danny screamed.

Suddenly, our two-and-a-half-year-old son, Adam, cried out as he stood in the adjacent hallway, watching the beating while tears streamed down his cheeks. My husband finally stormed out into the night, and I consoled Adam and put him to bed.

Danny and I were strongly mismatched from the beginning, and my marriage to him at age twenty resulted from my own rebellion against a loving, but controlling father. My rebellion hurt me most of all. My husband benefited from our union because he had a free ride during our brief marriage. Meanwhile, I made sure our son was well cared for in spite of the problems at home.

Long before we married, my husband had abandoned his given name and tagged himself "Babe" in an apparent attempt to bolster his lackluster athletic accomplishments. In the years I knew Danny, his immaturity didn't allow him to be an athlete of Babe Ruth's stature. The man I knew consistently quarreled with umpires and referees in team sports. In fact, by the time we'd been married a couple of years, he had quit or been ousted from more games than he'd completed. I once looked forward to Sunday afternoon baseball games where I could take Adam and enjoy being outdoors. But, Danny's on-field tantrums eventually caused me to plan other activities for Adam.

As a young adult, my husband lost one job after another. I was the family breadwinner at age twenty-one, while Danny spent most of his days picking up basketball or baseball games at the local gym. When he absolutely had to do so in order to appease me, he would look for jobs and manage within a few days or weeks to lose the ones he could obtain. Sometimes his bosses stated his performance was unacceptable. With other jobs, he faulted management's stupidity and quit. Meanwhile, I paid a babysitter to care for Adam when I went to my secretarial job each day.

In time, I dreamt of someone coming to rescue my son and me from our dismal circumstances. Fortunately, a kind landlord looked on us with compassion when Danny repeatedly told her we would be late with the rent. My salary didn't always stretch far enough to pay our rent on time while also buying food and funding my husband's leisurely lifestyle. As my courage to press him about working grew stronger, he became increasingly angry and threatening to me.

During one such argument, the floor pillows in our living room were easy targets for Danny's wrath. A full-fledged blizzard of white feathers filled the room as he ripped the pillows apart one evening. He screamed obscenities, and my tears flowed like the fountain in the swimming pool below our balcony. After trashing our living room, my husband left in a rage, only to return the next day expecting me to apologize for upsetting him. Thankfully, Adam had not been home during his father's pillow tantrum.

A few weeks later, while we were again arguing about Danny's free-ride attitude, he shoved me against the living room wall. My head flew back and hit the wall hard enough to wake our son, who slept in the next room. The noise and my tears upset Adam on this night, and in Danny's usual style, he flew out of the apartment after yelling at me for questioning his half-hearted employment efforts.

No matter what fate had in store for me, I knew my life wasn't on the right track. Any further evidence I needed came a couple of weekends later when Danny and I again argued about his perpetual laziness. The earlier-described beating followed. I was hurt physically and emotionally, but most of all, I was ashamed to be living in such conditions.

No one at work knew about what was happening in my personal life. When my boss questioned the bruise on my face the next day, I laughingly explained that my son accidentally hit me with a toy truck. My boss probably knew better because he'd been around Danny and observed his cocky attitude, but I couldn't acknowledge the physical abuse to professional people in the office. I invented excuses to avoid my parents for a couple of weeks because my father might have gone after my deadbeat husband with his hunting rifle if he'd known what had happened.

A couple of days after the beating, I had to tell my son "no" about something he wanted to do. Toddlers don't like hearing "no," but this time, Adam rounded his small hand into a fist and began hitting my arm, mimicking what he saw his father do to me two days earlier.

I knew the time had come for me to rescue my son. I wasn't sure where Adam and I were going to live, but we both were in danger if we stayed with Danny. I didn't feel courageous in choosing to be a divorced mom at age twenty-three. I knew I could support two people on my salary easier than I was currently supporting three, and I simply had no other choice if I was to regain my dignity and provide a safe environment for Adam in the years ahead.

That night, Danny overheard my confessions to a girlfriend about our situation and my plans to divorce him. After he confronted us, she agreed to stay with Adam and me for a few days, and she refused to leave me alone at all that evening. Thankfully, our mutual stand was enough to send him packing his clothes.

Danny called me over the next two weeks, even shedding uncharacteristic tears at one point, pleading to return to our apartment and the easy life he'd known. But, he wasn't willing to talk to a professional counselor who might have been able to change the conditions that existed in our home. I stood firm and refused to stay in the marriage.

Adam and I were lucky. Not all angry men go so quietly. But even if a more confrontational ending had ensued, I was finally ready to rise up and protect my son and myself from further violent behavior. Regardless of what the future held, the unknown path before us had to be a better choice. I now watch my son interact with his own two boys. I shudder to think how their lives would be if I had stayed in that physically abusive environment, and I'm thankful God gave me the strength to move on.

~Elizabeth Bogart

Facing the Music

The only man who sticks closer to you in adversity than a friend is a creditor.
~Author Unknown

"Ring! Ring!" The phone screeched at me for what felt like the hundredth time that day, for what seemed like the hundredth day in a row. It was a sound that once made me excited to hear from a friend, but now brought a queasy feeling to my stomach.

It wasn't a friend calling. It was one of the four credit card companies I owed money to... and they weren't calling just to chat.

I disconnected the phone and threw myself on the couch in frustration. Where did I go wrong? I was a college graduate. I had a decent job. I didn't go on thousand-dollar shopping sprees. I didn't even have a car or go on vacation. How had I gotten myself into this mess?

It all started when I was a freshman in college. It was a pretty elite college, three thousand miles from home. To say I was intimidated was to put it mildly. I was terrified. It seemed like my classmates all had so much more money than I did. (I wasn't poor, but we clipped our share of coupons and I certainly couldn't have afforded to go to this school without my scholarship.) They were all so much more worldly than I was, they'd attended fancy prep schools, traveled extensively, and had casual conversations about things I'd never even heard of. I felt out of my league.

So I tried desperately to get on an equal footing. I couldn't do anything about my background, but I could arm myself with the best tools to help me catch up academically. One of those tools was a new computer. I couldn't afford the $2,000 price tag, but when the company offered me a payment plan that would allow me to pay just $65 a month, it seemed like it was meant to be. I had a part-time job; I could afford it.

But, that wasn't the only expense. Books cost me around $400 per semester. Throw in the occasional coffee to help me study through the night, the rare weekend dinners with friends who didn't realize that $50 for a meal wasn't in every college girl's budget. (I'd get by with water and a cup of soup, but it was still $10 I couldn't spare.) I was desperate to fit in, to show that I was just as worthy of being there as everyone else, to pretend that I wasn't just the poor girl who couldn't keep up with the Joneses. The credit card offers that started arriving in the mail seemed like the only way I could make it through.

Despite all this, I never felt like I was acting completely irresponsibly with my money. The computer really did help me write my papers, and I would have had to buy the books either way. I didn't throw away hundreds of dollars on nights out, like some of my friends did. I didn't buy designer clothes. I took public transportation everywhere, instead of cabs. But, even with my best intentions, money I didn't have slowly bled away in $5 fits and starts.

And so, I found myself, three years later, hiding from my telephone, afraid to open my mail and unsure of how to help myself. Being in debt was embarrassing. I felt like I couldn't tell anyone, even my parents, because I was ashamed. I had a degree in economics and I worked at a mutual fund company — if anyone should know better, it was me.

I sat up suddenly. I was sick of the pity party. I was tired of pretending everything was okay while things got worse and I felt more and more hopeless. Something in me clicked. I knew I was a smart girl; it was time to start acting like one.

That meant facing the music. I pulled together all the credit card statements I had left unopened on the kitchen counter, and sat down at my desk to figure out what I owed once and for all. I took a deep breath and started to rip them open. I had to know what I was dealing with.

When I saw the numbers, I cried. I couldn't believe I had let it escalate to this point. But, a few minutes later, the tears cleared and I started to think rationally. The truth was that I had been terrified that the number would be much worse. Now that I had my (not so) magic number, I could do something about it. I went online and found a web calculator to help figure out how long it would take me to pay everything down, and I created a plan.

And, somehow, I stuck to it.

I'm not going to pretend that it was easy. In fact, it was one of the hardest things I'd ever done. For four years, I lived off the bare minimum it took to survive. Every extra penny went to paying down my debt. If I got a bonus or worked overtime, all that extra money went directly to my debt.

It was hard to live like a miser, but seeing my balances fall was liberating. The closer I got to paying everything off, the happier I felt. I hadn't realized how much my debt was weighing me down. As the amount I owed shrank, so did my stress. And, when I paid off my last credit card, three years after I decided to take control of my debt, I felt reborn. I was debt-free at last.

~Jennifer Lee Johnson

Welcome to Our Home

Stand up and walk out of your history.
~Phil McGraw

Those first few weeks at Ms. Dorothy's house are forever seared into my mind. I recall the first time I walked through her front door, tripping over a mat situated just beyond the entrance. I found myself sharing the floor with that mat, brightly labeled "welcome to our home." Standing to see the group of people I'd been told were my new family, I found myself unable to face them. Instead, I looked down at the floor, at a mat that tormented me with words I didn't want to read.

Welcome to their home. Welcome to their lives. Welcome to their rooms and their toys and their mother. All theirs, but I didn't want theirs — I had my own. I longed for my home. For my life. For my room and my toys, but most of all, for my mother.

I stood there, head hung low, as Ms. Dorothy introduced me to Dartanian and Sylvia, my new foster siblings. They showed no more interest in me than I did in them. They too were veterans of "the system." They understood, just as I did, that brothers and sisters, mothers and fathers, they change. Tomorrow, or next week, or in a month if it lasted that long, there would be a new family. So we had shells, all of us, fortified by one move after another, strengthened by betrayal and disappointment.

As though infectious, my silence became theirs. I lifted my head, looking first at Dartanian, then at Sylvia. Their eyes were as empty as my own, and their hearts, I knew, were just as hollow.

In the following days, I went through the usual routine that comes with a new home: a new school, a new doctor, a new therapist. New people who would tell me the same things. New places that would soon be forgotten. The days went on as usual, but with the nights came change.

More than a week passed before it occurred to me that I hadn't been crying at bedtime. For several years, that had been my routine. I kept everything inside during the day, suppressing thoughts of my family and my old life. At night, I relived my fondest memories: swimming in the red river with my older brothers, chasing my sisters with bullfrogs and crickets, sitting in my mother's lap as we rocked back and forth in that old wooden rocking chair, singing songs about babies in treetops and diamond rings that didn't shine.

I felt guilty for neglecting my nightly routine. In penitence, I brought to mind those memories I held closest to my heart. I was obliged to make up for the tears I'd so carelessly forgotten to shed. I felt that I'd betrayed my family in failing to lament their absence. To my dismay, no tears or overwhelming sadness accompanied the memories I replayed in my mind. This was not acceptable. I didn't know why at the time, but I simply had to cry. I had to suffer.

Despite thinking of things that previously elicited a torrent of tears, I could not cry. I know now what I did not know then. The tears and the mourning, and the consistency to which I applied my suffering, were ways of holding onto a family that I knew deep inside were lost to me forever. By crying, I kept myself emotionally attached to a group of people who were unable to reciprocate my affections. My emotions were so firmly rooted in the past that I was unable to experience happiness in the present.

That night, as I lay in bed, I took my first step onto a long path of healing and self-discovery. It is a sad truth that sometimes, though frighteningly difficult, we must relinquish parts of our past to live happily in the present.

~Daniel McGary

I Will Get Back Up Again

When you get into a tight place and everything goes against you,
till it seems as though you could not hold on a minute longer,
never give up then, for that is just the place and time that
the tide will turn.
~Harriet Beecher Stowe

When I opened my eyes, I saw four of everything. They were saying, "Open your eyes, Sarah, open your eyes!" So I did, but all I kept wondering was, why would anyone hang four clocks on the wall? I dragged my eyes left and saw four doors. Something came into view in front of my face, but it was out of focus—four out-of-focus faces. Actually, it was one face out of focus four times. It was my doctor, but I only knew that by his comforting voice, which said, "Sarah, the surgery is over, and you are okay."

Being diagnosed with a brain tumor is not something you can prepare for. It knocks you down like a giant wave at the beach hitting you from behind. You spin and flip and sputter and gasp for air. And then somehow, your head emerges from the water and you breathe again, with salt stinging your eyes and sand in your hair. You breathe and you walk toward the shore in tiny steps, hoping that another wave doesn't hit you.

I was diagnosed with a meningioma in 2004. Meningiomas are benign tumors that can still have dire consequences. They have a similar survival rate as breast cancer. Mine was discovered when a neurologist sent me for an MRI for daily headaches that wouldn't respond to medication. After the MRI, the technician handed me a copy of the MRI pictures. In the car, I pulled them out to look at them, thinking it would be neat to see what the inside of my brain looked like. In the middle of it, I saw a white blob. I picked up my cell phone and called my husband. "I have a brain tumor, and I think I'm going to die," I told him.

The neurosurgeon told me that there was good news and bad news. The good news was that I was relatively young, which increased my chances of survival. The bad news was that the tumor was growing in a very bad place, pressing against my brain stem. If the tumor continued to grow against the brain stem, it could compromise basic functions such as breathing and swallowing. Because the surgery was very risky, the doctor wanted to be sure the tumor was in a growth pattern before proceeding with surgery.

By summer 2005, it was clear that the meningioma was growing, and the risks of waiting outweighed the risks of surgery. My surgery would be done at Johns Hopkins with one of the best neurosurgeons in the world. I had faith in his experienced hands. My greatest fear was leaving my three little girls, ages three, seven, and nine. The neurosurgeon was honest with me about all of the things that could go wrong in surgery and that there was a possibility of disability or even death. I spent the last month before surgery making memory boxes for each of my girls, so that they would remember their years with me if something should happen.

So, early that morning, I had walked into the hospital with my husband by my side, not knowing what the outcome of my surgery would be. It took a minute for what the doctor had said to register. I was okay. I had made it through the surgery. The Surgery. That was why it felt like the right side of my head had a spike driven through it. But I was alive.

"Can you see me?" the doctor asked.

"Yes," I answered. "I can see four of you."

He chuckled. "Oh, I think one of me is definitely enough," he said.

The time in the hospital was a blur of pain and dizziness. After discovering I was allergic to the pain medications that were allowed after craniotomies, I was left to travel the ocean of pain on my own. I remember telling myself, if you can't get through it from one minute to the next, then get through it from one second to the next.

I had to have complete quiet and darkness. Any sound, smell, or sight jarred my damaged brain too much. My husband sat quietly by my bed for all those days, waiting for me to be able to bear voices again. Slowly, my quadruple vision went to triple vision and then to double vision. My unbearable headaches became bearable. They took the sign off my door that warned I was not allowed to move out of my bed without assistance because of vertigo. And I fought my way back to the land of the living, all because I was desperate to see my daughters again.

When I was released from the hospital, I still had double vision and an unrelenting headache. Memory and processing problems haunted me, but the sight of my house and my girls healed me in a way that I never could have healed in a hospital room. The road to recovery has been long, and it has been bumpy, but I have never stopped believing that I could do it. I didn't want that brain tumor to rob me of one more day.

I still go for MRIs every six months. The neurosurgeon is watching changes in the area of the surgery that may be re-growth of the tumor. There is talk about radiation oncologists and six weeks of radiation. I know there may be another wave looming, ready to knock me off my feet. But I am calm, and I am strong. I have learned how much strength there is in me, and I know that whatever knocks me down won't keep me down. I will continue to get back up again.

~Sarah Clark Monagle

After the Fall

Whenever you fall, pick something up.
~Oswald Avery

I wake up on a Thursday afternoon, after being asleep for a day and a half. I see the white ceiling of the hospital room and feel the IV in my arm. I ask my parents what happened and when they tell me, it all comes flooding back. Suddenly I remember the night I swallowed the three bottles of pills, and I begin to cry.

I am sent to a mental hospital where I will be kept "safe." Doctors are afraid I will try to harm myself again. My body just could not take any more abuse, especially after such a close call. I was inches away from death, and the nurses make it quite clear that they almost lost me. Had my father found me any later, they explain, I might have succeeded in my attempt.

Then they ask me a question. Why? Why had I tried to kill myself? I try to give them an answer, but I can't think of one.

"It just felt right at the time," I tell them.

This answer does not satisfy them, but they have no idea that I am being completely honest. I truly do not know why I had done what I did. I am asked the same question by countless people, and nobody seems to understand my reason.

While I am at the hospital I am given time to reflect on my actions. I spend a great deal of my time trying to identify what led me to overdose. Days go by and I still have no good answer.

Then a few days into my stay I am sent to a group therapy session, which is supposed to be a place where talking through problems with people who have shared similar experiences is supposed to help us through our struggle. The group leader asks me why I am in the hospital, and I explain that I am there for an overdose. He asks me if I was depressed at the time.

That's when it begins to come together.

"No, I wasn't depressed," I explain. "For once I wasn't. And in fact, I hadn't been depressed in quite some time."

I had struggled with depression since fifth grade, and I was now a senior in high school. Looking back, it's hard to remember a time when I was happy. Depression and sadness had found a way into my life and never left. The illness had a firm grip on me and wouldn't let go. It wasn't until a few months before that it had finally loosened its hold on me. For the first time in my memory, I had been happy.

Why then, had I swallowed all those pills if I was starting to feel better? Simple. Depression was comfortable to me. I hated it, but it had been in my life for so long that it had become what was normal for me. It was as if I didn't know how to live my life without the illness. The reason I had overdosed was an attempt to go back to a place where I was comfortable.

I explained this to the group leader, and he said something to me that I will never forget.

"Sometimes, it's easier to get up once you've fallen all the way," he told me.

Tears formed in my eyes and I began to cry. He was right. I had spent so much time battling depression, it was almost like I was struggling to stay standing up when I was falling down. Perhaps my attempt was really me hitting rock bottom—it could not possibly get any worse. Now I was ready to really stand back up. I was ready to move on.

Since then, my life has really looked up. Since making the decision to move on and leave my comfort zone I have actually gotten to a place that I never would have imagined I would find. I have managed to find happiness.

~Samantha Richardson

38

From Struggling to Successful

Your struggles develop your strengths. When you go through hardships and decide not to surrender, that is strength.
~Arnold Schwarzenegger

I will never forget Christmas 1985. A married woman with a one-year-old, I became a single parent overnight.

My husband had been traveling a lot on weekends. Instead of being on business trips, he actually was plotting and planning his new life in New York while we lived in California. He had mentioned over the last year that he wanted to move to New York. I was not ready to leave my family, so I never took those talks seriously. Perhaps if I had, things would have turned out differently, but I doubt it.

During that Christmas season, while the streets were full of the hustle and bustle of holiday cheer, I remained numb. He just left and abandoned me and our baby daughter.

I remember going to my parents' house and, without a doubt in my mind, telling them I was moving in so they could help me. But instead, my mom pointed me back to my house and said, "You are going to raise your child. I already raised my children. We will help you in any way we can, but we are not going to raise your daughter."

Of course, I was surprised, but in retrospect it was the best thing they could have ever done. They did, and have continued to, deserve the "grandparents of the year" award and have helped out whenever they could.

So, there we were in 1985—my daughter was a year and four months old and I was still numb, anxious, and feeling nothing short of a full-blown, diagnosable depression. I had just graduated with a journalism degree and was about to conquer the world in radio and TV news. That was squashed because I couldn't make a living at it.

I did the next best thing and got a job in sales, which eventually lead to working at a newspaper as a sales rep. It was perfect because the flexibility allowed me to be more available for my daughter.

My ex-husband would come out to visit our daughter on a regular basis, although once he was re-married and had two children, the visits became less frequent. In fact, our daughter would point to the hotel they stayed at when he visited and say, "That's Daddy's house."

It was cute, but at the same time it broke my heart. I wanted my daughter to have a daddy here, not 3,000 miles away. Not to mention, I was exhausted from having no reprieve like the moms who had every other weekend off when the dads took the kids. I was angry, frustrated, and resentful.

As I look back, I wish I had let go of those feelings, because they never served me well. It took me a long time to realize I was powerless over the situation, and holding on to the anger was detrimental to my mental health. Eventually, the light bulb went on and I was able to let go of a lot of those resentments. Although when Father's Day, birthdays, holidays, open houses, and father-and-daughter events came around, the resentments would surface again.

In the 1980s, there were fewer single parents and I received little support from the married moms. They just didn't get it, and it hurt, especially when they didn't invite my daughter to sleepovers or to go trick-or-treating for Halloween. It was as if my daughter and I had a disability, and there were mothers who even thought I was a threat. I was an outcast in the two parent world.

From 1985 to 1993, I became a serial dater. I also had a few short marriages in between—I thought getting married would complete our family. I know now they were huge mistakes. Although, at first, these short-term husbands were great with my daughter, eventually they wanted to take complete control of my life and my daughter's. These short marriages ended abruptly; however, today I am happily married. My daughter loves my husband, and he never had children, so she is truly the daughter he never had.

Then in 1994, after nine years as a successful salesperson, I went back to school to become a social worker. I needed something more fulfilling, and realized I wanted to work with single parents. So many agencies had been helpful to my daughter and me that I felt compelled to help others who were going through what we had.

Becoming a child custody mediator interested me because mediation helped my ex-husband see the importance of visiting our daughter. As a social worker, I had amazing opportunities to work in hospice and with individuals in recovery from addictions.

Most recently, I added life coaching to my psychotherapy practice. Two years ago, I took a leap of faith and opened my own private practice. I always had a little entrepreneurship in me. That led me to co-authoring *Conscious Entrepreneur*, which helps individuals follow their dreams, life purpose, and most of all, their passions. The book calls out to individuals who have a dream, "Don't be afraid. Do what you love and the success will follow."

This book led me to be an ongoing guest on the nationally-syndicated radio show, *Dr. Drew Live* with Dr. Drew Pinsky, discussing all sorts of mental health and life coaching topics.

And that experience led me to becoming a TV personality on the reality show *Celebrity Rehab 2* on VH1. I became the life coach to the celebrities living in the rehab, helping them move forward in their lives. It was not only an exciting experience, but incredibly rewarding. I was giving back everything I had learned and lived, and was able to see broken individuals build their lives again one step at a time.

As I look back, I wouldn't change a thing. I am incredibly proud of the person my daughter has become and the special mother-and-daughter moments we have shared. I revel in the joys I experienced during her childhood, whether it was watching one of her recitals or just holding hands at the mall.

She once wrote me a poem called "My Mother is my Hero," where she expressed such gratitude for all I did to make her life as great as it could be, as well as the lessons she learned along the way. I was just doing my job, yet she viewed it as unique and special. What mother gets that type of thank you?

No, I wouldn't change a thing, not now, not ever. My life has gone full circle—from young new graduate wanting to conquer the radio and TV world to a working single parent, to a multiple divorcée, to student, to happily married, to celebrity psychotherapist and life coach. It just doesn't get better than that!

~Sherry Gaba

39

Breaking the Cycle

Could we change our attitude, we should not only see life differently,
but life itself would come to be different.
~Katherine Mansfield

Dropping out of high school and becoming a single mom by the time I was eighteen years old was certainly not the dream I had for myself as a little girl, but that was the hand that I was dealt. I don't think I ever realized what a difficult journey it would be trying to become a successful adult while also raising a child.

As a young girl, I experienced sexual abuse as well as parents who battled an addiction to drugs and alcohol. Once I reached my teenage years, I found myself alone and becoming my own parent. By the time I had my son in 1989, I was depressed, 110 pounds overweight, and a high school dropout with no self-esteem. I could not even hold a job. By the time I was twenty-one, I had my second child, a daughter, but still struggled with obesity, depression and a poor work ethic. I knew I wanted a better life for my kids and for myself but I just could not find the motivation within myself to get us there. By the time I was twenty-six, I got a job at a hotel and had finally found a place that gave me the opportunity to grow and learn and start to feel like I was worth something. I was there for six years and had been promoted four times to be second in charge.

Today I am the General Manager of a fifteen-million-dollar company, have been named one of the Best 50 Women in Business in Pennsylvania, a top forty business professional under the age of forty, and have lost 140 pounds. My proudest moment was in May of 2007 when I officially graduated from high school at the age of thirty-seven.

How has all this affected my life as a woman and a mother? I have broken the cycle! My kids have watched me work very hard to grow as a person, a wife and a mother. They have seen firsthand what hard work, passion and dedication can bring into your life. My son is now twenty and has completed his first two years of college. I am so proud of where he is in his life. He is a hard-working, bright, funny, well-rounded young man and watching him grow, learn and become his own individual has been scary, wonderful and exciting all at the same time. My daughter is sixteen and is strong-willed and outspoken just like I am. I hope that I have taught her how to love herself more than anyone else will and to never settle for anything less than what will make her very happy.

My kids have been the motivators in my life. I worked so hard because I wanted them to have a role model that they could look up to. But I also wanted to show them that the blessings in your life are something you need to give back to others and that people are not defined by the mistakes they have made but by the content of their character. Being a mom is more than just feeding, clothing and providing a roof over your children's heads. They are empty books that we fill throughout their lives and you can never erase the pages.

I felt the need to show my kids the importance of giving back to others who are not as fortunate as we are. I started mentoring other kids, young people who lost their way and were dropping out of school, and young girls who have had babies in their teenage years and just need an understanding ear. I am also a mentor to women living in homeless shelters and transitional housing, teaching them life skills as well as work ethic and job interviewing techniques. In addition to all of this, I sit on three corporate boards and countless other committees. Somehow, in my crazy life, I still find the time to go home every evening, make dinner for my family and spend time with my kids.

When you have a love and a passion for your life and your children, you find the time to do it all. No complaining, no feeling sorry for yourself. I am now blessed not only with my two amazing children, but also with a loving marriage to their father, and a network of people who can say that I have touched their lives in some way.

~Aimée Urban

Sister/Survivor

The world is a tragedy to those who feel, but a comedy to those who think.
~Horace Walpole

When my sister, Judy, was diagnosed with breast cancer, of course I was worried about the outcome. But my experience as a nurse led me to believe the outcome would be good. She had been diagnosed early, her lymph nodes were not involved, and she was in good health otherwise. The doctor had given her an excellent prognosis. So why was I so worried?

Breast cancer surgery leaves surgical scars that are hard for some women to face. But I worried most about the emotional scars that linger long after the physical scars have faded away.

I was worried that just having to deal with the entire experience of having breast cancer could break my sister's spirit.

Judy is a strong, take-charge, independent, woman. But when she is faced with anything remotely connected with disease, blood, gore, or death... she totally freaks out. She walks away when people start talking about ailments, operations, or the mere mention of bodily functions. If a kid in the family says, "Look at my boo-boo," Judy covers her eyes and makes a face.

My sister complains about people who "constantly whine about being sick." She has been known to say, "I have to hang up now" if friends or family members insist on talking about their latest illness. She rarely acknowledges being sick herself.

Therefore, I worried that this was going to be a life-altering experience for her on many levels.

The cancer was discovered on my sister's very first mammogram. It was done when she was fifty-eight years old. "I knew I shouldn't let that doctor talk me into having a mammogram—if you go looking for trouble you'll always find it," she said. No one could convince her that finding the cancer early was a good thing. She blustered and balked but finally accepted the diagnosis and treatment plan. She would have her breast removed and reconstructed.

Judy's daughter accompanied her to the hospital. When the elevator arrived, my sister stepped back and let the doors close. "Thanks, I'll take the next one," she said.

My niece raised her eyebrows. "What was that all about? There was plenty of room on the elevator."

"There were sick people on that one!" my sister exclaimed.

Oh Lord, we're in for a long ride, my niece thought.

On the day of surgery, Judy looked petrified. That was understandable; all her worst fears had come to life. She had a dreaded disease. She was in a hospital... with sick people. She was about to have her breast cut off. To add insult to injury, they made her take out her dentures and go toothless in front of visitors and staff all morning.

In a little cubicle, a young doctor apologized for exposing her as he drew black marks on her breast. "Listen here, this doesn't embarrass me at all, it's being without my teeth that's embarrassing. In fact, more people have seen me without my clothes than have seen me without my teeth," she huffed.

Finally, they told her it was time to go to surgery, and the look in her eyes broke my heart.

"I swear to God, if I could go in your place, I would," I told her.

"And I swear to God, I'd let you!" she retorted.

When Judy came out of surgery, the entire family was there. Her son, Tony, went in to see her first because he was the most anxious. He was only gone a moment, then he came running out of her room in panic. We all jumped to our feet and ran to meet him.

He said, "Something terrible happened to my mom in there. I don't know what they did to her but she doesn't even look like herself. She won't wake up and her face looks like it's all sunken in!"

We raced into the room to find Judy heavily sedated, looking pale, hair mussed, and still without her dentures. My sister Jean burst out laughing. "When she wakes up, she'll put on her make-up, fix her hair, and put in her teeth. Then she'll look like she always does. She's fine!" A few hours later, Judy did just that and my nephew was relieved.

Judy was a trouper. She coped with her surgery and hospital stay (with sick people) amazingly well.

However, on the day of discharge she phoned me and said, "They left a tube hooked to a big drain thing inside me and they're sending me home with it! It has blood in it and they want me to empty it out every day. You nurses are used to this stuff. How do they expect people to handle these medical things at home?"

I assured her she would not have to deal with it. "I'll stop by after work each day to change the bandages and empty the drain. I know how you feel about gross stuff," I told her. When I arrived the first evening, she had already emptied the drain and changed her own bandage. She said, "I just couldn't see you driving sixty miles every day just to baby me. It's not like I'm an invalid."

Her recovery was smooth and rapid. The drain was removed and the incision was healing beautifully. Judy was soon well enough to resume our monthly luncheon trip. At the posh restaurant, she ordered soup. I cringed. She is especially buxom and frequently spills something (especially soup) on her bosom when she eats. It has become a family joke. We wait to see what she will spill at holiday dinners.

However, when the soup was served, she just sat there looking at it with this smirk on her face.

"What?" I asked.

She mused, "I was just thinking about something. If you were embarrassed when I dropped soup on my boob in fancy restaurants, just think how embarrassed you would be if the stitches broke and my boob dropped in the soup!"

It takes more than breast cancer to break the spirit of a strong woman.

~Joyce Seabolt

What Will Always Be

God gave us memories that we might have roses in December.
~J.M. Barrie

Midsummer's flowers fade with time
The petals turn to dust;
Just as hinges that now swing free
Will soon give way to rust.

And the picture we try so hard to preserve
In memory's crowded store
Eventually dims in twilight's mist
... And soon is there no more.

But ah, the joy and dreams still live!
Indeed, enhanced with time —
The senses reel with what once was
... What will always be mine.

So blow, winter winds; grow dark, oh sky!
What has been will live forever,
For what the heart binds to the soul
... No passing years can sever.

~Denise A. Dewald

Of Detour and Determination

People are made of flesh and blood and a miracle fibre called courage.
~Mignon McLaughlin

Shivering from cold and shock, I hold my son's hands as he lies on the snow in a spreading crimson pool, both legs jutting at odd angles. He's been caught as a pedestrian between two cars colliding on the icy highway, and I fear for his life. We lock eyes and somehow he stays conscious until medics arrive. As they load him in an ambulance, he manages to say, "Thanks, guys. I know you're doing all you can for me."

An orthopedic surgeon inserts metal rods in both legs, shattered from ankle to knee. The bones will heal, but because of extensive damage to muscles, tendons, and nerves, and gaping wounds that invite infection, the doctor gives Ben only a fifty-fifty chance of keeping his legs.

"I wish it were a dream and I'd wake up," Ben says, but he maintains a positive attitude toward his healing. He weans himself off heavy pain medications because he hates the feeling of being "half there." Six weeks after the accident, now late May, he returns to his junior year of high school in a wheelchair.

But his right leg begins to sag and gurgle, signaling infection. A doctor famous for "saving limbs" is our only hope of avoiding amputation. The doctor scrapes out infected bone, grafts a muscle from

Ben's chest to the site of the infection for increased blood supply, and puts a shunt in a vein next to Ben's heart, where massive doses of antibiotics will be pumped into his body twenty-four hours a day.

I'm terrified as we wait two long weeks to find out if the graft has taken. "Don't worry, Mom," Ben says. "I'm young and healthy. I'll heal."

When the bandages are removed, Ben's leg is pink, but extensively scarred. Still, he keeps his steady good humor. "My calf looks like a kidney bean covered with cheesecloth," he jokes to his rugby team.

In a third surgery, doctors take bone from Ben's pelvis and fill gaps in his legs where new bone has not formed. Beads of sweat on Ben's forehead and his deathly pallor reveal the excruciating pain of his transfers from wheelchair to bed. Yet he doesn't complain.

Still wheelchair-bound in early July, Ben takes on the rehab of an old VW bug. Daily, he slides from wheelchair to concrete garage floor and goes to work. He also finishes several projects to complete his junior year.

He begins turning wheelchair wheelies on the driveway. "Do you think you could do something safer?" I ask as he falls, pulls himself back into the chair, falls again. But he's determined to do whatever it takes to be physically active again.

Next, he assaults the hill outside our house, wheeling a little further uphill each day until he can go around the block.

He trades wheelchair for crutches shortly before school begins in the fall, and swings from class to class, his books and homework in a backpack.

I assume all is going well until the attendance office call about truancies, and fail notices arrive in the mail. "I need to be outside exercising," Ben explains to the vice-principal and me. "They want me to care who gets prom queen and king. I just care about walking again." He's courteous, but firm. Although I'm a teacher, I understand, and sign papers to withdraw him.

Ben works as hard at healing as any student works at maintaining a 4.0 grade point average. "Look, Mom!" he calls to me one day. "It hurts, but I can do it." Holding the crutches out from his sides, he puts his full weight on his legs. Tears of joy run down both our faces.

Soon, he uses a cane, his gait a shuffle because nerve damage has permanently affected every movement of his ankles and knees. After another four months, he feels steady enough to walk unaided, and then to ride his bicycle. "I'm getting there," he says.

He tries skateboarding again, wincing with pain and battling discouragement as he twists his permanently weak ankles and struggles to work around the limitations of nerve damage. Finally, he puts his skateboard away. Snowboarding is out of the question. He hikes, once again, into the woods he loves so much, but he can't go far, nor can he hike steep terrain. When he tries to run, the impact hurts too much.

One afternoon, he tells me he's been thinking about it a lot, and decided he's healed as much as he's going to. He expects chronic pain and breakthrough bleeding for a long time to come.

"I accept it," he says, but for the first time a black cloud of despair settles over Ben. How do I comfort my son, now broken in spirit as well as body?

He retreats more and more often to his room. His good humor fades, as does his desire to exercise. I suspect marijuana. "I'm worried about you," I tell him. "You're so negative these days."

"I'm fine, Mom. You're the one with a problem," he says.

I pray for my son and try to keep communication lines open.

One day, when he borrows my car to go to his counseling appointment, he rolls it. "I wasn't speeding," he says. When I see the car, ski rack torn off, the top, front, and rear dented, anger at Ben's recklessness mixes with relief that he's not injured. Obviously he's been speeding. How can he feel immortal when he's come so close to death?

"I'm afraid you're going to kill yourself," his sister, Tami, sobs. "What would we all do without you?"

When I ask Ben what he plans to do in the next year or two, his answer sears my heart. "How can I plan even a few months out? Life is so fragile. I might not even be around."

Ben's counselor advises that Ben needs time and support to heal from post-traumatic stress disorder created by the accident, not drug treatment. "It's hard to imagine what he's been through," he says.

Family and friends pray for Ben and gather around him with love and encouragement. He continues in counseling. After five months of struggle, he somehow finds, again, the will to move forward with his healing and his life.

"I'll try Merlo Station," he decides, and registers for his senior year at an alternative high school in our district. In classes of twelve to fifteen students and a community of support, he earns straight As. Once again he skateboards, battering and bruising himself hour after hour as he practices various tricks, working around his physical limitations. "I can do just about everything," he says. "It just takes a lot more effort." He snowboards again, though for shorter periods. He still can't hike steep terrain or long distances and he can't run, but with great determination he focuses on what he is able to do.

In June, fourteen months after his accident, Ben shuffles across the stage to receive his high school diploma. Our family cheers wildly. He's shown us all how to enter a dark place, reach into oneself for immense courage, accept the help and support of others, and emerge into the light.

~Samantha Ducloux Waltz

Tough Times, Tough People

Accepting the New Me

Acceptance of what has happened is the first step to overcoming the consequences of any misfortune.

~William James

Once Upon a Smile

We can let circumstances rule us,
or we can take charge and rule our lives from within.
~Earl Nightingale

It was easy being pretty with my large blue-green-grey eyes. My wholesome smile was never fake. My face never had the camouflage of make-up. That was "me" since childhood.

One morning in February 2003, I woke up and the right half of my face was paralyzed.

My right eye couldn't blink, my forehead was frozen, half my lips were in a set position, and my nose had one nostril pulled towards the non-paralyzed side. Without warning or understanding, my means of relating to people and the world was shut off.

My eye was taped shut to protect the cornea, and speech was difficult.

The neurologist said the longer the paralysis went on, the more permanent the problems.

An eye doctor suggested sewing the affected lid closed, and told me to get eye glasses because anything could fly into my eye, as I had no blink reflex.

I went for window-glass eyewear. On my nose, the frame looked crooked.

I pushed my straight blond hair behind my ears. My pretty face that had exhibited "me" with a constant and symmetrical smile now looked grotesque and reflected the stern-unmovable expression of people who show disdain toward others.

When I decided to take charge of this obstacle in my life, I first went to the supermarket. The stares were bad enough, but many people moved away from me as if I were contagious.

My speech was slow, as I had to think the words in my head and then decide on a synonym if a word began with a "b" or "p" because those required either use of cheek muscles or the ability to blow air.

I went out for dinner.

"You have a lot of courage to be out looking like that," I was told.

Cruel.

Another woman told me she had "a case of paralysis that went on for two whole weeks."

Contest; I'd rather not be the winner of longevity.

"Does it hurt?"

Curious, but not compassionate.

"How'd you get such a thing?"

Punishment.

A relative decided not to visit me, saying, "Your face might scare my children."

Callous.

I made others comfortable, because I, frankly, didn't have a quick enough answer for what spewed from their mouths. I said pat phrases like, "Life is too good to waste it," and "I'll make lemonade from this lemon," and wondered whether this would turn out to be permanent.

Eventually, some healing facial nerve fibers implanted themselves into the wrong muscles. The brain told the muscle to contract, assuming the nerve was connected to where it once belonged, only now that specific nerve was connected to a different muscle.

So when my brain thinks I'm smiling, my eye twitches, or when it thinks I'm blinking, the cheek muscle twitches with enough power that it's visible. I cannot blink the eye that's on the palsy side.

With nerve fibers rerouted, a whole new condition to live with opened up, and the communication shown by a face was permanently gone. The half-face paralysis with distortion and spasms was for the rest of my life, and I could expect added complications as years multiplied.

In the quiet of my room, the mirror heard my unspoken words as I commanded the eyebrow to lift, or lid to blink, or cheek to move, or lips to... Unresponsive commands... I realized that my face was a stranger.

I have dealt with this challenge, believing life is too valuable to have it dictated by others' stares.

For these six years, and for the rest of my life, I'll continue to go out among people and eat in restaurants. I make it seem less complicated, less uncomfortable, less awkward than it really is. I portray a person able to move in and out of circumstances without being encompassed by such, or even one bothered by, a face that is clueless regarding the "me" I am and had always shown.

For skin that never saw make-up to conceal even a pimple, I currently conceal my feelings and attitude under layers of jokes or distractions. I deal with humor, because the gift of life my parents gave me must be treasured as no other gift in my world.

The added gift of a caring and supportive family is beautiful, but I can give back with strength, courage, and being a consistent role model of a living-oriented person. Of course it isn't easy, but time gone can never be retrieved.

I do insist on being photographed in profile so my smiling side is the only part that shows, because that's how I still feel about myself. My family, in their memories, "see" the frozen part upturned as well.

~Lois Greene Stone

A Minor Inconvenience

Bridges become frames for looking at the world around us.
~Bruce Jackson

Laura is driving and I'm in the passenger seat as we approach the Highway 8 Bridge. That familiar sense of dread washes over me. I feel my chest tighten as I try to breathe slowly and methodically. I look over at Laura. She must see how panic-stricken I feel. I want to get out of the car, run as fast as I can to escape this fear that warns me I'm about to be carried off to that other world again.

"Mom... are... you... all... right?" Laura's voice sounds too deep. Her long drawn-out words echo as if they're coming from the far end of a cave. And her face looks distorted, as though I'm watching her underwater. She looks like she's swimming toward me, trying to rescue me from this drowning sensation as she reaches over to take my hand off the car door handle. Like a puppet, I watch her guide my hand to my lap.

"I'm fine. Don't worry about me. Watch the road." I try to say. But all these words stick in my throat, refusing to pass over my tongue.

I want to flee from this moment and get on with my life.

By the time it's over, we have crossed the bridge and are on the freeway. I take a deep breath and lean back against the headrest.

"Are you okay now?" Laura's voice sounds normal again.

I nod. Keeping my eyes closed, I take inventory of my

surroundings. I'm riding in the car. Laura is driving. We're going to the mall, her second home. I live in Chisago City now, not Lindstrom. We moved fifteen years ago. Todd is working from home today. Jenny is in college now. My seizures have returned. Collecting these fragments of information, I gradually reassemble the pieces of my life.

"What did I do?" I ask, as I open my eyes and look at her. I always ask.

Frowning, she assesses my condition with furrowed brow. I remember that she wants to be a nurse.

"You were moving your feet a lot. I thought my driving was upsetting you."

"It probably was," I tease. "I'm sure I was telling you to slow down." I smile and she laughs. "Did I say anything? I was trying to tell you that I was okay."

In the thirty seconds it took to cross that bridge, the seizure leaves me feeling as exhausted as a marathon swimmer who just completed her final lap and stands at the edge of the pool trying to catch her breath.

"No, you didn't make any noise. Why don't you rest for a while?"

"Then who would tell you how to drive?" I say, as I close my eyes and let my body go limp.

I'm relieved that we were in the car when this happened and not in a public place. My seizures are usually mild, and they come and go so quickly that most people, even my family, rarely notice that I've had one. But I worry about whether my behavior during my next seizure will cause strangers to question my intelligence because they've witnessed thirty seconds of erratic behavior. I've had too many embarrassing moments.

I wrote about my bridge experience for a class assignment. A woman came up to me later and thanked me for sharing it. Her husband had seizures but never talked about it. Hearing about my experience helped her understand what he went through. I understood her husband's reluctance to talk about epilepsy. People's misperceptions of the disorder can be more debilitating than the condition. But hearing her words of gratitude made me wonder if it was time for me to speak out.

When my husband's coworker learned I have epilepsy, he asked if I'd be willing to talk to him and his wife about my experience. Their eight-year-old had epilepsy, and getting the seizures under control was a challenge.

My heart went out to them. I remember what it was like to deal with seizures at that age. During a time when wearing the wrong color shoelaces can summon the ridicule of your peers, having seizures in school can be off the charts on the humiliation scale. Of course I would talk to them. I didn't know what I could say to help them, except that they weren't alone.

Growing up, my parents treated my epilepsy as they would any other daily routine. Morning conversation included: Did you brush your teeth? Did you take your medicine? Dinner conversations included: How was your day? What did you learn about? Did you have any seizures? Please pass the potatoes.

It was a part of our lives, but not the only part. I'm grateful for my family's acceptance of epilepsy as a minor inconvenience, something to be worked around. Not everyone sees it that way.

I'm told that my doctor was more upset about telling my parents I had epilepsy than they were at learning it. They were grateful for a diagnosis that explained what seemed like inattentiveness and excessive daydreaming; and that there was medicine to treat it.

Unlike diabetes or high blood pressure, epilepsy is not a popular disorder. As old as it is, it's still misunderstood. For many, there's still a stigma attached to having epilepsy. Children still taunt those who are different. Some kids who don't understand what a seizure is, or why it happens, grow into adults and employers who continue to have misconceptions about seizures and the people who have them.

People with the best of intentions have suggested that I might be possessed and have offered to exorcise any demons that might be controlling me.

Others who don't know I have epilepsy have questioned the intelligence of people who have seizures or whether they should have children. Until now, I never pointed out that I have managed to raise two healthy daughters and complete four years of college in spite of a seizure disorder.

My life has been occasionally interrupted by seizures and I've been inconvenienced by them along with the trial-and-error process of finding the right medication. While I'm mildly affected by epilepsy, today it's really no big deal. I'm more open about my epilepsy now — with individuals, families, even my state representative.

Just as my class assignment described my experience on a bridge, I want to help build the bridge that will lead to a better understanding of epilepsy. I want to encourage those who are still struggling, advocate for those for whom seizures are still a major hurdle, and effect new laws that could help them transform a major distraction in their lives into a minor inconvenience.

~Tracy Gulliver

Full Circle

Human life is purely a matter of deciding what's important to you.
~Anonymous

Having barely recovered from a spinal fusion, I heard my doctor say, "Glenda, you have Charcot-Marie-Tooth Disease, an incurable neuromuscular disease that affects your peripheral nerves. It will not affect your life span but could possibly put you in a wheelchair later."

I walked out of his office wondering how in the world this could happen. I was working two jobs, had a husband and two teenagers to care for, and I was only fifty years old.

It wasn't long until reality set in — I was forced to have one surgery after another on my feet. I can still remember the doctor's words: "Glenda, use the scooters in the grocery stores because that will save you a lot of energy, energy you can use for more important things like bathing."

I didn't know how difficult it would be to follow his advice. I live in a small town where I know a lot of people, and the first time I attempted to use a scooter, I couldn't bring myself to sit down. It felt like I was giving up. Instead, I walked through the store in excruciating pain! I didn't do that many times, though, until I succumbed to the scooter. In no time, I was driving so fast that one day I turned a corner and almost hit another customer.

I'll never forget the day I went to the post office after getting my first leg brace. I was attempting to get out of the car while keeping my back straight and moving the bulky brace at the same time. Another car had just pulled in beside me, and I didn't have a lot of room to open the door. I was having a lot of difficulty, and my frustration level was rising! When I looked over into the car beside me, I saw an elderly man putting on his oxygen mask. Humbled, I decided the brace wasn't so bad after all.

The first time I was fitted for a brace also sticks in my mind. An energetic man knelt at my feet and began putting plaster of Paris around my foot and leg. As he worked, dropping puddles of plaster on the floor, he talked casually about the weather. I wanted to lash out at the young man. Instead, I sat quietly and wondered what had caused my anger. I realized I was grieving the loss of my ankle. I didn't know it then, but I'd deal with that each time I was fitted for a brace.

With all of my surgeries, I began to feel overwhelmed, especially since my son was battling a huge problem of his own — an alcohol addiction. Between my diagnosis and his situation, which was causing car wrecks on a regular basis, things looked quite hopeless.

I knew I had to make some changes in order to survive. I looked at what I had working for me instead of what I had lost. I had always been an artist and had taken a creative writing class a few years before my diagnosis. I needed to simplify my life, so I decided to give up my job, which required me to travel a lot. I developed a plan. With my husband's help, I would make an art studio in a small building, once used for his office, that he no longer needed.

So, with a few coats of blue paint and a couple of window boxes for petunias, the building looked like a dollhouse. It was such fun working together on the building, and it also lessened my grief. Before long, I had my CD playing Beethoven while I brushed paint on my canvas. With the windows open, I could smell the wild honeysuckle growing near the edge of the woods. Sometimes, I glimpsed the geese as they landed on Lake Chatuge. I was grateful for my new peaceful refuge.

I'd like to say everything went well from that point, but life doesn't always happen that way. I ended up having a total of four surgeries on my feet, and learned to walk in braces and also use walkers, canes, and scooters. At times I felt at least a hundred years old.

Not only did I not know how to react to all of these changes, my friends didn't know either. No one knew exactly what to say to me. In order to get the rest I needed I had to set boundaries, and some of them didn't go over so well. Instead of dropping by for a visit, I asked people to call first. I also turned off my phone for a couple of hours every day. At first it felt strange being still. I'd always been on the run. It took about six months before I could accept not going to work. I still looked at the job listings for at least five years.

I also had to make some changes with my friends. At this time in my life, I needed to be around positive and encouraging people, not folks who would drain me with negativity. So, I worked at making new friends who had compassion, and let go of some who were negative. It was not easy. It was also not easy to keep a simple lifestyle, because there are so many expectations from other people. Ultimately, I realized if I ran myself into the ground, I would be the one who had to deal with the pain, and somehow that helped me make my decisions.

There have been many things I couldn't change, like my son's life. At this time, he has had six accidents. But, to my amazement, he is still alive. One car accident cost him a kidney, and it occurred at the same time I was waiting to have surgery.

Due to my physical pain, and his accident, I fell into a severe depression. With therapy and counseling, I am now feeling good again. I still go to counseling weekly.

I'm no longer in braces but I do use a scooter on a part-time basis, such as long shopping trips. A few days ago, a fellow asked me, "Glenda, how are you doing?"

I thought for a moment before answering, "You know, I believe these last few years have been the best ones of my life! Even though my life has had its challenges, having survived them, I've found what makes my life worth living, what is right for me and most importantly what is real."

In the wee hours of the morning, during excruciating pain, I learned to call out to my Maker for help, and he gave me the peace that passeth all understanding. I also learned that He is tough enough to endure my anger and is forgiving of it.

A few years ago, when I thought my life was over, it was actually beginning. I never dreamed I'd be writing these words, nor did I ever think my first poetry chapbook would be published last year. I can honestly say now, in hindsight, I am grateful for all of the lessons these challenges have taught me. They taught me how to live. I have now come full circle.

~Glenda Barrett

Bicycling Home

Most people never run far enough on their first wind
to find out they've got a second.
~William James

I f you had recently watched me bicycle sixty-three miles, you never would have guessed that I was a burn survivor who had to learn to walk again.

Holding onto my walker, I was Frankenstein's monster, my bandaged arms and legs jerking down the hospital corridor. I lurched down the hallway, dragging one leg forward, then the next and then, drooping against the nurse for support, I broke out into a cold sweat. Despair overwhelmed me. What if my legs remained stiff and inflexible? What if I had to spend my thirties behind a walker? How would I ever hike in the Oakland hills again, stroll along the ocean from Cliff House to the San Francisco Zoo, or bike twenty-five miles?

At age thirty-two, I biked, swam, or walked almost every day, sometimes doing two or three of these activities daily. A month before my accident, I schemed with a friend about doing a triathlon for fun. I had faith in my strength and endurance. I knew I could count on biking and swimming to get me through any kind of stress and make me feel whole and content.

All of this changed when a factory exploded as I was walking by. I had been on vacation visiting a friend in Boston. The only parts of my body not burned were my torso and feet. I had third-degree burns on my legs and second-degree burns on my arms, face, and neck. My doctor recommended skin graft surgery and shaved skin from my stomach to apply to the front and back of my legs, from my thighs to my ankles. I lay on my back, unable to move for a week, while the new skin attached itself to the little bit of old skin that wasn't burned.

I looked like a mummy, wrapped in miles of white gauze from head to toe. After some time, my mother tried to encourage me. "Eva, think of what you want your future to be." I wanted to be able to roll over and get out of bed by myself, bend my arms and legs, and walk again.

Close to a month after my accident, I was strong enough to move to a rehab hospital. I lay on a gray mat in the airy gym. My physical therapist asked me to push my legs against her hand. I winced. My legs were as rigid as wooden boards. "You can do it," she said. I threw my whole self into pushing and bent my legs one inch. Then another. It gave me hope. It was the first glimpse of my former self.

That afternoon, I sat on a stationary bicycle. My ankles wobbled, my feet were lead weights, my legs jerky. I gritted my teeth, straining my muscles to move the pedals. After ten minutes, I wilted. I lay still for hours.

On another day I walked outdoors, wearing a wide-brimmed straw hat, blue cotton pants, and a long sleeved butter yellow shirt. Clinging to the black metal railing of the steep staircase by the side of the hospital, I hoisted my right foot onto the concrete step, then my left. I stopped to catch my breath. I continued, step by step, huffing and puffing, till I reached the top. Breathless at the bottom, I collapsed into a wheelchair and closed my eyes. Later, resting in bed, a picture of myself swimming across a lake popped into my mind. When I told my dad, he said, "You'll get your endurance back, or move beyond it."

After a long recovery on the East Coast, I returned to the Bay Area, eager to bicycle through Golden Gate Park to Ocean Beach the way I used to. On my first ride I whizzed down the street and, before I knew it, I was winded. Prickles smarted my calves. Piercing pins and needles jabbed and stabbed my legs. I hopped on one foot, then the other, unable to stand still, as shooting pains stung my skin. Fraught with anxiety, I clenched my handlebars. What if I never got back my energy? What if I had to use a cane, walker, or wheelchair the rest of my life?

The accident traumatized me. Loud noises made me shake with terror. Balls of fire rolled toward me, flames as high as houses. The air reeked of smoke. I was certain an explosion would happen at any moment. It would trap me. My skin grafts itched like thousands of mosquito bites. I cringed when I saw my scars—dark purple, puffy snakeskin. My mother told me, "The important thing is you're walking again."

I was walking. With each step forward I let go of the flames, the roaring wind. With each step I let the aroma of crackly autumn leaves wash over me and let the odor of scorched hair fade away. With each step I told my legs, "You are strong. I'm proud of you for coming this far. I want you to be normal again without itches, prickles, or stiffness." I concentrated on bending my knees with each step.

I had to walk just the right amount. If I pushed myself beyond my limits or didn't walk enough, my skin was armor, unyielding and taut. I experimented with shorter walks, alternating with longer ones every other day. I stretched before and after walks. Gradually I lengthened both my stride and distance.

One of my doctors suggested pressure garments as a way to cut down on the prickles. The white tights pressed like boa constrictors against my skin. Within a few days I stood with ease and I walked and biked without the prickly pain tormenting my legs.

A major turning point came more than two years after my accident, when I went on a daylong, group cycling trip. My liveliness lasted the first half of the ride, but intense fatigue hit me on the return. On the verge of falling over, I did not know how I'd get back. I knew no one who could rescue me with a car, and even the nearest train station was ten miles away.

I stood still. I gulped water from my bottle. I drank more water. I forced the pedals millimeter by millimeter by millimeter. Pedaling felt like trying to move a brick wall with bare feet, but I told myself,

"You're making progress." I was. Teeny-tiny bits of the pebbly gray pavement faded away as I crept forward. I pushed my legs. My calves and thighs ached. Breathing hard, I struggled to rotate the pedals. "Pedal," I whispered. "Pedal. Pedal." I bent over, clutching the handlebars, grunting and sweating on the foggy, flat road. I shifted into first gear. My sneakers gripped the pedals. The pedals clunked forward. I gasped for breath. "Just one more time around," I told myself, when the pedals came full circle. "Just one more time."

I poured the last bit of my energy into propelling my feet forward and broke through the exhaustion. Energy surged through my body, swirling up through my legs, dancing its way to my heart, turning a pirouette when it reached my head. Exhilaration flowed over me. My endurance had returned.

~Eva Schlesinger

My Grandmother's Legacy

Pain is inevitable. Suffering is optional.
~M. Kathleen Casey

I was twelve when my grandmother died, her fingers so misshapen by rheumatoid arthritis they resembled claws. The same fingers that years earlier had kneaded bread, transformed flour and eggs into light, flaky pastry, and caressed my forehead when I was sick now lay useless and gnarled against the white sheets of her hospital bed.

Six years later, my own battle with arthritis began with a tingling, then numbness in my hands. I willed the pins and needles to stop, only to find the lack of sensation was worse. I rubbed my hands compulsively, trying to massage feeling back into them.

As I gazed down at my hands, they transformed from my own smooth, unlined fingers into claws—a legacy from my grandmother.

For years, the tingling and numbness came and went, following its own schedule. Worse during the fall and spring, better during winter and summer. Not enough to disturb my daily activities, but enough to remind me of my inheritance. I joked I would make a good weather forecaster. I could gauge the proximity and intensity of a storm by how much my hands ached.

Behind the joke lay fear—the vision of claws lurked in the back of my mind.

In my mid-twenties, I played squash. Quick twists and turns, constant pounding on the feet, and collisions were not uncommon. After a few years, I paid the price. Pain shot from my hip to my knee and I'd limp for a few hours. I traded in my squash racket for a TV remote and got my sports fix from watching games rather than playing them.

Once again, visions of claws danced in my head.

By my mid-thirties, my whole body ached. Getting up in the morning hardly seemed worth the effort since I'd be back in bed within hours. I slept a lot but never felt rested. My world shrank. I wasn't working, and it was hard to care about anything when all I wanted to do was sleep away the constant aches.

I tried one doctor and then another. The first doctor dismissed my complaints, too eager to hand out platitudes and anti-depressants. I was depressed, therefore I had a psychological rather than a physical problem.

The second doctor listened and acknowledged the depression as a side effect, not a cause. His diagnosis? Osteoarthritis, fibromyalgia, and scoliosis.

Along with arthritis, my grandmother had passed down a second legacy—a skeletal deformity in which bones in my lower right back were fused together. The result is reduced mobility and flexibility in my back, one leg shorter than the other, and lower back pain. The fibromyalgia, with its muscle aches and fatigue, I picked up on my own.

This doctor prescribed non-steroidal anti-inflammatory drugs (NSAIDS), though not without warning me of possible liver damage. I had to weigh improving my current life against damaging my future one. I chose the drugs.

I'd like to say I was "cured" immediately but that doesn't happen. However, getting up in the morning became less of a chore, the aches faded to a dull roar, and I could get through the day without an afternoon nap.

My world expanded. I read, took an interest in the news, and started teaching. Some days my hands ached from writing on the blackboard and my back hurt from bending over to help students, but it was manageable. The medication gave both my body and spirit a chance to rest and revitalize.

Visions of claws began to recede from my mind.

My mid-forties heralded a period of blossoming. I still taught, but added writing to my career path. Unfortunately, my career wasn't the only thing that blossomed. My arthritis progressed from mild to moderate, and pain spread from my hips and knees to my big toes, back, and neck.

I contemplated returning to bed, to let the arthritis win. Instead, I declared war.

I joined a gym and started a regimen of weight training and stretching. I worked with a personal trainer who modified exercises to meet my body's limitations while slowly pushing those limitations further and further. Over a period of months, I lost weight, gained muscle, and increased my flexibility. Since then I've added chiropractic sessions to help with the knot of pain in my lower back.

I still have mornings when I wake up and want to go back to sleep. Or days when my body creaks and groans. But most days I head to the gym and lose myself in the discipline of exercise. I've learned that sweat is a natural antidote to depression. Because of the stretching and strengthening exercises, I've cut my medication in half.

Right now my hands hurt because I've been typing too long and it's raining. But when I look down at them, I still see smooth, unlined hands, with a few "wisdom" spots that have appeared with age and experience.

This wisdom has taught me two things. One, arthritis is always going to be my constant companion; it doesn't have to be my master. And two, my grandmother's real legacy to me was not her arthritic hands or her fused bones—her legacy was her love.

~Harriet Cooper

48

The Love that Frames My New World

Oh, my friend, it's not what they take away from you that counts.
It's what you do with what you have left.
~Hubert Humphrey

My "careless" driving became the joke of the neighborhood. The third time I backed into the mailbox at the end of our driveway, I muttered another excuse trying to disguise the real reason for my ineptitude—I simply didn't see it.

"Yes, your retina is deteriorating," the ophthalmologist had said four years prior. He paused, then added coldly, "You need to prepare. There is no cure, and no one knows how long you'll have your sight."

By the time I reached thirty, my life had turned out better than a storybook. My husband's quick climb up the corporate ladder brought a special gift for me—the ability to stay home with my little ones. I took care of our three sons with delight and sighed with contentment at our perfect life, paved with success and prosperity.

Until one day my world began to shake. While my three-, five-, and seven-year-old sons wiggled in the back seat, I drove down a familiar street near our home. I turned on my blinker, glanced to the side before changing lanes, and unexpectedly, a loud metal clunk to my left startled me. Heart thumping, I glanced to see the car I'd sideswiped. It had come from nowhere. With the same shock, the effects of the retinal disease scraped pain into my life.

The bleak news from the ophthalmologist hovered over my sleepless nights. After years of experiencing increasing night blindness, my peripheral vision began to close in. I fought the notion I was losing my sight, but the evidence fought back, emphasizing the inevitable blindness that awaited me.

During nap time, I'd kneel beside my sleeping son's bed. With tears burning my eyes, I stared at his features—his long eyelashes resting on his chubby cheeks, his dark hair strands slipping down on his forehead and his lips that resembled his dad's. I engraved that image in my heart, not wanting to ever forget.

A few months swept by, along with more of my sight. I could only see what one sees through a keyhole. Struggling to see the phone book, I searched for specialists, healers, and herbal treatments. I inquired about transplants, even experimental developments in foreign countries. But, adding to my anxiety, all responded with negative answers.

The desperation also infected my family. My mom placed a large casserole dish of baked chicken on my kitchen counter. "I made extra for you and the family."

I heaved a pained sigh at the ugly reality that even cooking would be erased from the tasks I could perform. I wanted to thank her, but angry thoughts ricocheted in my head—angry and bitter at the unfairness of the whole thing. My sight loss affected all of us, bringing aching helplessness to our family gatherings.

I was losing something I valued, something vital for my survival. And I was losing it way too quickly. Finally, the day came when the faint light I saw turned to a dark gray nothing. And the prognosis that I'd be blind the rest of my life shoved me into an emotional dark prison.

For weeks, I'd cried out to God, prayed and begged umpteen times. With wrinkled tissue in hand, I dabbed my tears, held my breath, and in the silence heard the rumbling of my sons in the other room. Their world hadn't changed, but mine had been turned upside down. I still had to meet their needs, but no one could meet mine. They had a lifetime of possibilities, but mine had vanished.

Rather than bringing on despair, this comparison sparked something foreign and unexpected—the jolting realization that my blindness hadn't changed my role as their mom, nor altered my contribution to our marriage. Although sightless, I was still the same inside. A new sense of determination to care for them surged in me. I finally realized that, even though unable to journey on my own, their love would help me to navigate through life.

I vowed then to focus on their needs, to seek ways to still be their mom, and not to shuffle through life. Instead, I would take sure steps while holding the banner of victory. Shedding self-pity, I'd be the best mom I could be.

Though my world was dark, a renewed outlook shone light on my path. In the horizon, I perceived my family still together, thriving through tough times. And, using the white cane of perseverance, I'd still care for their every need.

To accomplish this, a willingness to readjust became my best tool. I sought rides from friends, relied on my husband to do the grocery shopping, found creative ways to still do the cleaning, cooking, laundry, and to monitor my three boys' busy activities at home.

One evening I came home from a prayer meeting. "Hey guys," I greeted them. "I'm home. Did you behave for Daddy?" I tossed my purse on the couch and scooped my three-year-old, Joe, into my arms, "I need a big hug."

"Need some help?" my husband offered.

"Nope, I'm home, and I'll take over," I assured him. "Come on, all of you. It's bath time." I rounded them up.

Instinctively, I counted the steps down the hallway and felt for the banister to head upstairs.

Once in their bedrooms, I pulled their one-piece pajamas from their dresser drawers. I reached in the closet for towels and then groped to find the soap in the tub.

While all three giggled and teased each other, in a matter-of-fact voice my three-year-old said, "Mommy has eyes at the end of her fingers."

I smiled at his unique reasoning. He was right. My fingertips had become my eyes—the effective sensors transforming what I touched into clear images in my mind.

My hearing also sharpened. I could differentiate their every sound, one voice from the other. I recognized each utterance, from their rambunctious screams to their faint whimpers. And each time they attempted to "trick Mom" by eating treats before meals, to their disappointment, my sense of smell tracked any aroma wafting from their direction.

Each trick they pulled became an opportunity to teach them to laugh, to find a sense of humor crucial when facing adversity, and to look beyond the circumstance into the lighter side of life.

The loss of my eyesight gave me the eyes to see the richness of a life with them—one that didn't need perfect health, a hefty bank account, or a bright and secure future. I saw more than that in the present.

I recall when I'd stare at my napping boy's face, fearing what I was losing. Now, I relish what I gained—a new portrait of life, painted with hues of possibilities, with vibrant colors dancing in my new horizon. And best of all, it's surrounded with love that frames my new world.

~Janet Perez Eckles

Walking Backward to Go Forward

There are many ways of going forward, but only one way of standing still.
~Franklin D. Roosevelt

My mother clutched the door handle and screamed as I veered towards the icy snowbank. We had made it successfully a few hundred yards from our driveway. My older brother, Jim, was home for Christmas so he took me to the parking lot behind the Triangle Movie Theater in Yorktown Heights, NY, and decided he would teach me how to drive in a way that was much less traumatic.

My recollections of Jim doing doughnuts in the dead-end street by Bedell Road in no way influenced my decision to put utter faith in his instruction. Jim was an excellent driver and had experience teaching me to navigate on wheels. His first lesson in riding a bike was so successful that he had to run down the backyard chasing after me so I wouldn't hit the apple tree. Jim now turned to me calmly and said, "Okay put it in reverse." I asked my obvious, "Don't you think that maybe I should learn to drive forward first?"

"No," was his reply. Tentatively and with frantic glances in my rear view mirror, I began to drive. I zigzagged, barely missing a lamppost at one point, and a few potholes at another. We did this for over an hour before I advanced to driving forward.

Despite the skills that Jim taught me, when I was twenty-four

I was involved in a near-fatal car accident. Among my injuries was a cracked pelvis. My orthopedic doctor was optimistic that I would recover without any difficulty walking, but as I sat in the wheelchair looking out my window, I was not certain. I became an immediate overachiever. I tried to stand as soon as possible, if only to have someone wash my hair. I played motivational music such as "Walking on Sunshine" by Katrina & The Waves and spent my mornings inching my way back and forth across my front walkway.

I tried to see the humor in the fact that I was twenty-four years old and had a walker. I promised myself I would use it as a clothes rack when I was fully healed (and I did!). The healing of the body is a miraculous thing, but something very odd happened while my bones were mending. The bones of my pelvis healed in such a way that at first I only regained movement to walk backwards in full complete steps. To go forward I could move about an inch at a time. If the doorbell rang or I had to walk a distance, I learned that I was much more efficient by turning around and reaching my destination by walking backward.

That healing process gave me time to reflect on my brief career, inexperienced relationships, and life in general. Everything thus far was backwards. I had been spent my time working towards goals that I didn't even want, developing skills I didn't want to use. When the time came, I stopped, turned and took some daring leaps forward. It didn't happen quickly, but I slowly made the necessary changes to point myself in the right direction.

Sometimes when our lives seem like we are driving in reverse or walking backwards, we are really learning the steps that will guide us into the greatest forward leaps of our lives. I just have to be patient and realize that sometimes putting one foot in front of the other doesn't go exactly in the direction that I planned. Sometimes, like a global positioning system, we have to go in every other direction but the path we need most, and then suddenly when the time is right, a voice will tell us exactly which way to go and we will leap forward on newly healed limbs.

~Susan LaMaire

A Good Sport

Life's problems wouldn't be called "hurdles"
if there wasn't a way to get over them.
~Author Unknown

My inner right thigh has a five-inch black and blue mark on it. I'm thrilled. Not because I enjoy wincing in pain every time I sit down on a wooden chair or because I am fond of the purple hue of my skin, but because I did something to earn that bruise: I climbed in a bathroom window after locking the keys inside the house.

This may not seem like a big deal to most people, but as someone who has muscular dystrophy, it is a gold medal in my personal Olympics.

Muscular dystrophy has taken away more than my muscle strength; it has taken away my confidence. I have been scared to try anything that requires a bit of athleticism. I am afraid of looking awkward, of falling down, of drawing unwanted attention to myself. Greater than my fear of getting hurt is my dread of discovering more things I can no longer do.

The last time I rode a bicycle, eight years ago, my thighs began to hurt so badly after three blocks that I had to get off the bike and wobble home. I haven't tried again. Some days my right arm can barely hold the weight of a dinner plate, so I've given up trying to bowl or play pool.

After several incidents of tripping over invisible bumps on the sidewalk and losing my balance while practically standing still, I started to redefine my persona. I buried the part of myself that was once able to throw a Frisbee the length of a football field; it was too painful to remember. I became an observer, not a jock. I read books; I didn't play soccer. I meditated and stretched. I made myself forget the pleasure of a tennis ball hitting the center of my racquet and sailing over the net.

But when a certain hunky outdoorsman named Matt came into my life, I was reminded of forgotten parts of myself. When he gave me the tour of his house, I was mesmerized by the weathered punching bag that hung from his basement ceiling. He handed me a pair of boxing gloves and left me alone with the bag and my fears. And I beat the crap out of that thing. I stopped every few seconds, afraid I might pull all the muscles in my back or wake up the next day too tired to walk. But as the rage and determination and sadness and joy all poured out, I kept on punching. My face got flushed and my body grew moist with sweat. My breath became labored. It felt like coming home. The next day I ached a bit, but it was that exquisite soreness that follows a satisfying workout.

Last week, I had dinner at my friend Felicia's house, when her friend Sam said, "I swam in the Bay today. I'm training for the Alcatraz swim."

"I biked for thirteen miles and then ran four miles around Golden Gate Park," Felicia bantered back. "That's longer than the triathlon I'm doing next month."

"Oh, yeah?" I piped up. "Well I climbed a ladder today. I was helping Matt work on his boat and I had to climb a ladder to get up there."

That confidence was still with me the day I shut the door to Matt's house, accidentally locking his house keys inside. My apologies could not make a spare set appear. His neighbors were out of town; his car keys and cell phone were trapped in the back bedroom.

We walked around the house like burglars staking out a property. The bathroom window was open a crack. My fingers began tingling with anticipation.

"Let me climb in the window," I said without hesitation. After all, I was the thinner one. I knew I could fit through the open window. I just didn't know how I'd do it.

Then that lost tomboy inner child of mine grabbed a black plastic bucket, threw it on the ground upside down, and stepped on top of it while leaning on Matt's shoulder. I maneuvered my left leg through the open window and straddled the sill sideways.

"Now what are you going to do?" Matt asked as I dangled three feet above his blue-tiled floor.

"I may not be strong, but I'm flexible," I said. "Lower me down real slowly. We can do this."

My thigh scraped against the ridges of the sill as I slowly slid down the inside wall. My left foot landed squarely on the gleaming tile. I felt the grace of a perfect ballet stretch, the passion of an all-out karate kick, the delight of my ten-year-old self jumping down from our crabapple tree.

There may come a day when I will not be able to get up a ladder or slide across a window frame, but today I can. And as I massage the tender rainbow-colored bruise on my inner right thigh, I know it is the mark of an athlete.

~Karen Myers

Living with Ghosts

It is far harder to kill a phantom than a reality.

~Virginia Woolf

How strange to call something "phantom" when it is so real. Despite its ghostly name, phantom pain is as real as it gets for an amputee. I have been plagued with the certainty of it these last ten years. For decades, doctors believed this post-amputation phenomenon was a psychological problem, but experts now recognize a physical cause for this pain—that it actually originates in the brain. At seventy-six, the phantoms still come and go with nary a warning, often with fantasies in which my hand and fingers move. Other times, the burning and stabbing leave me a whimpering mess, dreading the random daily onslaughts.

I mourned the loss of my dominant right arm as though someone near and dear had brutally succumbed. My surgeon warned that great pain often occurs a few days following amputation, that some people find the pain and delusions decrease over time, and others experience torturous bouts for many years. I wondered how the pain would haunt me, how intense it would be, how long it would last. I only know that when that devil hit during eight weeks in the hospital, it was the only time I allowed myself a piercing shriek.

I may never overcome the weird illusions as my brain still grapples with the amputation. If there's any merit to the torment, it has taught me great tolerance for pain of any sort. The accident and surgeries themselves were nothing compared to the bouts of excruciating pain that make me sit straight up in my bed from a sound sleep.

Since there are no wondrous drugs to soothe the agony, my doctor sent me to pain management specialists. Treatments dragged along for weeks and were dismal failures. Several medications yielded nothing but homesickness, thoughts that God had abandoned me, and a need to have my things and loved ones around me.

Antidepressants came next, then electro nerve therapy along with a host of further medications. I felt like a walking drugstore. I determined to keep my psyche intact rather than blundering around as a mindless zombie. Weather changes and fatigue were examined too, both proving unlikely sources of pain.

Spinal cord stimulation was offered—an electrical stimulator implanted under the skin, and an electrode placed next to the spinal cord. The nerve pathways in the spinal cord would be stimulated by electrical current, interfering with the impulses travelling towards the brain and lessening the pain in the phantom limb, leaving only a tingling sensation in the arm. Rather than trying out electrical gadgets via spinal surgery, I preferred holding onto hope the pain would lessen in time.

Stimulations of the brain, and even acupuncture, fell short versus my own ability to help myself by praying and by left-handed practice with crossword puzzles. For if all this pain originates in the brain, I resolved, maybe I should keep it busy enough to crowd out the ghosts. I was still alive, anxious to fit a prosthesis and get back to the business of living.

For a long time I dreaded family and friend get-togethers for fear I would embarrass us all, for without warning, I would grasp my hook and rock in agony. Uncontrollable tears gushed from me those first few years. How strange it was to spill that much water in mere seconds without sobbing aloud. My grandchildren were mystified and powerless to help.

Whereas I had nearly given up on artwork, needlework, and riding my ATV or snowmobile, the family jumped in to save my bacon. I persevered left-handed despite the awful news that rheumatoid arthritis had settled in. My play toys were equipped with left side handlebar throttles and a right side gizmo to fit various hooks. I continued pecking around daily on a computer, and even took hook in hook to crochet ski caps for grandchildren. Daily chores rarely spawn painful episodes, for the phantoms mostly prefer the quiet times. Along with skillful use of prosthetics, managing the burden has been the greatest challenge of my life.

There's no doubt about it, the severity and frequency of my phantoms has decreased some over the last few years. Moreover, I have learned to handle the demon within. Most of the time, nary a soul would even recognize the twinges and sharp surges going on up and down what's left of my arm. Mindful of the moments they too suffer, I shed tears for our troops learning to use the latest state-of-the-art limbs. How bravely our resolute heroes work to get back to their own business of living.

Recently, while spending days in our local hospital for rheumatoid therapy, I noted that the Pain Management Department was continually busy. Some of the patients were happy with results for various mental and physical afflictions. Others were like me—impatient and anxious. I know it is my own tenacious spirit and deep faith in all the things the good Lord has bestowed that allows me to cope with the intolerable. Now that they have haunted me these ten years, I tolerate the ghosts that defy my very soul.

~Kathe Campbell

Writing a New Dream

Renew your passions daily.
~Abbe Yeux-verdi

"Y̶ou'll be blind by the time you're twenty-five," a doctor at Children's Hospital predicted. "Your blood sugars are much too high."

I started hearing the phrase "diabetic retinopathy" at the age of six when I was diagnosed as a Type 1 diabetic. This condition causes fragile blood vessels to grow and rupture in the back of the eye, and can lead to progressive blindness. Due to the early onslaught of the disease, the risk of developing this devastating side effect was very high. The frightening phrase reverberated in my head to the point of obsession. The thought of going blind became my biggest fear, my worst nightmare and my eventual nemesis.

It consumed me. It devoured me. No matter where I was or what I was doing, it hovered overhead like a dark cloud, waiting for just the right opportunity to break open and shatter my world. As I sat in classes from grade school through business school and on to my job preparing cases for judges, the noose around my neck tightened.

Looking at everything through crystal clear vision, it was impossible to imagine a world without sight. How long would I hold onto my 20/20? When would it happen? Where would I be? The chilling words of that doctor from all those years ago haunted my subconscious. "You'll be blind by the time you're twenty-five."

Painting was my passion, my sanctuary. Losing myself in tranquil settings of picturesque landscapes filled me with peace and serenity. Painting was my haven, the only place I could escape where those threatening words couldn't reach me. But the minute I put my paintbrush down, there they were, sucking the life out of me.

As fate would have it, the first bout of blindness came when I was twenty-one. I had just put the finishing touches on my Tuscan countryside, a landscape dotted with vineyards of rich ruby red, deep purple and amber. But just as I sat back to admire my masterpiece, a huge splattering of black paint appeared on my canvas. Confused, I blinked several times, wondering where the paint had come from.

Slowly but surely, my brain received the message. It wasn't paint covering my canvas; it was blood covering my retina. My worst nightmare had just come true. I had just had a retinal hemorrhage.

Dumbfounded, the paintbrush slipped from my hand and rolled across the floor. I couldn't breathe. Feeling boneless and completely numb, I sank into a chair. Then the tears spilled. "No! Not yet! It's too soon."

"What happens now?" I asked my retinal specialist. "I see spidery webs everywhere I look. It's alarming. What can be done?"

"The hemorrhage is in the right eye," my doctor said. "Your left eye is fine. The blood vessels are leaking. The blood is internal. Eventually, the blood will be absorbed by the body. The main risk is that scar tissue can form which will hinder the vision permanently. Only time will tell how much vision you'll get back. But the good news is, you will never lose the sight in your left eye."

He was wrong. Precisely three months after my twenty-fifth birthday, I had a massive hemorrhage in my left eye, my good eye. For the next twenty years, vision came and went. I went through numerous eye surgeries in an attempt to keep my vision. And through it all, I continued painting through magnification. As long as I could paint, there was hope. But after one final operation, I lost the battle and all remaining vision. And I buried all dreams of painting. Despondent and disillusioned, I enrolled in a sixteen-week program for the blind and visually impaired. I learned mobility, personal adjustment and the use of a computer with adaptive software. A whole new world opened up to me through this program.

"Jaws and Window-Eyes are leading software for the blind," my instructor told me. "They convert components of the Windows operating system into synthesized speech. This allows for total accessibility to Windows-based computer systems."

"You mean I can use the Internet? E-mail? Microsoft with all its tools and features?" Hope soared for the first time in years. No longer would I have to use thick glasses to read or magnification to make print larger. I could type at the pace I once did and the disembodied voice would narrate what I typed on the screen. Amazing.

"That's right," my instructor said. "By learning how to use hot keys to control the mouse, you can use Microsoft Access, Excel and PowerPoint. Whatever you look up on the Internet will be narrated to you through modern technology."

For the next several years, I learned that when one door closes, another door opens. There is a plethora of opportunity available for the blind and visually impaired through the gift of technology. Not only do I have a speaking computer, but I have a speaking watch, alarm clock, calculator and glucometer to independently test my blood levels. Believe it or not, I even have a gadget that identifies money and color.

I went to the local college and obtained a certificate in medical transcription. I graduated top in my class with high honors. But my heart wasn't in it. Transcribing did nothing to fill my creative muse. But during my classes, my life took yet another unexpected twist when I discovered my passion for writing. And after a long and winding road—and three publications, a new dream has resurrected. Today, instead of painting my pictures on canvas, I paint my pictures with words.

~Sharon Donovan

Thrive

Worry never robs tomorrow of its sorrow, it only saps today of its joy.
~Leo Buscaglia

Not very long ago, I woke up one morning and discovered I couldn't walk. The doctor said that two vertebrae in my neck had quickly shifted, resulting in choking off my spinal cord. This was not the result of an accident. It came out of the blue. I had emergency surgery in Boston, but the spinal cord damage has left me disabled—physically. I can only walk for a few minutes at a time, and I can't lift my legs to climb even a curb.

At first I was stunned and depressed, and occasionally I still am. But I have learned so much from this experience. Naturally, I wish I had discovered these things without having a life-altering illness as the motivational force.

First, I've learned that we don't need to be a tower of inspiration to anybody but ourselves.

Sometimes when I read stories about people who have had terrible things happen to them and come out on the other side by doing something miraculous, I get down on myself in comparison. Like breast cancer survivors who go on to write inspirational books, or the amazing wheelchair-bound people who complete the Boston marathon with just the strength of their arms. Of course, people like this are spectacular. But when we try to measure up, often our self-assessments don't make the same heroic grades. My point is this: that is okay. For me, it's an Olympic moment when I take the garbage out, though it won't make newspaper headlines or give me an interview with Barbara Walters. But it is my marathon, my championship.

Another thing (I hate to even admit this to myself) is that when I was in the hospital for three days, there was something pretty comfortable about just staring out the window at the Boston skyline, knowing there was no possibility of business calls or children needing something, or laundry. It was enforced non-productivity.

Even before my disability, I could never allow myself to take time out by watching a TV movie during the day, unless I was either sick or doing something useful, like exercising. But I have learned that we don't need these excuses to take non-productive time for ourselves. And actually it is productive to take time-outs. We can simply sit and gaze at leaves as they fall, or a bee land on a flower, or do absolutely nothing and do it guilt-free. There's no need to justify seemingly useless activities by ironing or folding clothes or being sick.

I've also learned that present moment living is the only way to go. Will my vertebrae shift in other areas of my spine? The neurologist says it's "unlikely." But he didn't say, "No." I can choose to ruin my day by worrying about something that may never happen. Or I can choose to live in the present. I know this is very tough. I've always been a worrier about the what-ifs. But, you know, that list can be infinite. It includes car accidents, cancer, and on and on. My husband taped a saying from a fortune cookie to the front of our fridge. It says, "Don't trouble trouble till trouble troubles you."

When I first became disabled, I'd hate it when I'd go to a restaurant and a server would say, "Watch your step." I hated it because I couldn't accept the fact that I could barely walk. I was in denial and wished everyone around me would be too. When my husband installed a safety bar in the shower, I was angry and defensive. "I don't need that!" I said. But I did and always will. I'm no longer in denial. I can't be. Now, when someone warns me about a step, I don't take offense. I appreciate it. With or without an illness, it never diminishes us to receive help. People want to help others. It makes them feel good.

Lots of life is about perspective. Problems have a vastly different hierarchy now. If the kitchen's a mess, I don't really care. If my blouse isn't ironed and has a few wrinkles, I don't care. If I pull a muscle or have a cold, it's annoying but not the end of the world.

I wish it didn't take this experience to teach me not to take so many things for granted. When my pal Julie and I were heading to our table for lunch, she suggested we stop to let others pass. As a woman scooted by us, Julie said, "I bet she doesn't appreciate that she can walk like that." Now I appreciate my legs, though they're wobbly, and my arms that work fine and my family, friends, pets, hot breakfasts, and pizza with extra cheese. Oh, the list is endless!

And finally, I've discovered that coping and thriving are two very different things.

When I think of coping, I think of Band-Aids. Of course at times they're needed, such as to protect a scratch from getting further nicked. Coping means to me the same as managing—making do, not letting things get worse.

Thriving is a different story. Thriving means, in my mind, not just protecting ourselves from further hurt, but enhancing, and actually making things far better.

I look at people who deal successfully with problems, whether they be physical, emotional, or situational (such as loss of a job), as those who cope or those who thrive.

At first I just coped, but eventually I decided that wasn't enough. Although, it's not easy at times, I aim to thrive. I'm not just pleased when I've moved up another notch on a physical therapy machine, I'm elated. Now, I want to use my skills and experience to help other people going through similar problems. I want to turn this around so I don't focus on my disability but instead marvel at my abilities.

The shifting of my vertebrae took away my chances of running, climbing, or walking more than a few yards at a time, but it didn't touch my often-frightened though rarely stoppable determination to thrive.

That part was left intact.

~Saralee Perel

Tough Times, Tough People

Fired!

*He who is outside his door
has the hardest part of his journey behind him.*

~Dutch Proverb

54

The Moment
My Life Began

Turn your face to the sun and the shadows fall behind you.
~Maori Proverb

Monday morning, 8:15 A.M. is when it happened. I lost my job. Not just any job, my first real job. This was my first professional experience outside of graduate school. I worked almost two years before my vice president called me into her office to relay the life-altering news.

It didn't take long. In fact, I kind of knew it was coming. I just sat there listening to the sad tone of my boss' voice and the other vice president who accompanied her as they talked about how much they'd miss me, how sad they were, what my severance options were and how they knew whatever I did, I would succeed. The more they spoke, the more I started to drift into a moment of complete surrender to my faith.

Just a week prior to the news, I was in Hawaii enjoying a vacation with my close girlfriends. During our weeklong getaway, we decided to skydive. I had always been a planner—a control freak—and yearned to let go of that characteristic. As I fell from the plane, I let go of all my worries and just lived in the moment. I didn't worry about deadlines, relationships, the things of this world. Instead, I took in the beauty of the sea, the mountainside and the unexplainable peace that comes from just floating and having no clue what the next moment will hold or feel like.

It was in my boss' office that morning that I reverted to the feeling I had as I took a step of faith and fell. Fell and let go of all things in my control, and trusted that life isn't about me and my plans. Instead it's about following what I believe to be true and trusting the one I believe created me.

That day was the first day of the rest of my life. I often tell my old co-workers that the day I lost my job was the best day of my life. It's the day I stopped living in a nine-to-five box and started living life as it was meant to be lived: adventurously.

The next couple of weeks were trying. But I couldn't let circumstances get me down. I was a woman who yearned to enjoy life, and no matter what my income now was, I was determined to make that dream a reality.

Two weeks after I was let go, I found myself surrounded by middle school students on a bus heading to North Carolina. I had always wanted to volunteer with youth, but never had the time due to my job and prior commitments. But since I was no longer constrained, I went on a weeklong trip as a chaperone. I was blessed to get to know some amazing girls as we shared a hotel room, and even more blessed as I watched these kids perform for various non-profits throughout the city.

Next, I went to camp as a leader. Again, I developed relationships that would benefit the middle and high school students. I was in fellowship with them, along with growing internally myself. But even more exciting things were on the horizon.

I had always wanted to go overseas on a mission trip, and in fact there was one I was very interested in. We would set up a sports camp for orphans in a desert town clear across the world. The kicker? The trip was scheduled for the same week as my biggest event at work. I could never have gone.

I applied for a passport and started to prepare for the trip. My new passport showed up in July, just days before I was asked to accompany a group of teenagers to the Dominican Republic on another mission trip. The trip would be free, since I would go as a leader and there was nothing holding me back.

My life only continued to get better. I travelled across the country. I visited London for the first time. I learned about culture, others, and myself. I had made a commitment to myself in the beginning of 2008 to make it a year of no fear, and for the first time in my life I had a free schedule to play with. I had no classes, no meetings, no work.

I had gone to school to be a writer, I was born to be a writer, and for the first time I could take the time to be a writer. My job interviews focused on writing. Continuing my education was also a big dream of mine, and I enrolled in online courses for another graduate degree. I was chasing my dreams at a time when the world was telling me to be depressed and settle for whatever I could get. The loss of my job opened doors I never would have foreseen or even attempted to venture through.

~Michelle McCormick

55

They Won't Eat Us!

To fear is one thing.
To let fear grab you by the tail and swing you around is another.
~Katherine Paterson

I got a pink slip. Sounds sexy, right? I wish I could say that it was the slinky, sassy kind that one might find in a Victoria's Secret catalog. But given the state of our economy, you probably know what kind of pink slip I'm really talking about. After all, pink is the new black in this economy.

I can't say I'm surprised. I've had my eye on the market. I've also worked in the corporate world long enough to know how these things work. It literally comes down to the dollars and cents of the matter. It's not personal. It's business. So over the past few months I have braced for this moment, if not dared myself to embrace the opportunity that will come with my severance package.

However, convincing my nerves to look on the bright side has been an entirely different story, especially on that somewhat sobering morning when I was sequestered in a faraway conference room to receive the news.

On the long walk to that conference room, where a senior leader from New York awaited me, I called to mind a profound conversation with my three-year-old niece, Lexi, just a few days before. She shared a story about this dinosaur café her dad, my baby brother, was taking her to for lunch in Orlando where they live.

"They won't eat us," she kept repeating in her sweet little voice. "They" being the dinosaurs.

I wasn't sure who she was trying to convince, herself or me. Funny, but those were the words that saved me on that seemingly grim morning.

"They won't eat me," I mumbled to myself as I walked the green mile toward my impending fate, shuffling my feet like a kid on her way to the principal's office. The truth being, I wasn't all that convinced that they wouldn't.

All I knew for sure was that little Lexi was onto something beyond her three tender years on this planet. When you think about it, no matter how big the proverbial meat-eating dinosaurs are in this life, they won't eat us unless we let them.

So after working nineteen years for a company I loved, with people I loved even more, I felt numb sitting in that conference room face-to-face with the next chapter of my life. In a big way, after months of much fear and uncertainty, it was somewhat of a relief to finally hear the words out loud and to be assured there is life after a layoff.

Believe it or not, there is a certain freedom that comes packaged in the truth and in the distinct knowledge that, in the end, they won't eat us!

~Natalie June Reilly

The Glass Slipper

Simplicity makes me happy.
~Alicia Keys

We're middle-class America, working hard for our dreams, working hard to help our children dream.

My husband, Tom, used to be a banker. I was a teacher. We started a family in the 1980s and bought a home, based on only one income. I quit work to raise our children, Adam and Lauren.

We saved and invested. We chose not to buy a bigger home. No cars for the kids when they were in high school. We bought college bonds instead, and socked away more money to pay for college. We were responsible parents. We planned for the future.

I was living the fairy tale: a house, two kids. No dog—Tom doesn't like them. But the shoe fit. The glass slippers fit.

Then the word "deregulation" entered our lives.

The bank Tom worked for merged with another, becoming bigger.

"But if there are fewer banks, how is that helping competition?" I asked him.

"Some say it will, some say it won't," he said. "Time will tell."

The word "recession" entered our children's vocabulary as Tom's bank merged again, becoming even larger. It merged again a few years later. Then again. Now it's a giant.

Each merger Tom was awarded with a pay cut.

Each merger reduced our health care benefits.

Each merger had a Reduction In Force.

In 2003, we inserted the term RIF on my husband's resumé. We both sent out our resumés. My job as an adjunct English instructor brought in abysmal pay without any health care benefits. But when you're fifty, it's not so easy changing jobs.

In the midst of sending out resumés, my husband urged me to start writing.

"You love to tell a story," he said. "Write your novel. This is the time to do it."

I started writing chapters as I hunted for jobs on the Internet. Guilt filled me. I sent out more resumés.

Support came through the help of friends. Tom was offered a job as a vendor setting up displays at home improvement stores. Less than half of the pay he used to receive, but it was an income with health care benefits.

We rejoiced.

Three years later, the company went under.

Thanks to another friend, Tom secured a job as a contractor with AT&T. We had to pay for our own health care, but it was a job.

In September the following year, the contractors were let go.

All of our careful financial planning helped us stand up in this climate of downsizing, but taking our family on a vacation to Mexico or Hawaii was no longer an option. All we could afford was a week-end in Michigan, which we did do as a family. We now viewed steak as a luxury, but realize chicken is better for us anyway.

Our kids are in their twenties now, so a thinner Christmas would be no big deal to them.

The fairy tale had changed.

But had it really?

It was only in my mind that our Christmas tree should be surrounded with presents. What I was used to. What I saw as a kid. What I thought I had to keep creating for my own kids.

I shook my head and breathed deep, staring at my feet inside the glass slippers. I was still trying to fill the slippers up.

Then the light changed, helping me to see my feet more clearly. Who decided to make Cinderella's dream shoes out of glass anyway? They must never have seen skin pressed against glass. It's not very pretty.

That's when I decided to take my glass slippers off.

As the fresh air reached between my toes, my mind cleared. I remembered the feel of the sand under my feet from our recent trip to Michigan. My college-age children laughing as I hopped and leaped over the stinging-hot sand. We all laughed at each other as we realized we were the whitest on the beach. We glowed on the outside and within. My children never complained about sharing cars with their parents in high school, nor did they complain now about sharing the hotel room in Michigan.

I thought I needed to provide palm trees, an ocean, and perhaps a dolphin.

I should have known that our laughter was enough.

Back home, friends asked how we got our kids to go on a vacation with us.

"We've always done things together," I told them. "When Lauren was sixteen, the two of us shared the family's first cell phone."

Lauren and I laugh and can't believe we did that, but we were both happy to help each other. I now see that we had invested in family bonds back then, not just college bonds.

Our present is filled with simple needs.

On weekends, my husband and I have a bonfire in the backyard, holding hands, soaking up the heat. Who needs the sun in Mexico? We have heat and smoke in Illinois!

Our daughter comes home for the weekend from college, and shares her exploits around the campfire.

Out of college, my son now lives at home rent-free. We prefer he sock his money away in the bank, planning his own financial future, and easing our minds in the process.

I serve chicken dinners at home surrounded by candles. And my husband falls asleep on my lap as I watch two Jane Austen flicks for our Saturday night date.

As I write, I discover one of the many notes of encouragement my husband has left me, supporting my writing. We have cut back these last few years to help our children, but my husband has never cut back on his support for my dreams. He believes in me, so that makes him my Prince.

I used to wear glass slippers, but I walk on the sand now, barefoot and smiling. I burst out laughing as I realize sand is an ingredient in the recipe to make glass. I've downsized, too.

~April Heide-Kracik

Nickel Walks

Success comes in cans, failure in can'ts.
~Author Unknown

You've seen beer cans and soda cans lying pell-mell at the side of the road, the metal cylinders that litter every town's highways and byways, tossed by drivers who can't be bothered to find a garbage can. Well, next time you see one, say a prayer of thanks for the litterbug because that tossed can may change a life.

There was a time when my husband was out of work, a recession was in full swing, and we had two small boys to feed. We exhausted every possibility for job opportunities, cut expenses to the bone, and depleted all resources. Every day would dawn with hope that it would be that particular day which would bring a job and income. Day after day—nothing.

I knew where all the Goodwill stores were and developed an eagle eye for finding nearly-new jeans, shirts, and jackets for the boys. It was a gala event when Mommy brought home "new" clothes to replace the holey pants which little boys create. The smiles on their little faces took away the sting of what I needed to do to clothe them. I felt like I had struck it rich on the days when clothes with blue tickets were half-price.

Rummaging through dented cans on the clearance shelf in the back of the grocery store became a family sport—a far cry from throwing anything and everything into the shopping cart without a thought about price. Gone, too, was a quick stop at McDonald's. Had we actually eaten out twice a week once upon a time? Did we waste all that money on greasy food just to get the must-have collectible toys? Canned beans never tasted so good.

Chances of finding a job were slim to none in New England in the early 1980s. Our high spirits disintegrated and we became panic-stricken. In desperation, I knew I had to keep going for the sake of our children. Despite my own promise that I would never ask for help, I held up my head and walked into a government office to apply for food stamps.

Sitting and waiting my turn, I wanted to bolt outside and never stop running. Embarrassment turned into anger when the apathetic clerk looked over my application, snapped her gum, and stated in a disinterested voice, "Oh, sorry. You DO qualify for food stamps, but you have to sell your car before you can receive them." Without missing a beat, she turned away and called on the next hapless applicant. Stunned, I explained that we needed our car to look for work. We didn't live near public transportation and there would be no possibility of obtaining employment without a vehicle. Without even looking, the clerk muttered, "Sorry. Next?" With that, I was dismissed.

I stumbled into the bright sunlight and swore that I would never again ask anyone for help. Never again would I be humiliated. But, the problem remained. How could I feed my family?

Knowing I needed to clear my head, I began to go for long walks. The fresh air felt good and I began to sort things out in my mind, looking at our situation from a different angle. Despair was futile, so praying was substituted for complaining. I prayed for the blessings of being out of work, for having a husband who was trying to be a good provider, for people who had less than us, for healthy children. Some days I was pretty low and could only thank God for having a pulse, but I made the conscious effort to have gratitude every morning when I walked.

Trying to avoid traffic on our country roads, I edged over into the brush and noticed all the cans on the ground. I could cash in each container for a nickel. A plastic bag tucked into my pocket became a necessity and then two bags became the norm. Soon there were dozens of sticky, dripping cans rattling around to redeem for enough money to buy a gallon of milk! A few more days of collecting and a loaf of bread was my trophy.

My goal each day was to see how many "nickels" I could find. Every week there would be enough to buy a staple, but, most importantly, my attitude improved, and being out of work wasn't the major disaster which I had initially perceived. I began to experience the beauty around me which money couldn't buy: Canadian geese honking their way across the sky, skunk cabbage poking its verdant crowns through crusts of snow, the sweet smell of lazy, early morning breezes—signs of spring and hope and new beginnings.

That was more than twenty-five years ago, and today we face economic uncertainty and massive unemployment again. Last week I saw a man rummaging in the underbrush gathering up cans. He became beet-red when I shouted "Hello," and he began to make excuses as to why he was picking up the dirty containers. I waved away his explanations and said, "A nickel is a nickel," and I bent over to help him fill his bag.

~Irene Budzynski, RN

Crisis, Opportunity, and Change

When written in Chinese, the word crisis is composed of two characters.
One represents danger and the other represents opportunity.
~John F. Kennedy

I was in my late forties and I was happy and healthy and had a great job. I was a single mother and I was quite proud of myself for what I had accomplished. I not only owned my home, but I also owned two rental properties. I had experienced great financial success throughout my professional career so I was not quite prepared for what I was about to face.

The day that I was laid off was actually the catalyst that propelled me to make life changes. I was completely blind-sided when I was laid off in January of 2007. I worked in the financial industry and always had a well-paying job—not having a job was foreign to me. I not only had extensive work experience, but I had an excellent work ethic and interpersonal skills, which I knew would help me land another good job.

I started my job search immediately. There was no reason why I could not get a good job. I had a great resumé, I interviewed well, and I was always able to establish a great rapport with anyone almost immediately.

After a few interviews, I had a feeling I was not going to land the right job anytime soon. I am not sure if this was due to the impact of the economic crisis in the financial sector, or if it was because I needed to make changes, or possibly a combination of both.

Since I had no idea how long I would be without a job, I put myself on a very strict budget. I only bought the essentials and I cut out all entertainment. I felt very sad for my son because this crisis was affecting him too. I feared using up my savings, so I decided to sell one of my properties. It was on the market for six months and only two serious buyers came along, but due to the credit crunch, they were unable to obtain loans, and I was unable to sell.

I had to stay positive. I knew I had to depend on God's guidance now more than ever. I had a responsibility to my son and my mom who was staying with us temporarily. My mom came to stay with us after my father died in October 2006.

In April, a few months after I was laid off, my mom became very ill. She began experiencing excruciating chest pains. We were constantly at the hospital or with her doctor. Shortly after that, my autistic son began having behavioral issues in school. I became consumed with worries about my mom, my son, and finding a job. I began to have frightening dreams. I prayed for guidance and for strength to deal with everything that I was facing.

My unemployment benefits were about to end and I seriously wondered how I would make ends meet. Since I was also living on my savings and watched them deplete every month, I looked at what other funds I could access. After some careful thought and meditation, I decided to liquidate a small IRA account. If I budgeted carefully, I knew this would get me through at least another year. I knew this was a good decision because I felt a sense of calm.

Since I was allowing my inner voice to guide me, I made a conscious decision to start enjoying life once again. I also shifted my focus from my job hunt and money worries to my son and my mom. My mom was getting better and I began to feel good about myself again. During my quiet moments, I was saying these words, "I have money for everything." I started to take my family to dinner every once in a while. I took my son to the movies, the park, for walks, and to visit friends. Overall, I spent a lot more time with him and with my mom. This is something I would not have been able to do if I had been working.

One morning after I had said out loud, "I have money for everything," I looked at myself in the mirror and a little voice said, "This is your life now." Emotionally and spiritually I accepted it, but logically I still wondered how this could be. I had to pay my mortgage and my bills. How could I do this without working? I prayed for more guidance and faith. I knew that my situation was temporary and that my break would come soon.

My mom went back home to South America in March of 2008. My son and I got used to having her around, and we felt all alone when she left. Now was the time to find a job. I needed a job where I had the flexibility to spend time with my son. I decided to get a job in the school district, possibly at an office in one of the school sites so I could have the same time off he had.

After five failed interviews I almost gave up. Even though I interviewed well, they felt I was over-qualified.

I saw a part-time job as a teacher's aide and I decided to apply for it. I knew it was only part-time, but I felt compelled to apply for the position. I had a bachelor's degree in sociology and during my college summer months I worked with children in a head start program. I felt this somehow qualified me for the job.

Three months later, I received a letter from the school district advising me that my application had been accepted. However, before they would even consider me, I had to go through their process of testing, background check, medical exam, and an initial screening interview. Their screening process consisted of a group interview conducted by a few teachers from the school district. If I passed those components, I would then go for a second interview that would determine whether or not I would be hired.

Lo and behold, I was hired. I am now working with children and I love it. It is certainly a shift from the corporate world, but I am very happy.

Due to the economic crisis, interest rates fell to a record low. This positively impacted the loans I have for my two rental properties.

The interest rates fell dramatically, and my rental properties became income generators. My part-time job and my rental properties are now providing me with income to live on, and I have more time to spend with my son. He and I are much happier.

I know that this is just the beginning of my recovery. I know that better times are on the horizon and I am looking forward to those times.

~Pat Hurtado

The Humorous Heroine

*It is often hard to distinguish between the hard knocks in life
and those of opportunity.*
~Frederick Phillips

"Annie," he said, "it's time to move on." I had heard rumors about layoffs, but my head reeled. I had given twelve years of my life, working weekends, working late, covering multiple positions, and generally nurturing the company like it was my own. Yet it had been bought out by a financial conglomerate and so, like many others, I was gone. Within a month, over ten percent of the staff would be dismissed. It was musical chairs played to the tune of a corporate funeral dirge.

My upbringing had taught me that if you worked hard, you'd be rewarded. I always gave my best effort, putting my personal needs last. My ex-husband had taken advantage of this character trait, and now, I realized, so had my company. A corporate acquisition, coupled with numerous layers of executive incompetence and extravagance, and again my faith was shattered. A bitter lesson learned twice.

I was a single mother of two boys, struggling to pay a mortgage. We were already running on a tight budget, no fancy vacations or meals out, still paying off an expensive divorce. At least, I had reasoned, I was working and feeding my kids. Now I felt dizzy, rudderless.

In a way I was relieved to be rid of the job. My kids were happy I was out. "You never liked that job anyway, Mom," my older son said. I was surprised he had noticed. I guess it showed more than I realized. Yet, like any parent, my primary goal was to provide for my family. I figured my heart's true calling could wait until my kids were well established and out on their own.

Still, I had my boys, a bit of savings, and a resilient attitude. I thought of J. K. Rowling, author of the *Harry Potter* series. A single mom in desperate straits, she had written an incredible series of books, pulling herself up by her own bootstraps, out of the gutter and into the gold. It would be a long shot, but maybe, I reasoned, I could do the same.

I'd been writing stories about my childhood and posting them on my blog. As the daughter of two city people who had moved to the country and started a farm, I had an unusual upbringing, full of wacky happenings and unusual situations. The stories were popular, and for years people had encouraged me to write, so I mused — why not put them all in a book? My parents would soon celebrate their fiftieth anniversary. This could be a nice gift for them and for me, if I could get it published.

I always wanted to write for a living but never dared make the jump and leave my day job. What a time to follow my star, but the timing was beyond my control. So I rolled with it as best I could. Every day I spent hours writing the book, then scouring the want ads. No success in my job search, but finally the book was done. I started pitching it to agencies, gaining interest, getting turned down, re-pitching, re-writing, and never giving up.

Around the same time, I met a man who was pursuing his ambition of becoming a country music singer/songwriter. What a pair of dreamers we were! Still, he had tremendous talent. I helped him craft his biography, a web page, press releases, stories for the local newspapers and music magazines, and eventually his first CD. Finally he signed a recording contract. I was thrilled for him, and happy to have helped.

Yet the thrill rang a little hollow. Again I had put someone else first. Yes, I loved him dearly, but this was the classic female faux pas. We're natural nurturers, helping others succeed and grow. I had to focus on my own dream. My livelihood, and that of my children, depended on it.

I wrote for newspapers, magazines—any publication that would have me. I wrote humorous stories, amusing anecdotes, light-hearted tales that would ease a worried world. These were especially troubled times for the print media since, in a financial downturn, the first thing most companies cut is advertising. It seemed everyone was panicking, hunkering down until this fiscal tornado was over. Still, I reasoned, the world needed a hero. Or at least a heroine with a sense of humor.

"I saw your column in the paper," my son's teacher said. "I loved it! I read all your stories. They make me laugh. Please keep writing!"

"I saw your Thanksgiving story in the newspaper," my accountant said. "Hilarious!"

Sure, I thought. I'll keep writing. But my financial hourglass was quickly running out of sand.

Then something strange occurred. I had read about it happening before, during the Great Depression. I first noticed it with the film industry—annual revenue was, surprisingly... up! People were tired of hiding from bad times. They wanted to escape, at least for a couple of hours. While they weren't taking big vacations, they still needed to get away from it all. They did this by going to the movies in record numbers. Tiny breaks from reality, but sorely needed. Could it be the beginning of a turnaround?

One afternoon I stopped by a bookstore. It was full of people. Literary agents responded, and inquiries for my manuscript increased. My new book was humorous, light, and odd—could it help people forget how difficult times were? I was convinced it was only a matter of time before it sold. Still, I was afraid to hope.

In the meantime, my boyfriend's record company sent him on a concert tour. Before he left, we had a heart to heart talk. Even though we'd be apart, we promised to call every day and stay in touch. He'd be back soon enough. Whatever we would face, we would face together. With renewed strength and confidence, my stories began selling. More newspapers picked up my columns.

"Laugh and the world laughs with you. Cry and you cry alone." I'm fine with that. I write to ease the tough times, help people see the lighter side. Now I can share it with the world. And I've never been happier.

Quite a quirky fairy tale ending! But thank you, tough times. You freed me from a soulless job and shook me out of my comfort zone, enabling me to find true love and follow my heart's work. I wouldn't have done it without you.

Life isn't always what you expect it to be. Sometimes that's a good thing.

~Annie Mannix

For Richer or Poorer

You have succeeded in life when all you really want
is only what you really need.
~Vernon Howard

M y husband lost his job on November 3, 2008. That was
the day before the U.S. Presidential election and I was
in France on business. The South of France. Cannes, to
be exact. I work part-time for an IT research and consulting firm, and
they flew me over there for a big event. I had been looking forward
to the trip, and the election, for months. I didn't plan on sobbing my
way through the week after David lost his job.

I never would have pegged myself as reacting with such drama
and desolation. But I was totally surprised. Totally. Sure, David had
felt some concern in early October when his small marketing agency
realized year-end results wouldn't be what they had once expected.
But he'd had the conversations with his boss, hypothesized with colleagues about who might get cut, and he kept coming back to a con-
viction that he was safe. I believed him because he believed himself.

When I called home that first night in France to say goodnight
to the kids, my mother-in-law (who had flown in from Florida to
watch them while I was out of town) broke the news.

I was speechless. And felt so unprepared. We hadn't planned in
any way for such an event. Our mortgage was high. Our bills were
high. We lived comfortably in a beautiful colonial in Connecticut,
but we both worked and needed both our incomes to survive.

Between the time difference, my work schedule, and a lurking mother-in-law, David and I found little space for the kind of quality conversation we needed. I asked him to call the housecleaner and tell her not to come Thursday or until further notice. He could tell her why. I hated to pass down the loss of income but that was the reality for all of us.

That week in France, it rained every day, the election came off great, the food was fabulous, and I was miserable. How would we get by? Would David find another job? I couldn't get past my fears because I couldn't talk to David and hash it all out, coming to some emotional and financial stability to get us by.

When I returned home that Friday, we were in a fog. The kids pounced and we circled the obvious, hoping to get back into our groove before tackling the tough stuff. Then David's sister called.

"Listen, I know you just returned from your trip but I'm wondering if I can come down with Aliya tomorrow and spend the night. We'll watch the kids and you two can go out."

"Yes! Thank you," was all I could manage in reply. Debra and her daughter were more than welcome. And a little time together was just what David and I needed.

When we finally arrived at a restaurant (our last hoorah) and sat down, everything seemed instantly better. As it turned out, David was doing just fine. He had immediately posted his resumé online and was working his network and social media sites to develop job leads.

I breathed a sigh of relief.

"We can make it three months and then we'll have to dip into savings," I put forward.

Neither of us liked this prospect but all of a sudden, our focus had narrowed to a small core of priorities. After my solitary distress overseas, I had moved into a deep survival mode and my goals were simple:

1. Spare the children worry or distress over our circumstance.
2. Don't let this beat us—not as a family, not as a couple.

My thinking was that as long as my family was safe and healthy, we'd be alright. I am not so attached to my house, my car (a minivan) or any material aspect of our lifestyle that I fear its loss more than the security of our foursome. Period.

This simple reality allowed me to keep my darkest fears in check. What was the worst that could happen? Foreclosure? Bankruptcy? These were a long way off and probably unlikely. But I knew that all the other little fears leading up to them (cleaning the house, no extra cash for babysitters and nights out, no vacations, perhaps even Spam) were what could cause levels of anxiety and stress that would take a toll on us.

I also found a freedom in my bare-bones mindset. I was accustomed to the constant pressure to upgrade everything. I had fallen into the mode of constantly assessing our décor, clothes, and lifestyle for what could be improved. Perusing the endless stream of incoming catalogs was a leisurely way to check up on what else we needed. And the endless needs and wants put pressure on our budget.

In truth, I felt poorer when we thought we were okay financially, because I always felt we needed more. When David lost his job and we cut all spending, I looked at everything we did have. Looking at what we might have to cut, I realized we had so much. More than enough. Believing that we could survive if it all was taken away, I discovered our bounty.

So I said to David and myself, "I'll worry in March." We spoke with our financial advisor and he moved some savings into easily accessible CDs. If David didn't find a job by March, we'd start dipping in.

Until then, I'd be damned if I wasn't going to enjoy all this free time with my husband. We were used to the typical workweek schedule where we were both so exhausted by early evenings, after putting two preschoolers to bed, that we barely had time or energy for a conversation or, well, you know.

It took about three weeks for us to work out the kinks in his being home and tangling up my typical daily schedule with the kids. Then we found our balance, and our groove.

We had fun! We enjoyed a long lunch out or two, sang Christmas and Hanukkah songs for Charlie's preschool class, and shopped for holiday presents in the middle of the day. David left most mornings to work at the library, and he scheduled lunches and coffees with people from his broad work and social network. But he was available if I needed him home to watch Sophie while I picked up Charlie, and this gave me a much needed break.

And by Christmas, David had a new job. A promotion! He would start January 5th. We popped a bottle of champagne to celebrate. We couldn't believe his good fortune given the dire economy and job losses surrounding us. But David worked hard to find the job, and his skills and personality were a good match for the small, growing agency. All of a sudden, I wanted him home longer to play and help out. We hadn't hit March yet, so we were still in the honeymoon stage we'd created out of his job loss.

As it stands, David has started his new job and he loves it. I miss him already. And I'm trying to keep the priorities I discovered last November.

Through all this, I learned that while I may not have control over whether either of us loses our job in these tough times, I have plenty of control over how we adapt to what life throws us. My family's spirit and togetherness aren't dependent on how much money we have. And those are riches I don't want to lose.

~Heather Pemberton Levy
(originally published on www.EconoWhiner.com)

Downsized

Moving on, is a simple thing, what it leaves behind is hard.
~Dave Mustaine

"This is your thirty-day notice."

Everything slipped into slow motion. I felt the blood drain from my face.

"It's a money-saving decision." My boss looked away and twirled his pencil. "By combining departments we can save on management costs."

I wondered what I had done wrong, if I had unknowingly crossed an invisible line that pushed me out of existence.

"It's nothing personal," he said.

It felt very personal. We sat in silence. I could feel his relief when I finally stood to leave.

"What are you going to do?"

I had no idea.

My husband was sympathetic. Words caught in my throat and came out in a near whisper. No matter how hard I tried, I could not bring myself to speak of it to anyone else. Not my mother or my sister, not my adult children. The hurt was too deep. Not even the benefit of a pink slip; just a casual remark on a Friday afternoon that ended my career.

My devotional reading that morning had been Psalm 37:25 (NIV). "I was young and now I am old, yet I have never seen the righteous forsaken or their children begging bread." I felt forsaken in spite of the Psalm.

I stayed indoors the entire weekend, unable to eat or talk with anyone.

On Monday, the facility buzzed with the news. Swirling emotions exhausted me and I counted the hours until I could punch out and go home. Then I counted the remaining days until I could leave forever, marking my desk calendar with a pencil. It seemed impossible I could survive twenty working days, the embarrassment and shame, the rumors.

Without future projects on my desk, there was little to do. I dared not complain; I needed every cent I could scrape together before unemployment cut my wages in half. There were bills to pay. How would I manage?

I had worked hard to get to the place where I didn't have the physically demanding job of working on the floor, the rotating shifts, the lifting. At fifty-one, I had physical limitations beyond my control.

I wanted to remind everyone that I was Employee of the Month only three years back, that two months ago I received a glowing evaluation. It was hard when co-workers sympathized with me and terrible when they were unsympathetic. But even worse were the people who said nothing at all. I felt like I was on death row or had something contagious; people avoided me, not knowing what to say. Perhaps they were sympathetic. Maybe they felt I deserved to be cut. Maybe they were afraid if they commiserated with me, their own jobs might be in jeopardy.

I packed my grandchildren's photos beside my electric pencil sharpener, my continuing education information, my Employee of the Month plaque, and my personal reference books that cluttered the shelf above my desk. It was too soon to take my personal things home but I couldn't stand to see them in the office that used to be mine. I cleaned out file cabinets and cupboards, worked on paperwork, and finished up a stack of employee evaluations.

A friend told me how God had given her a verse when she left a job with less-than-friendly feelings. "If people do not welcome you, shake the dust off your feet when you leave their town, as a testimony against them." Luke 9:5 (NIV)

Shake the dust off my feet? Not me! I cared too much about my work to leave with a bad attitude.

"Think about it," she said. "Maybe it just means it's time to start something new."

I did have a secret ambition. For years I had spent my free time working on a historical novel. Vacation days were filled with writing conferences and museum visits. Maybe this loss was God's way of making my other dream possible, the dream of being a writer.

But even the lure of other possibilities didn't take away the agony of losing my job. Every day I clung to the comfort of my devotional book. Each day the assigned Scripture spoke to me and gave me strength.

It would soon be over. I investigated unemployment insurance and perused the want ads. So what if I had been employee of the month? Now I was unemployed, unsure what my future held.

My boss called me one afternoon. "When is your last day?"

"March 19th." He should know.

"It doesn't make sense for you to quit in the middle of the month."

I wanted to remind him that I hadn't quit. Maybe he had changed his mind and would let me keep my job. My heart pounded with anticipation.

"Would you consider working through the end of March?"

My heart sank. Everything in me wanted to refuse, to throw it back in his face. He hadn't thought through the merger of the departments and wasn't ready for me to leave. Surely God couldn't expect this of me. Each working day was agony. I wasn't sure that I could do it for two more weeks.

I felt God's promise that He would help me, gulped back the anger and agreed to stay until the end of the month while sending up a desperate prayer for strength.

Late into the evenings and early mornings I sat at my computer, finding solace in my writing. A magazine sought essays for an anthology. The response to my submission was positive and immediate. Poems and short stories crowding my desk were taken out and polished. Friends in my writing group urged me to submit them to magazines. I applied for a writer mentorship program and wrote a grant request for a novel workshop. For once, I would have time to do the things I wanted.

At the same time I felt such anguish about my job loss, I felt a growing exhilaration about new possibilities.

Finally, it was my last day. My devotion that morning spoke of Christ's temptation in the wilderness when the Holy Spirit led him into the desert to be tempted by the devil for forty days. I picked up the calendar and counted the days from the first notice to my last day on the job. It was exactly forty days.

This realization put things into perspective and gave me strength for that final day of work when my mascara washed away before I even got to the office for all the goodbyes. I was exhausted. It was over. I had made it with God's help.

The next morning, my designated Scripture passage was Luke 9:5 (NIV), "If people do not welcome you, shake the dust off your feet when you leave their town, as a testimony against them." It was no coincidence.

Someone once told me that with every closed door, God opens a window. It was time to let go and start anew. Mentally I shook the dust off my feet and turned on my computer.

~Candace Simar

Tough Times, Tough People

With a Little Help from My Friends

I am of the opinion that my life belongs to the whole community
and as long as I live, it is my privilege to do for it whatever I can.
I want to be thoroughly used up when I die,
for the harder I work the more I live.

~George Bernard Shaw

No Disability between Neighbors

I want you to be concerned about your next door neighbor.
Do you know your next door neighbor?
~Mother Teresa

"Mom," Cody said one morning. "Can we go see the big, giant machine over there?"

"Yeah!" his younger brothers piped up. "Can we, Mom? Please, please, please?"

With a sinking feeling, I knew what machine they were talking about. The backhoe was on the lot nearest ours, leveling the land around the new gray-bricked home quickly taking shape.

We had moved to the country to get away from neighbors. Now it looked like neighbors had found us. For a while there, big machines shattered the quiet, tracking large clumps of mud in the road and annoying us to no end. I sighed.

"Okay guys, let's go," I relented.

We watched from the road as the man skillfully manipulated the backhoe, digging and leveling the lot. A white sign was posted at the edge of the road.

"Doris Morgan," the sign boasted.

My husband, Stephen, was the first to meet her. He was working in his garden when he lent his wheelbarrow to her for yard work.

"Well?" I asked him. "What's she like?"

He shrugged his shoulders and replied, "She seems real nice. Hey, did you know her son and his construction crew built her house?"

"Really?"

"Yep. He's in a wheelchair because of some car accident. That was him on that backhoe."

"What?!"

What appeared to our untrained eyes as an ordinary task was accomplished by a man paralyzed from the waist down, who had mechanically adapted the backhoe, along with other large machinery and vehicles, to fit his needs.

It didn't take us long to warm up to our new neighbor. Doris Morgan was a real estate secretary who retired after three major back surgeries and heart problems. Miss Doris, we affectionately called her.

Slight in stature, with the stamina of a twenty-year-old in spite of her medical problems, Miss Doris has a heart that fills the world. We began house sitting for each other, and in exchange for helping plant her grass, Miss Doris baked cookies for us. We grieved with her when she lost her sister one Thanksgiving. When I was away on business, she made casseroles for my husband and kids. Stephen mowed her lawn whenever he had time. The favors volleyed back and forth between our households.

Stephen rang her doorbell one evening. It was nearing the end of Valentine's Day, and he was clutching a vase filled with flowers he had arranged earlier.

"Yes?" he heard her ask on the other side of the door.

"Miss Doris, it's me—Stephen," he said.

She cracked the door open with a questioning smile.

"These are for you," he said, handing her the vase. "I know this is a bad week for you, but we didn't want you to think we'd forgotten you on Valentine's Day."

She began to cry and hugged him. "Oh, Stephen, you are such a sweetheart."

The week of Valentine's Day was the anniversary of her beloved husband's passing. She made a sacred point of withdrawing from the world during that week. And we made a point of connecting with her during the hardest time of the year for her.

Doris Morgan was honored for all she does for her son, who relies on her on his bad days. She does his taxes for him, babysits his rental properties, cooks, cleans, and shops for him when he is unable to, and nurses him through the hard times.

"God don't give me more than I can handle," she declared.

Truly the sound of a mother's love.

It's been almost five years since Miss Doris moved into the home her son built. One can see her outside with our boys trailing behind her in her gardens.

The neighbors may have found us. But what we found instead was family.

~Jennifer Oliver

Choosing My Own Path

Biology is the least of what makes someone a mother.
~Oprah Winfrey

I know everything happens for a reason, but do I really believe that? What has happened in my life should not have happened.

I thought my mother was good at being a parent. She was there to listen when I told her things and she got me surprises when I was sad. But what was she really doing? She was lying to me all the time.

She hit me even when I was doing what she said. She left me and my younger sister for days without calling or telling us she was okay. I thought she was just being a parent and taking vacations to get some free time without us kids bothering her 24/7.

My mom would also take me and my younger sister to random houses, get way too high, and leave us there to fend for ourselves. She's lucky neither of us were raped or killed.

During all this, I took care of my sister by myself. I made sure she ate three meals a day, bathed, and made it to school. I watched her to make sure she was never hurt, and, most of all, I was the only one that stuck by her side through everything. I was her mother-figure for more than half of her life.

To this day, my little sister will never fess up to what has happened in her life. She covers it all up like nothing wrong ever happened, and she is still momma's little girl. But my mom will never be able to make up the time she has wasted.

She is always trying to buy our love back, but I will not accept it or allow her to treat me the way she has before. She wants me to forgive and forget, but I'm not seeing it happen. Maybe one day when she shows me she cares about how I feel and puts effort into being a part of my life, maybe, just maybe, I will forgive her. But I will never forget what she has put me through.

Sometimes I try to forget everything just for my own good, but it replays over and over again in my head.

It kills me to know that the woman who gave birth to me did this. She put all four of her children through the worst thing possible for a child to experience. Now it is affecting not only one of us, but all four of us.

My older sister is twenty-two years old and still trying to get the love she never had from my mom. Yet, my mom is not giving it to her. She is only making her suffer more.

My brother is seventeen years old. He is still trying to forgive my mom. He is in jail now, because he followed her path and did everything he could to get into my mother's life. He did drugs with her, sold her drugs, or just gave them to her to make her happy. He protected her when she was being hurt by men she got involved with. He got hurt by defending my mom. He even beat his own father up for her, yet no love was found. He was let down by her and still is being let down.

For me, I am fifteen, almost sixteen years old, and I am always trying to find love from her. I talk to her about many things that I will not share with anyone else, and she lets me down by telling other people and judging me or hurting me. I always wish my mom would just love us kids the way we love her, but what she has shown me since she's been back in Washington is that she is doing nothing right. She's not going to be able to fix her problems and show us she really cares about our lives by doing what she is doing.

My little sister is thirteen years old. She is trying to get involved with my mother as much as she can. She calls my mom to make sure they are still having their weekly visits. She does what my mom should be doing, but my mom is too busy with other things to get involved in our lives. It's not because she is busy with work or financial things, but because she is too busy getting high and doesn't remember things.

My mom has been into meth for about twenty-five years, and I don't think she is going to escape her addiction. No one in my family sees what I see. They are all blinded—to the extent that they won't accept that my mom is a drug addict.

Recovering from all this abuse, I have grown stronger. I am not going to follow my mother's steps. I'm going to be who I want to be, not who everyone else wants me to be. I hope my little sister doesn't go down the same path as my family, but I can't change anyone but myself. So I'm changing the path of my family history, and I hope everyone else realizes they're not doing anything good for themselves.

I'm proud to say that I am not going to be like the rest of my family, and I am going to achieve a lot in life. I'll have good things in life and I will be happy. Doing drugs will not make you happy. It's escaping life the easy way, and hiding from reality because you can't face it.

My motto is live life to the fullest. Don't do anything you will regret because it will stick with you through your life. Think before you act and make the right choices. Follow your gut feeling and do what your heart tells you is right. Don't trust anyone but yourself, and keep your personal things to yourself or they will get around.

The love I need will find its way to me in a better way. Not the way my mother finds love. But when there is really love around me, I'll know it's there and real.

Now, I am a ward of the state and with a foster family that I love more than anything. They give me what I need and want, and they are always here for me one hundred percent. I wouldn't want to be anywhere else in this world. I am proud to call these two my parents, Monique and Diane.

~Alexis Ludeman, age 16

Drive-through Giveaway

If everything comes your way, you are in the wrong lane.
~Author Unknown

I n 1984, my husband lost his job in San Diego, California. He wasn't eligible for unemployment benefits. We had two young sons to feed. I worked full-time as a bookstore clerk, but I earned minimum wage, which at that time was $1.50 per hour. Plus, I was pregnant and at that time didn't know I was carrying twins.

One Saturday, we were out of more than money. I opened our refrigerator, and the empty shelves seemed as barren as the Arctic Circle. I closed the fridge. The only valuable possession we had left was a late-model silver-gray Pontiac Trans Am.

I'd picked up a flyer, where a local church advertised supplemental food boxes, free to anyone who needed one. There was one hitch: this was a drive-through giveaway. You stayed in the car while a volunteer handed a box to you through your window.

My husband felt humiliated. "No way am I telling the whole world that we're begging for food," he said, folding his arms against his chest. Instead of the usual sunny weather, it had been raining all morning, so our sons sat building with Legos on the floor.

My husband had grown up disadvantaged, so I couldn't blame him. Five-year-old Nate looked up from his blocks. "I'm hungry, Mom. What's for lunch?"

Three-year-old Chris chimed in. "I'm hungry too."

The mother in me knew I had to put food on the table for the boys. And I didn't know it at the time, but I was eating for three. "Fine," I said. "I'll go." I grabbed the car keys and started out the door. I stopped. "Chris, Nate, want to ride with Mommy?"

Both boys zoomed out and buckled into their car seats.

At the church on that rainy Saturday, I queued up in our silver Pontiac Trans Am, the only vestige of our former abundant life. The Trans Am rumbled to the rear of a line of battered station wagons and junk heaps. The rain stopped, but the scene was dreary, and most people looked as if they had nothing to smile about. As we inched forward, I felt all eyes on me. Everyone seemed as frozen as my fridge.

I wanted to explain to all the other poor folks that I only looked well off — that my car was more a burden than a blessing, that it was all we had left. Appearances, I wanted to scream, can be deceiving. Instead, I kept my mouth shut and thought of all the cars I'd ever owned.

My first set of wheels had been a Chevy Malibu my grandmother donated to me when I was a poor college student. That car had cloth seats and air conditioning. I felt proud.

The Malibu seldom broke down, and if my husband hadn't wrecked it (don't ask), I'd probably get to drive it in heaven. The Chevy gave way to a miserable parade of awful transportation — from VW buses that caught fire to a rusted-out Oldsmobile we called Betsy.

Now I sat behind the wheel of the fanciest model I'd ever owned. The Trans Am, with its sleek lines and cool louvered rear window, idled in a very long line, with the kids getting antsy and my pride long gone. Nate asked, "Mom, why is everybody staring at us?"

I couldn't bear to look, slouching down further in the bucket seat. They begged me to roll down the windows, and I did, if only to keep them quiet.

But our boys hadn't heard of car status or shame. They hung out the open windows, yelling and waving.

"Hi mister!" Chris shouted to an elderly gentleman in his red and white Rambler.

"Cool bike!" Nate said to a young man on a scooter. One by one my sons greeted folks who were either down on their luck or there to help others.

Cars inched forward, some cutting their engines in between advances. Along the way, the Rambler died and wouldn't restart. Several men helped push it through the line, and then jumpstarted it for the old guy. By the time we got to the head of the line, people were smiling, talking together, laughing. I wished my husband had come along, if only to see that many others were struggling too.

Finally we reached the place where a volunteer stood ready to hand me my food box. The boys continued their banter, until the volunteer remarked, "Your kids are so happy, it makes standing out here worthwhile."

I smiled. "Thanks," I said. The others in line now felt more like family than strangers. We were all in the same predicament.

When our twins arrived a few months later, we traded that Trans Am in for a car that seated six. Before Food Box Saturday, I believed people judged me based on what I drove. I'm sure some thought I took advantage, because the Trans Am made me appear wealthier than I really was. Yet once the ice was broken, nobody judged.

With the groceries safely tucked in the backseat, Nate and Chris waved back at those still waiting. It was raining again. I closed the windows and sat up straight for the drive home.

My children taught me there's no shame in reaching out to others, even if all you can offer is a smile and a cheerful hello. We're all in this together.

~Linda S. Clare

Staying Warm
in the Dark

We cannot live only for ourselves.
A thousand fibers connect us with our fellow men.
~Herman Melville

While spring in Alaska can be exciting, the spring of 2008 is not one I would like to relive any time soon. Mother Nature gone awry can be rough. But even the darkest disaster can possess a silver lining, a happy surprise or two.

On April 14, 2008, my husband, Shawn, and I overslept. When we did wake, it was to a silent and shadowy home. Peering out the window, the world was shrouded in white. All our neighbors' homes were dark. The power must have gone out during the night, not too unusual for this time of year.

What we did not yet know was that by the end of the week many of our friends and neighbors would be unable to afford their electricity. Everyone living in Juneau would undergo a test of determination and courage.

Juneau, the capital of Alaska, has no road access. The town is located on a remote section of land guarded by glaciers, ice fields, craggy mountains, and the Pacific. Visitors and locals enter Juneau by plane or boat. The main source of Juneau's electrical power is from Snettisham, a giant lake well outside of town. A man-made waterfall generates power which is carried through miles of cable.

This magnificent power line is held high above tall trees by stately towers over some of the most rugged terrain on earth. Traversing down the mountains, another section of cable more than two miles long is buried beneath the salt water of Gastineau channel and finally ends in Juneau.

Eventually, we learned that during the early morning hours a tremendous avalanche galloped down the peaks that carry these electrical cables. Twelve minutes of roaring snow charging down a mountain can do a lot of damage. The furious boom of snow clouds, rushing boulders, and uprooted trees seemed endless.

A helicopter was dispatched to assess the damage. Personnel discovered that one cable tower was entirely knocked down, while four additional towers were mangled.

As the helicopter circled to leave, a second avalanche crashed down the mountain, resulting in seven towers requiring repairs.

And nature wasn't finished with the capricious spring antics. On April 17th, a record-breaking twelve inches of snow was added to the melee.

Alaska Electric Light and Power provides up to ninety percent of Juneau's power. Their back-up plan was about to endure a rigorous test; the diesel generators were fired up. Within hours, electricity was restored. That's the good news. The bad news was oil and diesel prices were rising to $4 a gallon and would likely go higher.

Dire predictions had Juneau requiring an estimated 100,000 gallons of diesel to burn each day. Nearly a quarter of Juneau's homes rely solely on electricity for heat. Few homes have wood stoves.

AELP estimated repairs could take up to three months, and diesel power could be five times the cost of hydropower. The normal kilowatt rate of 11 cents would be increased to 55 cents. Some scoffed when they read this. They didn't laugh long.

Shawn and I were not laughing. We were scared. Our standard electric bill ran about fifty dollars. Could we afford to pay $250 a month for this one utility? Our heating bill was already skyrocketing with the rising cost of oil. I was recovering from a series of surgeries, and we were relying on one income.

For a time, fear reigned. Then, we remembered we could change our attitude. We considered what else we could change; there was plenty. To our happiness, the town of Juneau also rallied.

Through strict and voluntary conservation, diesel usage for the generators was reduced from 100,000 daily gallons to about half. Soon, overall electrical usage was down by more than one-third.

The mayor, in an open letter to Juneau, thanked folks for their frugality. He informed us water is the single largest draw on public electrical usage. Pumps to move water, water treatment, and daily consumption require enormous amounts of power. So we decreased water usage as well.

The City Assembly brainstormed for solutions. They petitioned the state for $25 million in disaster aid. However, one of the requirements for "disaster relief" is loss of life. No lives had been lost, and the request was denied.

The city officials opened an account for low-income families to apply for energy assistance. Thus, families who could not pay their electric bill would receive the financial aid.

In our home, we searched for ways to conserve energy. We purchased fluorescent bulbs to replace incandescent. Because April has abundant light, we were able to make welcome use of daylight.

Shawn strung an impromptu clothesline between two trees in our south-facing backyard. Smug, I drove to the store to purchase wooden clothespins, anticipating the joy of hanging wet clothes in the fresh air. Chastened, I came home empty-handed. Every single store in Juneau had sold out of clothespins!

Undaunted, we hung wet clothes over the line when the weather allowed. When it rained, a common occurrence in Juneau, I laid clothes over every flat surface inside the house.

Other measures we took included lowering the temperature of the water heater, which already had an insulating blanket. We unplugged every appliance not in current use to avoid a passive draw of electricity. We used the microwave oven whenever possible.

In the community, laundromats had a fine increase in business. For a few dollars, a family could wash and dry their clothes, while enjoying a warm and well-lit environment. Everyone dressed warmer and delayed packing up the winter jackets, mittens, and hats.

Businesses turned off half the lights in the stores and turned the heat down a little. The three public libraries enjoyed increased usage. To save energy, each library closed one day a week, on rotating days. The downtown library shut off one of two elevators. The public swimming pool closed the electrically-heated sauna.

Neighbors walked together in the evening after work instead of plunking down in front of the television. Commiserating on shared deprivations often brought a smile and a sense of togetherness.

My friend Cathy summarized, "We are all shivering in our dark, unheated houses, eating raw, cold food, and wearing dirty clothes." Being too close to the truth made us laugh even more.

AELP conducted repairs around the clock, taking advantage of the many hours of daylight. While repairs were estimated to take about ninety days, to everyone's joy and appreciation, on June 1st, six weeks after the avalanche, Juneau was off generator power and back on hydropower.

The surprise mentioned above? Nine months after the avalanche occurred, it seems Juneau saw a dramatic, if temporary, rise in the birth rate. Apparently there are lots of old-fashioned ways to stay warm in the dark.

~HJ Eggers

Good Old-Fashioned Sharing

Friendship isn't a big thing—it's a million little things.
~Author Unknown

I t wasn't that I was embarrassed my husband was out of work. The situation was what it was. It's just that we are private people and don't share our problems easily with others. So when he lost his job, we just acted like nothing had changed and no one seemed to notice.

It didn't take too long, maybe two weeks, and my kids' friends noticed that Kyle's dad was home a lot more. When asked about it, I told my good friend and neighbor, Tammy, we were out of work and looking. She then told me that her husband had been applying for graveyard shifts all over town because his company was going under. I was shocked! We were constantly doing things together and I hadn't a clue they were struggling.

I didn't feel like we were the only ones going through this anymore. I always knew that others were struggling with the economy in a downturn, but now I had a comrade to share my woes with.

Knowing what they were going through, I wanted to help them, even though we didn't have much ourselves. So, I became the reconnaissance shopper. I scour the coupons and ads, and match things up to pay half-price for many items. I call Tammy when I get done with my planning session and offer to pick up things for her at the discounted price. It seems like our money goes even farther because we are willing to share.

It goes the other way too. Tammy and her husband have given us enough wood to heat our home this winter. They have the tools to cut firewood and they did extra for us. It has been a huge help to reduce our gas bill to almost nothing.

There are other examples of helping each other. I taught Tammy how to make bread and rolls; she watches my kids when I go to job interviews; I make dessert for Tammy's family party; she drives my kid to the bus stop in a snow storm... and the list goes on.

I don't have much to give but I can give of myself. I can have charity, love, and hope in my heart, and the more I give those away, the more I get them back.

~Tina Jana Earl

Heartbreak and Compassion

If you want others to be happy, practice compassion.
If you want to be happy, practice compassion.
~Dalai Lama

Lori is my dearest friend in the entire world. We became close years ago when we both received our cancer diagnoses, Lori with ovarian cancer and I with thyroid and uterine cancer. We have tried to live each day with hope for the future.

During the past three years, Lori has had two major surgeries and three long regimes of chemotherapy. She lost her hair with the first chemo and developed agonizing mouth sores during the later chemo regimes.

In December of 2007, Lori chose to stop chemo. Though tests showed no sign of cancer, she began to feel increasingly dizzy. Walking became a chore. She continued to lose control over her hands and legs in the following months, and I began my campaign to convince her to travel with me to the Mayo Clinic Hospital in Scottsdale, Arizona, my home away from home for my own cancer treatment.

In May 2008, Lori and I found ourselves on the road to Arizona in my car, our suitcases and her wheelchair stuffed in tightly. Scottsdale is hot in May, hotter yet in June, but during our first week there I pushed Lori up the winding road from our hotel to the Mayo each morning and back again in the late afternoon. I took Lori each day to the appointments and tests that had been scheduled by the three doctors who were managing her case—an expert in internal medicine, an oncologist, and a surgeon.

Within days we were on a first-name basis with the other patients in the waiting rooms, who, like us, talked quietly or read books and magazines while waiting for their names to be called for their appointments. We were all fearful to some degree about what the future held for us and yet we asked after each other and shared words of encouragement.

Joe was seventy-one years old. His wife Dorothy was sixty-nine, and had been recently diagnosed with kidney cancer. Dorothy was frail and Joe looked after her every need. They held hands as they sat in the waiting rooms, she in a wheelchair and he as close as he could move his chair. It was obvious that they adored each other and would be lost without each other.

Stan was elderly, perhaps in his seventies. His wife had died years earlier and he was alone. He had been diagnosed with lung cancer weeks earlier at home. He had come to Mayo for help. Though he was alone, he was amongst friends as we all asked about his progress.

Mary was recovering from a hip replacement. Her husband walked by her side everywhere she went. Mary needed to use a walker while she was recovering from surgery. She was also blind, with a seeing-eye dog. The dog was confused by the walker, but he still attempted to guide Mary through the hospital during the day and through the hotel in the evening where they stayed down the hall from us.

Chad was fifty-nine. He was going through radiation and chemotherapy for prostate cancer. He was alone and he did not mention family. You would never know that he was sick by looking at him. He was so darn handsome and he was always smiling. He had the kind of smile that spread across his entire face, including his eyes.

We spent that first weekend in Scottsdale at the mall. That's where we found the wigs. We bought matching wigs and wore them back to the hotel. Our Mayo friends who were staying at the hotel laughed so hard.

By the second week of our stay at Mayo the summer heat was oppressive. We turned to the shuttle van drivers at the hotel for help in getting us to and from and from the hospital. Walking had become a chore. The hotel van came complete with a wheelchair loader in the back, so Lori could be rolled on and lifted into the van with little effort.

In that second week, following days of blood tests, X-rays, CT scans, MRIs and examinations, we were finally given Lori's diagnosis of paraneoplastic syndrome. Normally our body activates cancer-fighting antibodies or white cells, known as T-cells, to combat cancer. With this syndrome, instead of attacking only the cancer cells, the body also attacks similar proteins throughout the body, including those within the brain. Lori's immune system was destroying her brain.

Paraneoplastic syndrome is so rare that Lori and I sat together with the oncologist as he called around the world searching for any case where the syndrome had been successfully treated. The diagnosis was grim. Lori cried. I cried.

We were quiet on the ride back to the hotel that afternoon. I am certain that the van driver knew that we had received some very bad news as he watched us in the rear view mirror, our eyes red and our faces tearstained. Lori and I remained in Scottsdale for one more week, as the doctors worked to develop a possible treatment plan for a rare disease with no successful treatment identified to date. The doctors were kind and patient and they seemed to want to desperately help Lori.

Our fellow patients, who we had come to know so well in the waiting rooms, took Lori under their wings, offering to help us in any way possible. They were battling cancer of the liver, bone, breast, brain, pancreas, ovaries, prostrate, and a whole host of other terminal illnesses, and yet they all shared their concern and kindness with two women a long way from home.

Lori and I returned home last July, where she began the treatment that Mayo had set up with the local oncologists. Her weight dropped forty-five pounds and in the ensuing months she lost most of her motor skills, including her ability to read, write, and walk. I continued to encourage Lori to fight to live, but we both knew that the odds were against her.

Ironically, not long after we returned from Mayo, it became apparent that I too was losing my battle with cancer. I am at peace with that. Cancer is not able to kill our friendship, a friendship that quite possibly might not have developed had cancer not brought us together. Cancer is not what defines who we are and we will not allow it to conquer our spirit.

During these past months, as Lori and I came to terms with our health and future, we have been blessed with the kindness and compassion of family, friends, and strangers. Thank you.

~Kathrin Fleming

Love Versus Adversity

Friendship makes prosperity more shining
and lessens adversity by dividing and sharing it.
~Cicero

The stock market collapse of 2008 hit my husband, Tom, and me at the worst possible time in our lives. We were both retired and in our late fifties—too old to re-enter the job market (what few jobs were available) and too young to receive Social Security. We didn't even have a second car or any gold jewelry to sell to raise cash (as a financial guru on the *Nightly Business Report* had suggested).

Because we had retired early, we were already living lean. We shared one car. If I needed some clothes, I went to the thrift shop. I bought groceries on sale and stockpiled them in our basement.

In January, 2009, I met with my three best friends for our quarterly dinner. 2009 was to be a special year for us—we were all turning sixty. One friend suggested the four of us go away for a "60th Birthday Bash" to a bed & breakfast. It would be a fun chance to celebrate friendships that have endured forty-five years.

Tom and I had agreed we would deal with the pain of losing much of our retirement money by cutting back on vacations and eating out. Excursions were to be limited to destinations within a few hours of home and hotels where we had earned free nights with our credit card points. But I felt this trip with the girls was important.

At dinner one night, Tom listened as I detailed the plan for the girls' special weekend—restaurants, soaking in the spa, shopping, etc. He looked at me intently. He didn't say "no," but he didn't say "yes" either. We continued eating in silence and I thought about our new financial arrangement. "You know," I said, "maybe I won't go. This little trip could end up costing a couple hundred dollars." Then Tom admitted, "It really wouldn't be fair for you to take a vacation when I have to stay home."

I knew I had made the right decision. Tom and I were a team. I understood his feelings completely and bore no resentment. As much as I loved my friends, I loved my husband more. The next day I sent my pals an e-mail saying I was sorry, but I wouldn't be able to go on the weekend getaway.

A few weeks later one of my friends, Marilyn, called. "It just won't be the same if you're not with us on this adventure," she said. "Life is so short and this may be our only chance to travel together." Grandkids were starting to arrive. We didn't really know if we would all still be living in the same city in a few years. "I have a deal for you," she said.

Marilyn had just moved into a condo and I had offered to divide my perennials and grasses, fill in the empty spaces in her flower beds, and give her some pots for a container garden on her porch.

"I know you offered to help me with my landscaping. Since you're doing that work for me, I want to pay for your room on the weekend away. And breakfast is included."

A lump formed in my stomach. I knew she shouldn't be offering to do this. She, also, was retired and couldn't be that secure financially. I didn't know what to do. I was grateful for her generosity and deeply touched. But it didn't seem like a fair trade.

"Gardeners love to give their plants away. That's what we do," I said. "It's no big deal for us." But Marilyn was adamant that this was her way of paying me for my help. So I thanked her and said I would talk to Tom.

After I told the story to my husband, he had no problem with me going on this trip. In fact, he actually seemed happy for me. Maybe he just needed to know that I was taking our "change in lifestyle" seriously and willing to stick to my end of the agreement.

As I happily look forward to the "60th Birthday Bash" with my best friends, once again I am reminded that the bonds of love, be it for a spouse or friends, are much stronger than the chains of adversity. Always!

~Kat Kitts

One Boulder at a Time

Fear dances with courage.

~Ever Garrison

Every day I stepped off the school bus I repeatedly looked over my shoulder. Beads of sweat broke out on my forehead, and the two blocks to my house seemed like miles—agonizing miles.

I hoped my life would return to normal after school started in the fall—but it didn't. I tried to pretend that nothing had happened. I wondered, is life ever going to feel safe again? Only a couple of my closest friends knew that summer I had been raped by a serial rapist. And I certainly didn't want anyone else to find out my world had turned upside down.

At fourteen I should have been excited about school games, dances, and other activities with friends, but I didn't want to attend anything. My classmates couldn't help but notice the change in me. I felt like people were looking through me and knew my terrible secret and saw my shame.

While playing basketball during PE, I couldn't conceal the red blotches that broke out on my arms and legs. My friends asked questions like: "Is it catching?" "Does it hurt?" or "What's wrong with you?"

Finally, I told them, "My doctor said it's hives, probably an allergic reaction to something."

Actually, my doctor said the hives were caused from stress brought about by being traumatized. He put me on tranquilizers and told me to stay out of the direct sun, but that didn't stop the nightmares.

Weeks passed, the questions stopped, and I finally began to feel better. Then news reached us that an arrest had been made. My nightmares returned.

A couple of days later, as we walked down the hall to the room where the line-up would occur, my legs started to shake. I cried, "I can't go in there. What if he sees me?"

Officer Jones put her arm around me and said, "It's okay. The men in the line-up can't see through the glass partition."

I pointed to my attacker.

A couple of months later a court date loomed over me like a dark cloud. I realized that during the trial I'd have to face the man who had stolen my innocence. The thought terrified me. Once again, my stress levels climbed, and the nightmares and red hives returned.

Then an unexpected source of comfort came when I joined my church choir. The words in the hymns soothed my shattered nerves. One of my choir friends invited me to her house for a slumber party.

My mom encouraged me, "Karen, go to the slumber party, I know you'll have a good time. You'll be safe there."

I took my mom's advice and went to Lynn's party, and for the first time in a long time, I felt excited. We sat in a circle and told scary stories while the fire crackled in the fireplace. Our sleeping bags were strewn across the floor. Their family room was separate from the main house, which gave us a sense of independence. Laughter filled the room. Then Sally suggested, "Why don't we sneak out at midnight and go for a walk?"

"Yeah! That sounds like fun," Lynn agreed.

My throat constricted. I shouldn't have come. Now what was I going to do? The friendly environment had turned threatening. I could feel my body tremble as I said, "It's not safe to wander the streets at night."

Sally asked, "Why not?"

The girls grew silent and waited for my response. Tension mounted so thick one could almost envision slicing it. I leaned forward and said, "Because..." My throat went dry and I paused.

Lynn broke the silence. "Everyone is asleep, so what's the problem? What can be dangerous?"

All eyes were on me without understanding that a battle raged inside my mind. Fear played a game of tug-of-war with my heart, but I knew the time had come to share. I took another moment, sighed deeply, and began. "Last summer while I was babysitting my brothers and sister, a stranger came to our house. He said he was a contractor and had come to measure the floor in the family room. I knew my parents were talking about remodeling that room, so I didn't suspect anything when I led him downstairs. I found out too late that he was a serial rapist."

I paused and took a deep breath as tears ran down my cheeks. "It's not safe on the streets in the wee hours of the morning."

After I shared my story, the room filled with an eerie silence, and we all settled down to sleep. No one went outside. I understood that my friends didn't know what to say to me, or how to deal with the pain of my experience, but I felt a sense of relief, as if another huge boulder had been removed from my shoulders. By telling my story I felt I had helped keep my friends safe.

I thought, perhaps, I'll find the courage to face my day in court after all. Maybe life can become normal again one boulder at a time. I took a deep breath, relaxed, and went to sleep.

~Karen Kosman

70

A Certain Samaritan

Have you had a kindness shown?
Pass it on!
Let it travel down the years,
Let it wipe another's tears,
Till in heaven the deed appears —
Pass it on!
~Henry Burton

My parents divorced in 1963, when I was eleven years old. One year later, my father stopped providing any type of financial support for my three sisters and me. My mother was on her own, working to provide for her family of girls, one of whom had severe developmental delays.

Times were definitely challenging then. I remember the threatening calls from bill collectors, the sound of my mother crying late at night, and those few evenings when flour and water pancakes made for a very meager dinner. But the memory that surfaces much more strongly than all of the others is one in which I learned a dear lesson about caring and sharing.

To support our family, my mother worked during the day in a local newspaper office. In addition, several nights a week, she sold women's clothing at home-based parties.

Driving home late one night, she sat stopped at a red light. Weary from her work, she did not see the speeding car racing up behind her, its driver oblivious to the stoplight. The other car crashed into the back of my mother's car at sixty miles per hour.

It may have been her weariness that saved her life that night. Her limp, tired body was propelled from her seat into the back of her station wagon. The car was crushed into an accordion of metal around her.

Amazingly, my mother survived with only bumps and bruises, cushioned by the clothes she had hoped to sell. But her car did not survive, and the driver of the other car was a young man with no insurance. I remember the look of anguish on my mother's face as she worried about how she was going to get the money for another vehicle.

The next day, I saw our neighbors, the Claytons, walking down the hill from their home. They handed my mother an envelope with $500 tucked inside. I remember my proud, tough mother protesting that she couldn't take their money. There was no way she could possibly pay them back.

Mr. Clayton smiled at her protests and then gave her a powerful admonition. "Don't worry about paying us back. When times are better, just help someone else who is in need. That will be payment enough."

My mother took his counsel to heart. A year later, she returned from a long bus trip to a neighboring town where she had been selling advertising for a local publication. As she walked through the door, huddled close beside her was a young woman holding a crying baby. My mother ushered them into our kitchen and proceeded to put together a few simple things for a dinner for our guests.

As the night wore on, the young woman's story unfolded. She had run away from an abusive husband, taking only her young child and a handful of possessions. She had only enough money to get as far as our city. When my mother met them on the bus, she knew what she had to do.

My mother made them a makeshift bed on our living room couch. Later, I saw her open her purse and hand the young woman enough money for the remaining bus trip to the distant city. I knew that was all the money she had, yet I saw such a look of determination and joy upon her face as she handed it freely to the girl. I listened as the young mother tearfully called her parents, telling them she was coming home.

Through the years, times continued to be tough for my mother and our family. In spite of this, again and again, I saw her reach out to help others however she could, whether it was with money, time, or another form of service.

It has been several decades since our neighbors came down the hill with their gift. I try to follow their and my mother's example, helping a little here and there. I'm hoping that my own children will in turn learn the sweet lesson that I did all those years ago from a dear neighbor and mother. I hope that they will see that even when times are tough, acts of kindness and generosity can make such a difference.

~Jeannie Lancaster

71

Lifeline of Hope

Remember, we all stumble, every one of us.
That's why it's a comfort to go hand in hand.
~Emily Kimbrough

The smell of fresh-cut grass tickled my nose as I watched my husband walk toward me. He clutched a letter in his fist. I turned off the weed whacker.

"They're sending someone out here to get our stuff," he said.

"Who? What stuff?"

"Because of those taxes they think we owe them, they're putting a lien on our assets."

"What assets?" I asked. "What can they take that would be worth the trip out here?"

I took the letter and glanced at the official state seal. A long, difficult battle to exonerate ourselves was proving to be futile. Due to a glitch in their system, a state we lived in for a short time was trying to collect taxes that were already paid.

Pink apple blossoms flitted around us, the joyful swirling a stark contrast to the moment. We should have been happy; the bankruptcy we filed seven years prior was finally off our credit reports. But instead we found ourselves in a pit of debt with no options other than once again going bankrupt, and we desperately wanted to avoid that. This letter sounded like a shovel crunching the soil. We were being buried alive.

The sound of the phone ringing drifted across the yard. I ignored it. It would just be another creditor and I knew too well what they would say. Another threat of a lawsuit. Another threat of garnishment. I didn't have the energy to deal with them.

"I'm going for a drive," my husband said and walked away, the gate banging behind him. I watched through a blur of tears. The pressure was affecting our marriage, our children, everything.

The stress was overwhelming. But greater weight came from the shame and regret we felt from once again finding ourselves in this situation. We had made poor decisions with credit after we had resolved not to. We didn't want to shirk our responsibility, but we couldn't see any other way out.

A few days later during Bible study, I asked the ladies to pray for us. I wanted God to meet our needs and to give us wisdom to handle this mess.

After study, two dear friends approached me. Each of them stuck a small piece of paper in my hand. I started to look, but they stopped me.

"Just take it home. We want to help."

"Oh, I can't," I said. I was embarrassed to be in a place where I needed money from someone else. One look from them was all I needed to know that I had no choice. I hugged them and prayed blessings for them.

In my car I unfolded the checks. Both women were seniors. One spent her days caring for her quadriplegic husband and the other lived on a phone company pension. This was far more than they could afford. I wept all the way home.

My husband sat with a pile of bills in front of him when I opened the door.

"Look," I said, holding out the checks. My husband took them as he looked at my face.

He looked at the checks and inhaled sharply. "Why did they give us this?"

I thought his pride must be wounded since mine had been.

"I just asked them to pray for us and then they gave me these."

He looked at them for a while. "This will pay our electric. They can't cut us off now."

I took a breath and whispered a prayer of thanks. They had given us something far more valuable than cash; they gave us hope.

We were able to climb out of the pit, with God's help, and we are stronger for the journey. But it was the hope offered by two generous friends that strengthened us to lift our heads and begin the climb.

~Kay Day

Tough Times, Tough People

Chapter 8

Tough People

*The difference between perseverance and obstinacy is that
one comes from a strong will, and the other from a strong won't.*

~Henry Ward Beecher

Lessons in Suffering

The human spirit is stronger than anything that can happen to it.
~C.C. Scott

There are rich lessons to be learned in suffering. For many, pain can open up the interior life to divine inspirations, understandings, peace and compassion. The suffering soul instinctively is drawn to like souls.

Lara and I initially met when I was a Eucharistic minister at a local hospital. She was recovering from surgery after her second bout of cancer. Her initial cancer diagnosis took place in her twenties with thyroid cancer. Now some twenty years later, she was recovering from a lobectomy for lung cancer.

After communion, Lara looked at me curiously and asked, "So what's your story?"

It was obvious that I had a story. I understood all the medical jargon, could render practical nursing advice, yet got around with Lofstrand crutches and was dispensing communion rather than nursing care. I briefly explained that yes, I had been an RN for twenty-three years before multiple sclerosis took its toll. Now I ministered a few hours a week at the same hospital I had worked at for years.

She nodded knowingly. There was an underlying aura of peace and surrender about her. "We just do what we can," she said softly.

A few months later, while sitting in a quiet church pew, I heard a wheeze coming from behind me. The soft noisy breathing was melodic, not labored, but had definitely been birthed from trauma.

I turned slowly around and smiled at the pale woman behind me. It was Lara.

"Beat the big C again," she whispered before services began. "Want to go out for coffee and celebrate?"

And so began our decade-long friendship.

Lara's calm demeanor, and her ability to live in the now, inspires courage. She has relied upon her inner strength and wisdom to weather long storms. And what she found through her suffering, she wisely passes on to her divine sisterhood through friendship, generosity and quiet listening.

"So much of life is destiny. Lessons to be learned. Obstacles to overcome," she says. And if my tone turns bitter, referencing someone I felt has done me wrong, Lara shrugs. "It's sad when people don't meet our expectations," she says simply.

I have never heard her say a mean word about anyone. "Criticism, negativity, nastiness just sap away all your positive energy," she says. "It hurts you more than the person you are talking about."

I know she's right, but I haven't evolved to the point where she is. Lara has a respect for people — her fellow women — that feminists would envy. She doesn't need to be political about it — she lives it. Women are equals and treated with respect without jealousy, criticism, envy or judgment. She accepts where you are at, who you are with, and what you are doing.

Lara has a remarkable ability to step back from the toxicity of life. Her spirituality is forgiveness and compassion. Religious politics makes her sad, politics in general even sadder. But she tries not to dwell on society's ills. She advises prayer, then release. Detaching from the outcome of events, she admits, took years of prayerful reflection.

"I had cancer not once, but twice, for a reason," she sighs. "I beat it twice for a reason, too."

I asked her what the reasons were. She shakes her head. "I'm not sure. But someday it will be clear to me."

Nurturing herself, her husband, children and grandchildren is done more by her presence than her words. Lara speaks simply, listens deeply, and seldom argues. Occasionally she'll give her opinion on something, but you are not bound to agree. Indeed, our friendship often lapses into periods of serenity and silence. There has never been any awkwardness about it. Silence soothes the heart.

The few disagreements we have are quickly resolved. "It's amazing how months of chemo can put all of life into perspective," she says. "You really get a sense of what's important when you routinely lie in meditation while toxic chemicals run through your system."

Radiation treatments suppressed her bone marrow for a while, slowing production of blood cells, leaving her anemic and tired. Our outings continued but became abbreviated. When my MS involved vision problems, she'd be my driver no matter how tired she was. It wasn't discussed much. She'd just pick up the slack.

Being a cancer survivor has mellowed Lara. By her own account, suffering has made her more whole and more defined as a human being. I didn't know her before the cancer began, but can attest to her dramatic spiritual growth and healing. And I can see how the growth and healing affect all those around her.

From life's trauma, Lara has found the ability to quietly spread love.

~Diana M. Amadeo

73

Making the Best of the Worst of Times

In the middle of every difficulty lies opportunity.
~Albert Einstein

I was eleven years old when my grandparents, who raised me, and I fled our Soviet-occupied country, Hungary, in the fall of 1947, landing in a refugee camp in Austria. Our only worldly possessions were the clothes on our backs. We had lost everything because of World War II, but we were alive. And for that, we were grateful to the Lord.

The refugee camp housed hundreds of destitute refugees like ourselves. Although dismal and cramped, we were provided with a roof over our heads, donated clothes to wear, and soup and bread to fill our hungry stomachs. So what did it matter that we didn't have a penny to our names?

But it mattered a great deal to my grandfather. He hated living off the charity of others, hated not being able to provide for his family as he had always done in the past. Feelings of helplessness overwhelmed him, and he spent a great deal of time praying, or "having conversations with the Lord," as he would call his prayers.

Just beyond our dismal camp was a beautiful natural world of mountains, a crystal clear river, and farms dotted with grazing animals. The river was the Drau River, and Grandpa and I discovered it on a summer day while taking a ramble through the countryside after Grandpa said he had a dream directing him to take a walk.

"You can enjoy the water, while I get busy with something else," Grandpa suddenly announced with a gleam in his eyes.

So, I splashed around in the shallow, clear water while Grandpa walked up and down the bank. Then I noticed he was cutting some branches from the river willows growing profusely along the bank. Soon, he had a large armful of them and we headed back to the camp.

"What are you going to do with them?" I asked him curiously.

"I will make some baskets," Grandpa replied.

"And what will you do with the baskets?" I asked, suddenly remembering his hobby used to be weaving.

"I will try to sell them to the Austrians."

Soon Grandpa found some old boards and bricks, and set up a worktable in front of our barrack. Then, after laboriously peeling the willow branches, he began weaving his first basket. A large crowd gathered around to watch him, and some boys volunteered to get more willow branches for him.

"Thank you. And when I sell my baskets, I'll pay you for your help."

Within a week or so, there were six beautiful baskets ready for market. Grandpa hung them on a long stick, flung them over his shoulder, and off he went to town, looking like a hobo peddler, much to Grandma's embarrassment. He returned just before dark minus the baskets. He had sold all of them! Then reaching into the bag he was carrying, he pulled out something for me. It was a new storybook I had longed for, that I had seen displayed in a book store window on one of our walks through town.

"Oh, thank you, Grandpa," I shrieked as I threw my arms around him. "I can't believe you were able to buy it."

"You are very welcome. And never forget, with the Lord's help, and some will and determination, you can make the best of the worst situation." Then he reached into the bag again and pulled out a ball of red yarn and a crocheting needle, handing it to Grandma. "I remember how you always liked to keep your hands busy, Terez. This will help." Grandma had tears of joy as she fingered that ball of yarn! Then, just before he went off to pay the boys who had helped him, he announced proudly, "And I have orders from people for many more baskets."

Grandpa continued with his new venture all summer and even gave free lessons in weaving to anyone interested. After he sold the next batch, he bought himself a fishing pole and a large frying pan. Then, building a fire in the rock circle he had arranged, he cooked up a large batch of fish he caught in the river and shared it with our neighbors. It was most unusual to have the aroma of frying fish wafting through the camp—where barracks were lined up like soldiers and helpless people lived their lives in them, hoping and praying for something better.

My dear Grandpa was a wonderful gift-giver. He gave me the book I had my heart set on—along with a lesson for life about making the best of the worst situations. And that lesson has served me well in my own life.

~Renie Burghardt

74

Ziggy

Be kind, for everyone you meet is fighting a hard battle.

~Plato

Times were tough in our household. My husband was out of work and there was no sign of anything promising for him. Our son had been in a diving accident and was recuperating at home after two surgeries. In addition to going to nursing school full time, I was working three part-time jobs just to put food on the table for our family of five.

After a rather meager meal one night, I answered the ringing phone. With no introduction, a quiet, deep voice asked, "Do you need food? Come to my place and I can help you." Directions followed and he clicked off. No in-depth conversation or queries as to our financial situation. It was up to us to decide whether or not we trusted a voice on the telephone.

I was desperate. With barely any food in the cabinet and no prospect of a job for my husband, I knew I had to take a chance, swallow my pride, and accept the bizarre offer. Was there a catch? Were we the victims of a scam?

It wasn't an easy task to get to our benefactor's home. Miles of wooded, winding roads led to more wooded, winding roads. Someone must have played a cruel joke on us. Just as I had made up my mind to turn around, gritting my teeth over the waste of precious gas used on this wild goose chase, a mailbox appeared in the headlights.

The simple white, raised ranch home was easy to miss. Set on a knoll, a bank of trees hid the front of the house, but the blazing lights from the open garage beckoned me. There was no car in the garage. Instead, lined up in orderly rows were tables filled with canned food, bags of bread, packages of diapers, laundry detergent, everything needed to maintain a home.

A craggy, nondescript gentleman greeted me with a minimum of verbiage. Not much different than our phone conversation! "Look around. If you see what you want, help yourself." He handed me paper bags and turned away to another bewildered new arrival, passing along the same message. This couldn't be real!

I guiltily filled the paper sacks with what we absolutely needed and gratefully thanked the elderly man. "Be here next week. You'll run out by then," was his reply.

My head was spinning. I had three bags of groceries given to me FREE by someone I had never met before, and he had told me to return for more. Who in his right mind did such a thing? Well, it seems that this Angel of Mercy, Ziggy, did. Widowed and retired, he wanted to do something worthwhile in his golden years to fill his time. Daily, he drove his pickup truck and begged for usable items and canned goods from local grocery stores. He delivered most of the booty to the shelters and food banks. He stocked the leftovers in his garage and sought out folks like us who had fallen on hard times.

I never knew what our weekly menus would be until the boys and I had "shopped" in Ziggy's garage. We ate canned ham, stew, oatmeal, or corn ninety-nine different ways, feasting like royalty. With our bellies full, we could focus on paying necessary bills with what little money we had. A major stress had been lifted that winter while my husband looked for a job.

Once in a while I stop in front of that house where Ziggy used to live. The garage is gone, but I can still hear that little man saying, "Look around... help yourself." Yes, Ziggy, I did look around. I saw a gentle spirit who gave what he could to a young mother and her family that needed a boost. Then I helped myself to what I wanted: a renewed belief in the kindness of strangers and gratitude for hope which had been dimmed. You fed our bodies and our souls, and the world is a richer place because of you.

~Irene Budzynski, RN

Riding Home

People who are homeless are not social inadequates.
They are people without homes.
~Sheila McKechnie

On the way home. The train's gentle rocking is slowly lulling me into a sleepy haze, despite the fact that I am standing with what feels like a building in the bag on my back. I turn slightly to alleviate some of the pain in my shoulder and see the door opening at the end of the car.

An obviously homeless man slouches through the sliding door, bringing with him the reek of stale urine and unwashed skin. He's dressed in a heavy, decrepit coat dotted with stains, ripped jeans, and mismatched flip-flops (despite the fifteen-degree weather on the streets above) that reveal sore-laden feet and black toenails. Behind him he drags a bag that looks thirty times as heavy as mine, filled to the brim with a plethora of odds and ends.

He shuffles down the length of the car slowly, asking for spare change in the polite, experienced voice of a person who has done this before. I glance down as I do a quick check of my pockets, hoping for spare change to give him that won't leave me bankrupt for the remainder of the week. I come up empty and lift my head just as his path crosses mine. Shrugging apologetically, I tell him I have no change, expecting him to move through the door next to me and continue on to subsequent cars.

Instead he stands and stares at me, saying something quietly.

As I strain to hear, I realize he is asking me to take him home... and love him.

Suddenly money doesn't matter to this man who lives in poverty, without even enough money to purchase socks to stave off the chill. He wants love. Not food, not clothes, not even a blanket. Just affection.

I feel worse than I did about finding empty pockets on my person. The man in front of me wrinkles my nose with his smell, is standing too close, has only the bag with him, and none of it matters. I wonder why he can't have love like everyone else.

He tells me I'm beautiful and begs me to take him home with me. My heart cracks and I can't even think of the proper words to say besides "I can't, I'm sorry."

His face crumples and he asks me, "What's wrong with me?" The answer is on my lips before I realize that it's true.

I let him know that I'm not good enough for him.

Long after the man has left the train and I have found my way home, I think about the answer I gave him and wonder why it felt so right to say. I realize that I wouldn't have requested love over money or food... the fact that he could appreciate something so simple and intangible is more than I ever could have expected of myself.

He taught me the power of love without even meaning to.

~Myla Seabrook

Super Strong Mom

Mother love is the fuel that enables a normal human being
to do the impossible.
~Marion C. Garretty

My mom is the greatest mom ever! As I grew up, I saw her as my hero for all the things she would do for me. I remember when she would fix my baby dolls or when she helped me color pretty pictures when I started elementary school. I remember in middle school, I would see her do things that fathers were supposed to do, like fix the car without caring how greasy her hands would get. Now that I'm in high school, I see how she is strong but sensitive at the same time. She looks at life with a positive attitude no matter what the situation is.

One day I came home from school and saw papers on the kitchen table and my mom sitting with a worried face looking at my dad. My dad wasn't working at the time because he had broken his arm. I had heard my parents talk about money issues a couple of times before but I never asked about the situation.

"What's going on?" I asked.

"We have to be out of the house in two weeks," my mom said. She had her elbows on the table and one hand over her forehead. Then I realized this was a serious problem. That very day, she made phone calls and started to look for a place to rent.

We had no money and no idea what we were going to do. I read the papers on the table; it said we had lost the house because we hadn't been paying rent. I was surprised that all this was going on and my dad seemed to be doing nothing about it and my mom never said anything about it. It seemed like everything was falling apart, but my mom seemed as if this was making her stronger.

That whole week she tried her best to find a place for rent. Besides the fact that we had no place to move to, we also had nothing to eat since the food my dad had bought the month before had run out. Even though she didn't show it, I felt my mom's pain and how much it hurt her to not be able to provide a good shelter and food for us.

After that whole week of seeing her struggle, I came home and she had a smile on her face and was cooking, which was really weird because she doesn't like to cook. I assumed there was good news and asked her, "So what's new?"

"We are starting to move today," she said with a smile on her face. "There's a place near your school and thank God they allowed all of us even though the place is pretty small." I could tell she was relieved and happy. At that moment, I admired her so much.

My mom is the greatest mom ever. I would not know what to do without her. Times like these are moments that make me admire my mom's strength. Some people might give up in bad situations. My mom looks at bad moments in life as a test, or a chance to make her stronger. When things seem to be the worst, she makes every-thing seem so easy to fix. I want to be like my mom when I have children of my own. I thank God for giving me such a wonderful mother like her.

~Brenda Barajas, age 16

Burned

Every day may not be good, but there's something good in every day.
~Author Unknown

I had just finished watching the twentieth anniversary of *The Oprah Winfrey Show*. Previous guests appeared and picked their own favorite guests who inspired them, and in some cases, changed their lives.

I will never forget the woman who had face cancer. She said she used to feel sorry for herself, until she saw the show with a beautiful young girl who was hit by a drunk driver. The girl had caught on fire. Her face had literally melted away. The story really hit home.

My mother had been burned over seventy percent of her body in a house fire two years before. I'll never forget the phone call that I received at work that cold January morning.

"Is this Ms. Dixon?" The voice on the other end of the line sounded distant. "I'm calling from the Vineland Police Department." I lived in South Carolina. My mom and brother lived in Vineland, New Jersey. I knew it was something tragic.

"Your mother is Naomi Cook? I'm sorry to have to tell you this, but your mother has been flown by helicopter to Philadelphia... there was a fire in her house. She is critical."

The drive to New Jersey was the longest of my life. The whole way there it seemed that every memory of my childhood came back. Warm cookies and loads of love is the only way I could describe my childhood. I recalled how my mom walked me to school when

I was very young. Once, there was this little boy who was taunting me. When she heard him calling me names, she went right up to his mother and in no uncertain terms told her that her son better knock it off. That's how she was. She didn't put up with any guff, not from anyone. She was tough, and she taught me how to be the same. Yet she had a heart of gold when it came to the ones she loved.

When I arrived at the burn center, I honestly didn't know if I was prepared for what I might see. I was right. My mom was wrapped from head to toe in bandaging. She looked like a mummy. All that was showing were her eyes and nose. I broke down and sobbed most of the night.

The next few months my mother fought her way back from the brink of death. She was kept in a drug-induced coma because of the pain from the burns. During this time, she survived two bouts of pneumonia, the constant infections that plague burn survivors, numerous operations, and skin grafts. The medical teams that kept her alive were incredible, and the fact that she hadn't succumbed to these horrific injuries was nothing short of a miracle.

Four months after the fire, the doctors felt it was time to bring my mother out of the coma. To help bring her around, the doctors suggested playing her favorite music and talking to her. The children from the Sunday School class that she taught all drew her pictures. I had them all over the cabinets in her room and explained each one to her in detail. After one particular long night at her bedside, and two weeks of waiting, I began to lose hope. Would she ever come out of this? Was all of this in vain?

The next morning, as I came down the hospital corridor, one of the nurses from the night crew jumped up when I went past her. "Good Morning!" She was awfully cheerful.

One of the male nurses who especially watched over my mom came up to me. He linked his arm in mine. "Did you have a good night?" He was upbeat too. He pulled back the curtain that protected my mom's room. "She did." My eyes filled with tears. My mom was being helped into a wheelchair by two of the physical therapists. In the course of the night, she had awakened. When she looked up and saw me, her face lit up, and she smiled. Everyone present in the ward started to clap. "Mom! Oh, Mom." The tears streamed down my face.

It would be a long, long journey down the road of recovery. But, my mother did recover. To say it was a lot of hard work on her part would be a gross understatement. She had to re-learn how to walk, talk, eat, dress herself, all the things we take for granted. Not to mention living with the disfigurement of the burns. She did all of it.

I won't lie and say that there weren't times when it would have been easier for that fire to have taken her away from us. It was inhumanely painful dealing with the physical affects as well as the emotional. People often would stare at her. There was a time I took her to the grocery store. An insensitive man outside asked, "What happened to her?" I quickly rushed her inside. I just wanted her to have normalcy. I didn't want anyone to notice that there was anything different about her. I wanted people to only see the inside, to know how much this woman was loved.

While she was resting on a bench near the checkout line, a little girl, maybe five or so, came up to her. She had a Band-Aid on her finger. "What happened to you?" The little girl asked innocently. I was in a panic. I couldn't get to her from the line. Mom had to handle this one on her own. "Oh, I was in a fire, but I'm doing a lot better now." My mom smiled at the girl. Holding her bandaged finger up, the little girl said, "Do you need a Band-Aid? My mommy has more." The sincerity was heartwarming. "I think this boo-boo is too big for a Band-Aid, sweetie," Mom joked. Then she looked over at me and smiled. For a brief moment, she had that familiar twinkle in her eye that I'd missed so much since this whole nightmare started. She was Mom again. It was just a quick glimpse into the past, but all the love and memories poured into that one moment and it has stayed with me and sustained me after all this time.

That fire was never able to take away my mom's willing and determined spirit. In spite of her dire circumstances, Mom touched the heart of everyone she came in contact with. Whether they were young or old, healthy or sick, she would tell them her story of how God spared her life from the fire.

I have tried, however difficult, to carry my mom's great attitude about the fire throughout these years. No matter what life brings to me, I try to remember to see the glass as half full. I owe it to my mom, who never gave up.

~Lisa Wright-Dixon

Marks on the Heart

A leader leads by example, whether he intends to or not.
~Author Unknown

"Your son Joseph has autism."

I dug my fingernails into the arm of the chair, feeling that at any moment I'd sink into the floor. That wasn't the diagnosis I'd expected to hear from the doctor.

A short time after his third birthday, Joseph's speech progression slowed. My husband and I were both concerned, but not overly alarmed. Our older son, Jonathan, had a speech delay at this age. Joseph would have speech therapy, empowering him to overcome this obstacle, just as his brother had. But autism? I shook my head. The doctor was wrong.

Across the room, Joseph rummaged through a toy box. He giggled as he pulled a plastic phone from the heap. I suppressed my laughter. As usual, my son's joy was infectious. He was too happy. All the autistic children I had ever seen had been withdrawn. There was no way Joseph was autistic.

"That can't be right," I insisted. "Look at him. He's happy. He can read words too advanced for his age." A lump formed in my throat as Joseph, smiling, climbed into my lap and wrapped his arms around my neck. Tears ran down my face as I felt his breath on my cheek, his heart pounding against my chest. In my eyes, my child was perfect. Now a total stranger was telling me he wasn't.

"And video games. He can buy games on my cell phone," I sobbed.

The doctor cleared her throat and said, "Joseph is what we call 'high-functioning autistic.' That means he's of average intelligence or above.

"But," she continued, "there should be no excuses. Treat him like you would a typical child, or you'll let autism cripple him. Do you understand?"

The only thing I understood is that I had plans for Joseph. He'd be a leader, leaving his mark on every life he touched. Now those goals were slipping away, faster than water through a sieve.

In the following weeks, I floundered in a sea of depression. I doubted my ability as a parent. I berated myself, believing I would've noticed the symptoms earlier if I'd have spent more time with Joseph and less on my writing. And it didn't boost my self-esteem when people said: "My goodness, what did you do while you were pregnant?" or "I guess it's genetic. From your side of the family?" No matter what was said, they made it obvious I was the one to blame for Joseph's condition.

I hated going out in public. It was then Joseph acted the most autistic: yelling spontaneously, rocking back and forth, and slapping his face. All of which drew stares and whispers from onlookers. I hated them all, especially the ones accompanied by well-behaved, typical children. And I detested myself for not wanting to be seen with my precious son.

As a means to de-stress and maintain my sanity, I took nightly walks. One night, as I had so many times in the past, I looked to the heavens to soothe my troubled heart. As I gazed at the stars, twinkling like gems against a canvas of black velvet, I realized something. It wasn't my fault. I didn't cause Joseph to be autistic. I couldn't have done anything to prevent it. I could only move forward and do what I could to help my son overcome his disorder.

I stopped placing blame on my husband, and began working with him, researching different programs and placing Joseph in occupational and speech therapy. I read everything I could, educating myself and other people on the disorder.

I began to see Joseph as he really was, a perpetual, mischievous ball of energy, not much different than other children his age. I marveled over how he lived every second to its fullest, not caring what people thought.

Once, in the grocery store, he burst into gleeful, spontaneous yells. Cringing as passersby gave us cold stares, I tried in vain to silence him. "Oh let him holler," an elderly woman said, breaking into a toothless grin. "He's just making a joyful noise, that's all. Warms my heart to hear him."

Joseph pondered things I took for granted; the way a raindrop left a crooked path on the window, the swoosh of wings as birds took flight. Even the setting of the sun left him in breathless wonder. Following his lead, I too began to marvel at the little things in life, and I couldn't believe what I'd been missing.

As it was, Joseph hadn't strayed too far away from my goals. My little leader was leaving his mark on every life he touched, especially mine.

~Debbie Roppolo

Hope Is a Choice

The road that is built in hope is more pleasant to the traveler than the road built in despair, even though they both lead to the same destination.
~Marian Zimmer Bradley

Hurricane Katrina was one of the most devastating tragedies in American history. When Katrina slammed the Gulf Coast and ravaged the city of New Orleans in August of 2005, I was working for HUD in Oklahoma City. One day, our quiet office housed a team of twelve foreclosure specialists. The next week, our staff grew to more than three hundred Katrina Disaster Relief reps. Our job: assist affected homeowners with mortgage issues and aid those on rental assistance with relocation efforts.

At the time Katrina hit, I had my own personal issues. The demands of taking care of my aging father as well as my son who was having trouble in school were wearing me thin. Coupled with the overtime that the disaster required, I left the office most days emotionally drained. How could I help others when I was struggling myself?

Since our hotline was given prominent media exposure, we handled thousands of calls per day, many of which had nothing to do with housing needs. Evacuees had limited contact with the outside world since their cell phones had died and their laptops had floated away. Sitting for days in crowded makeshift shelters miles from home, they waited and waited—just for a chance to use the phone. Our phone lines never quit ringing.

I spoke with countless victims who were desperately trying to locate family members lost in the flood. They all needed assistance with housing, food and clothing. The monumental task of rebuilding or relocating was overwhelming. I listened to story after story of horrid details: families who lost every piece of furniture, every article of clothing, every picture ever taken. Cherished mementos and every remnant of their past—gone forever.

Very few had jobs to which they could return, so paychecks quit coming and money ran out. Devastation set like concrete. It took weeks before any federal assistance was available to the majority. Some received none.

At times, I would just wipe my eyes and say, "I'm so sorry." That was it. What else could I say? They knew I hadn't suffered like they had. They knew I was in a dry office building somewhere in Oklahoma City. I still had my home... my job... my family. Bottom line—my life hadn't been ransacked like theirs had. Many days I wondered how I could think my issues were relevant considering what they faced.

Even though we were there to help, the trauma made some callers demanding, rude or belligerent. Some were impatient and hysterical. Some were suicidal. Normally, I was sympathetic and enjoyed helping others, but with all the negativity, it was hard to stay positive and encouraging. Just when I thought I had heard it all, I got a call from Brenda.

Brenda was a single woman in her early fifties with no children. She was all alone and had been living in a crowded shelter in Houston for the past month. Due to the number of hurricane victims who had been evacuated to Houston, there was no way to know how much longer it would be before temporary housing was available. When I asked her how she was coping, this is what she said to me:

"I've heard that my house is still underwater and at this point, I have no idea if rebuilding is even a possibility. The hardest part of all of this, though, is seeing the elderly suffer. The young have longer to recover, but many of the elderly have no other resources."

I swallowed hard. How would I react? Brenda was hit hard but her heart still overflowed with compassion for others.

"I know that recovery lies ahead," she continued. "I believe that if we were the ones chosen to endure this hardship, then God will give us the grace to endure. The destruction of our city has given birth to a spirit of unity."

I was speechless. For the past several weeks, I had been the one trying to offer encouragement.

"My hope isn't based on my circumstances," she continued. "My hope is based on my decision to hope. Hope is a choice."

Wow, I thought. What am I doing here? She should be the one that callers speak to. Never had I heard such unrelenting faith in the midst of loss. Brenda had stored trust and confidence in her spiritual pantry for a rainy day. And what a rainy day it was — no pun intended.

Moments later, we finished our conversation and I logged information on my screen about our call. As I reviewed the data I had just entered, I noticed a typo. When I hit the backspace key to correct my error, the realization hit me: Brenda couldn't edit her past. Her tragedy was impossible to revise. There was no delete button, no escape key to press. The only thing Brenda could change was her attitude. She had been involuntarily transplanted, but she made a decision to thrive, not just survive.

As I finished logging information about our call, I closed the file and marveled at Brenda's choice — the choice to focus on her future beyond the storm.

I still had my home. I still had my family. So that day, sitting in my office staring at my computer screen, I shifted my focus. If Brenda could endure such a tragedy and resolve to maintain hope, I could too. I've never faced calamity like Brenda had faced, but if I ever do, I hope I react with a fraction of her confidence and faith. So thank you, Brenda from New Orleans. Thank you for showing me how to maintain hope — even in the face of adversity.

~Christy Johnson

Spitting in Death's Eye

Most folks are about as happy as they make up their minds to be.
~Abraham Lincoln

Within a few months, I was reeling from three disasters. At only fifty-six, my father died a painful, prolonged death by cancer. He spent his last six months slumped in depression. One of my closest friends was misdiagnosed, and died after an unnecessary operation due to a slip of the scalpel. Ron was forty, and left behind a young wife and two children. Finally, my divorce had wrecked my emotions and finances, and, worst of all, my ex-wife had taken my two daughters to live 300 miles away. It felt as if the roof of the world had collapsed on my head.

In my career as a professor at a community college, I had met many people who were supposed to lie down while life flattened them, but who refused to cooperate. Poverty, single parenthood, learning handicaps, and abusive parents were common. I relished helping these people find themselves and succeed. But with my own troubles weighing on me, I began withholding the extra attention and care they needed. There was no sympathy left in my tank. I lost patience and dismissed their problems after comparing them with mine.

Then Roxanna showed up in one of my classes. Fifty-five years old, but looking sixty-five, wiry thin with blue veins spider-webbing her skin, she wore canvas sneakers and rock star T-shirts. Once she might have been beautiful, but her hair was dyed too red and her cheap false teeth chattered when she spoke quickly.

During a class discussion of alcoholism, one young man declared he could control his drinking. Roxanna spoke up. "I'm a recovering alcoholic. I know about controlling drinking. When you hit the gutter, I'll show you around the neighborhood."

Another time, she announced she was currently on welfare. "You think it won't happen to you. But I used to have too much money for my own good. Nice house, a Lexus, every hot gadget. All gone, kids!" She clapped her hands as if knocking dust off them. "You know what? Losing made me a better person. You think college will make you rich and then you'll be happy. But watch out for money. It can make you poor!"

Later that week, during a discussion of marriage, she declared she was a romantic woman—which brought snickers from two young men behind her. "Hey!" She spun to face them. "You have to be romantic to get married four times—especially twice to the same guy. Number one and three. He got me with his eyes." She sighed. "Number five is going to have a hook nose and knobby knees—maybe a heart condition. And just a little money. He won't cheat on a woman. You write that down, honey," she said to a twenty-year-old woman beside her. "Hunks break your heart. They think they deserve a pretty girl. Find a man who will be grateful for you."

The boys howled with laughter. After class, I told her that the young men loved her.

"Yeah, like a mother—dammit!" Then Roxanna told me that she was six months out of cancer chemotherapy. "I want to counsel the terminally ill—if I'm not one of them. I can take death," she said. "I've spit in his eye more than once." I believed her. Mr. Death better watch out. This woman was not going gently into the night.

I was amazed one person could sparkle with such limitless enthusiasm after so many disasters. And inspire the rest of us. She electrified the class with energy, drew out the slumped, baseball-capped dudes in the last row, and stirred debates while making us laugh. She pounced on ideas like a fish hawk and made everyone in the room eager to participate. We had a mission in life and a time limit, and hardships were part of the curriculum.

When she was in her alcohol highs, floating on money and attached to handsome men, Roxanna had been unhappy; when she had to fight to live, when she had a chance to shine in usefulness, when she did not know if the next week or month would be her last, Roxanna learned to live with zest and fullness.

I can't say Roxanna alone turned my thoughts around, but she weeded out my excuses. Losing money, marriages, health, and her youth had not depressed her but had woken her up. Life was about doing something, not complaining or comparing what you're going through with others. Those who live—really live—fight back with humor, tenacity, and passion. That's what my student taught me.

~M. Garrett Bauman

Tough Yet Tender

We must embrace pain and burn it as fuel for our journey.
~Kenji Miyazawa

She was just a baby when the first illness attacked. My sister, Kris, spent that Christmas in the hospital with some kind of viral infection. I was only five, but I remember the harried look on my mother's face—worry turned outward.

Kris made it through that illness and grew up. But she was always smaller than I and fighting some sort of problem. Sometime before puberty, she lost the sense of smell, which actually became a family advantage. Whenever any of us had the flu, we called Kris. She couldn't smell the vomit and cheerfully cleaned up the mess.

During college, Kris had to drop out for a year. Migraines sent her to the toilet to throw up in the middle of the day. Doctors couldn't explain the severe headaches, and Kris endured tests that made her head pound. Finally, an X-ray revealed a hidden tooth under her jaw. After the extraction, the headaches eased.

In spite of frequent illnesses, Kris maintained a weird yet delightful sense of humor. If my brother or I bothered her, she retorted, "Make like a tree and leave." She often reversed words in phrases, such as, "I want a fudge hot sundae" or "Call the vet and get that medicine some cat." One Saturday afternoon, as we watched Bonanza, Little Joe helped Hoss get up after a saloon fight. Kris laughed and quipped, "He's not my brother. He's heavy."

Always surrounded by friends, Kris became the encourager of

the neighborhood and the family—the person who sent funny cards and always had a joke to share. She returned to college and finished her physical therapy degree.

We missed her when she moved to Africa. This young woman who knew pain helped make prosthetics at a mission school and taught handicapped children how to walk. We met Kris in Europe one summer and laughed our way through eleven countries. Kris led the way through the Palace of Versailles and climbed up to Crazy Ludwig's castle—ignoring the pain in her weakened knees. Her spirit never wavered, and she returned to Africa for another mission term.

But even in the middle of her important work, her body betrayed her. She contracted hepatitis and then TB. Treatment was mandatory, as Kris worried she might infect some of her patients. She left her beloved Africa and returned to the U.S.

We were glad to have her home, but watched her grieve the loss of her calling. She soon rebounded and found places to help. She became an animal PT and helped disabled dogs walk again.

Endometriosis caused an early hysterectomy, followed by months of shingles that were painfully persistent. Yet Kris attended family ballgames, graduations, and band concerts. She never complained about her illnesses and quickly earned the title imprinted on her T-shirt, "Our Favorite Aunt."

Later, after we both reached fifty, a degenerative disc gave Kris a painful limp. I watched my sister begin to age, but marveled that she still found joy in the simple things of life: feeding birds, reading mysteries, and cheering for her sports teams. Kris fought morning fatigue, daily pain, and the persistent torture of those shingles.

Rheumatoid arthritis is the latest challenge, and Kris takes chemo to fight its progression. It bothers me to see her limp, but I marvel at her strength. She still manages to drive to New Mexico every summer for our family vacation. She walks along mountain trails and beats us at *Uno* games, laughing the entire time.

I wish I could take away my sister's pain, but the challenges have strengthened her and helped her empathize with others. Her tender heart cries for the children she rehabilitates through Home Health, while every suffering animal finds food in Kris's barn. She makes a good living, but a great portion of it goes back to Africa as Christmas gifts and monthly support. Her empathetic spirit comes through her voice. Whenever I call her, I hear the warmth of a woman with a pure heart.

Strangers might look at the curved spine and the limp, wondering what is wrong. But so much is right with Kris that the illnesses seem just a minor hindrance. She's much more than the sum of her defective parts. She's my sister — my hero.

~Rebecca Jay

Maestro

Happiness is a thing to be practiced, like the violin.
~John Lubbock

I kept seeing my father, suitcase in hand, his back towards me as he left through the front door. He left as though it were just another day and he would be back in a few minutes. But, he wouldn't be back. It amazed me how he had left us so easily, without a thought, without so much as a backward glance.

Where do you go to fix a heart that has been so ruthlessly destroyed? Now, I understood all those songs that asked that eternal question about how to mend a broken heart. According to them, the answer was time.

We had decided on a little diversion, a little Christmas holiday to speed up the healing. We went to Mexico to visit some of my mother's cousins, Catalina and Raymundo, who she hadn't seen since she was a teenager.

I can't remember what I was doing before I saw Cousin Manuel. I just remember that when I did see him, I was horrified.

They brought him into the house on a slab of wood pulled by a rope. I can still hear the squeaking sound the metal wheels made as Raymundo pulled him carefully over the threshold. Manuel wore a plaid shirt under a plain, dark brown vest. His back was supported by a manmade prop, much like the ones behind picture frames, only much larger because it was made to support the weight of a human being.

Cousin Manuel had no legs. His trousers were folded under

his body. His shirt was cut away at the armholes to reveal stumps projecting about four inches from his shoulders with a few fingers protruding from them. This is the way he had come into the world.

My eyes were wide with disbelief. I wasn't ready to see anything like this. I wanted to close them and run. And he was smiling. How could a person who was cursed with such a deformity be smiling?

As I tried to sleep that night, questions about Cousin Manuel filled my mind. Did he live with Catalina and Raymundo? Did he have his own room? How did he eat? Who dressed him? How does a person who is half a person live from day to day? Curiosity began to replace the pain I was carrying around inside. There was something about his presence that had nothing to do with his physical condition.

The next morning, I was rubbing the sleep from my eyes when I heard the most lovely sound. I immediately thought of angels and heaven. It was the sound of violins.

I heard voices and the slight shuffling of feet. Then the noises stopped. There was a pause. I tiptoed to the shutters, the morning sunlight streaming in through the slats, and opened one side very slowly, just a crack.

Outside our room was a large patio. I could see the backs of students, approximately ten to sixteen years of age, standing with their violins tucked under their chins. Poised. Ready.

The sound that came from their instruments transported me. For the first time since my father walked out that door, I forgot the pain. I felt as though someone was caressing my soul, as though my heart was being embraced by something from another world.

As I listened, I strained to see the face at the podium. The instructor's voice was soft, serene. The students would stop and start at his command. I saw a sea of long and short hair, hands lovingly holding their fragile instruments, their attention completely captivated by that voice, faces focused on him.

Then, I saw two young men come forward and say something to him, ending with the word "maestro." I heard the squeak of the wheels and saw the empty slab of wood before I saw them lowering the maestro onto his makeshift cart. The tenderness with which they did this left a lump in my throat.

When the mind questions what the eyes see, it searches for a logical explanation for it. My mind could find no logic for this, for a man without arms or legs coaxing such sweet sounds from these budding musicians, a man many people would consider useless, an invalid, a cripple.

My mother was awake. She put her hand on my shoulder. She said nothing. I knew she was in awe too. We watched the maestro smiling up at the young students who had lowered him. Each student thanked the maestro with a quiet, reverent bow, violin case at his side. One of the young men began to pull his cart, the metal wheels clacking against the cement.

Suddenly, I was ashamed of myself. I hadn't seen him. My eyes had seen him, but my heart hadn't. Now, I was forced to see who this man truly was.

The day we left, Cousin Manuel came to say goodbye. He was smiling as always. And he was sorry to see us leave because he had a special invitation for us to attend his wedding the following week.

He was the same person coming through the same door in the same way he had the first time I had met him, but now, I was the one who had changed. My heart embraced him. I knew why his students had such a deep respect for him. He may have been half a person physically, but he was a towering example of the strength of the human spirit. He was a testimony to overcoming adversity, transforming it into something he shared with others, something they would remember throughout their lives. He had literally turned his misfortune into music.

As we left, I felt within me the assurance that, with time, my mother and I would indeed be whole again. I knew this because the maestro had unknowingly taught me a lesson. This time, as I boarded the bus for home, I returned with the maestro's smile in my mind and his music in my heart.

~Leah M. Cano

Tough Times, Tough People

For Richer or Poorer

*If two stand shoulder to shoulder against the gods,
Happy together, the gods themselves are helpless
Against them while they stand so.*

~Maxwell Anderson

83

My Parents' Worth

What this world needs is a new kind of army—the army of the kind.
~Cleveland Amory

After travelling thirteen hours from my home in Munich, Germany, and circling the Nashville airport waiting for the snow to let up, I finally landed in the middle of a brief but ambitious blizzard. It was going to be a different Christmas. This year I knew I was coming home to a country and family changed by crisis, each doing their best to cope with their own blizzards.

"How is she?" I asked my father and gave him a big hug.

"Pretty well," he said, helping me with my suitcase. "She has some pain in the arm where they took the lymph nodes."

He filled me in on my mother's condition as we poked along with the other snow-frightened drivers. The blizzard had caught so many off guard. When we finally arrived home, my mother greeted us at the door, decorated with tubes and round, plastic drains peeking out of her pajamas here and there like ornaments. She'd just had the mastectomy the day before.

"You look like a Christmas tree," I said, always looking for the hilarity in a crisis.

"I feel like one. Your mail's on the table." She turned to go into the kitchen. "You'll have to pour your own tea. I'm not supposed to lift anything."

I got my tea and sat down in the kitchen to talk about turbulence and bad airline food and to open the stack of letters my parents always collect for me — a bouquet of alumni newsletters, credit card approvals, and mutual fund quarterly statements. Staring at my most current statement, I tried to wrap my head around the fact that, at least on paper, I was worth about thirty percent less than I was last Christmas, the last time I'd sat in front of this stack.

"Uhhh..." I said to my wealth manager, otherwise known as Daddy, who'd just taken his seat at the table with his super-heated coffee. It was bubbling like a lab experiment.

As I'm sure he'd repeated a hundred times that month, he proceeded to calm my fears — so eloquently expressed — by outlining the last four economic valleys in U.S. history and their subsequent upswings. His coffee had long since gone cold by the time he ended the lecture, owing mainly to the fact that my father speaks in slow motion. (We call him Slow Joe.) It was, however, exactly what I needed to learn about America's current financial blizzard: 1) things might get worse; 2) they will get better; 3) it might take a while.

"And you're still worth just as much to me," said my wealth manager — which was comforting in its lighthearted humor, but wasn't this just a tad off topic?

It suddenly hit me that if I, with my pitifully small molehill of cash, was worth thirty percent less, then my father, with his considerably larger mountain, was suffering from devaluation on a much grander scale; and it did cross my mind that some of this dwindling Mount Moola was, or would be, my inheritance. I raised my finger to broach the subject, but before I could embarrass myself with the crass question, "Just how much of my inheritance have we lost?" the phone rang.

An old friend was losing her home. The bank had given her until the end of the month, but by the end of the day, my parents had rallied the troops — better known as their Sunday School class — and come up with the payment. None of the people in the class knew the woman, and none was under the illusion that this would save her home; but the money would buy her another month to figure something out.

I knew my parents would be there to help her do just that. You see, they have always been staunch believers that the Church should help when it can. Dinner-table discussions have often focused on what's wrong with the world and whether the Church should be more active in getting things right. My father, a red-tie-wearing Republican, and I, an expatriate living in Germany for the last thirteen years, rarely see eye to eye on anything political. We talk and talk until my father withdraws to his office to play solitaire and I retreat to the gym.

This visit was different. There was no time for theoretical political discussions, no musing about what was wrong with the world. This year I witnessed my parents—compassion and generosity—in action. I watched as my mother, still in her pajamas and in pain, phoned friend after friend, explaining the woman's predicament a dozen times until well into the evening hours. My father, a military man, chose the e-mail blitz. A bit stunned by all the action around me, I sat back and learned.

In the two weeks leading up to Christmas, my father orchestrated other mini-bailouts: A friend's car required urgent repairs, a client in distress needed someone to talk to—and who would have thought this person would be his wealth manager? Each time the phone rang, my father hit the ground running with his step-up-to-the-plate attitude. The blizzard seemed to be getting worse. In fact, December was such a busy month that I almost forgot to buy Christmas presents.

They turned out to be simpler this time. I got socks; I needed socks. We bought one another books; we love authors. One gift from my parents was a donation made in my name to the Nashville Rescue Mission, a charity that provides food and shelter to the homeless. It's the gift I'll remember most fondly. In fact, everyone received this present from my parents, even the small children, who didn't quite know what to do with the worthless slip of paper. It wasn't a Tennessee Titans sweatshirt or Nintendo. It didn't taste good.

"We thought we'd try something different this year," my mother said, her voice a bit wobbly. Was she worried that we'd be disappointed?

"You just don't like shopping," I laughed.

She laughed, because she really does hate shopping.

Joking aside, I knew what she meant, but I had a sneaking feeling that this form of fire-brigade generosity was nothing new for my parents.

A teacher by vocation, I like to think of myself as a good student, and on this visit home I was fortunate to learn a few new lessons: 1) People of action, like my parents, will love us through this financial blizzard with their mini-bailouts; 2) I'm a bit silly, which I'd suspected on numerous occasions; and 3) my parents' worth is infinitely greater than the sum of all their investments.

~Christopher Allen

84

Interesting Times

A moderate addiction to money may not always be hurtful;
but when taken in excess it is nearly always bad for the health.
~Clarence Day

My dad once said to me, "May you be born in interesting times." He shared this with me whenever I brought him my latest tale of woe. He would just lean back in his office chair and smile as I cringed.

Through good fortune, good planning, and the grace of God, two years ago my wife and I started working on our finances. Coupled with my father's sage advice and something Nancy Reagan once declared to the world — "Just say no!" — I began my quest to learn more about my spending habits. If I had known the can of worms I was about to open, I'm not sure I would have been so eager to start learning.

My problem was controlling the way I thought about money and personal finances. There is an old joke about a college kid who kept writing checks; a few days later, his checks were bouncing everywhere. Shocked, he exclaimed, "I can't be out of money! I still have checks left to write!" That story, funny as it is, explained my life. Part laziness, part learning disability, with some dyslexia mixed in, but mostly it was my recklessness with money that kept me spending.

My misunderstanding about money comes from not knowing. For instance, I believed the prices I paid in a convenience store were the same as a grocery store. Or I would call my bank to see how much money was in my checking account and then spend what was left without accounting for the checks which had yet to clear. Eventually, the bank made a smart decision and stopped my check-writing privileges.

The issues I had with money were such that when I talked to my dad about how badly I wanted to get married, he advised, "Your job, Joe, is to find a woman whose holes in her head fit the rocks in yours." I laughed, but kept his sage advice in mind. I did find that special gal and she married me, baggage and all.

My wife came from a long line of frugal souls. She had a savings account when we first met, but unfortunately, I took care of that. Every winter, I made sure we had new ski equipment and every spring, new bicycles. Of course she shared her misgivings when I brought home the new items, but I didn't listen. I only had my eyes on the new shiny toys.

I finally realized I had to come to terms with my emotional ties to money and spending. I had to "just say no" to therapeutic shopping. But the power I felt when I made any purchase—whether it was a dollar or a thousand dollars—was the same. It was awesome how I felt, especially when walking up to the counter, bantering and interacting with the salesclerk, while making my purchase. I liked how I felt and looked forward to coming back.

But here's the worst part of my issues with money: loose change in my pocket gave me a rush. For years, I collected that change, depositing it in a jar on my dresser. When full, I secretly dumped the contents into a tote hidden in my closet. And I didn't spend the money. Why? The answer is scary: a good addict needs his stash.

Yes, those coins were my stash. It defied logic, but in my case, it was true. Having a stash and hoarding money were all classic signs of addiction. The irony was that I was a rehab counselor, and it was my job to see the signs of addiction. For me, those signs came home to roost when I had a heart attack. Before the attack, I had become a sneaker with my hoards of money, but I kept spending our "other" money. I even hid money around the house, just like a good addict hiding booze or drugs. My wife and children didn't know about my stash.

It never occurred to me until later that this behavior probably caused the heart attack. I told a friend about my money hoard and showed him where to find it if anything ever happened to me again. Dumbfounded, he said, "You're kidding. You have that much money and your wife doesn't know? She's a great woman. Tell her the truth and show her the money."

I told her. The stash is now tucked safely away. I still don't understand all the feelings I have associated with spending, but I'm learning. For the first time in our marriage, I've gone two complete years telling the truth about how much money I make. Up until that point, I compared myself with others. I would look at their outsides and judge my insides by what I saw. If I didn't measure up, I'd go spend more money just to do so. But now I don't feel the need to judge myself with such harshness. The last addiction we give up is the hardest one. I sincerely pray that this is the last addiction for me, because I'm not sure I could survive digging as deep into myself again.

I'm glad I was born in interesting times. It gave me the chance to learn a lesson on spending.

~Joseph T. Lair

85

Camping on the Couch

Life begins on the other side of despair.
~Jean-Paul Sartre

Fighting back the tears, I faked confidence. Kristin was six, Kara was four, and we were pretending to camp. The living room sleeper sofa was pulled out and we were giggling as we shined flashlights in each other's faces under our pretend tent, a warm blanket.

It was January in North Carolina and it was cold and snowing outside. The temperature indoors was not much warmer because our electricity had been cut off. Camping in the warmest room of our home was the only way I could think of to shield my children from the realization that we had no lights or heat.

We happened to be alone because my husband was working. There had been times before when money was tight, but this was different—it would be a turning point in our lives. I was genuinely scared about what would happen if we didn't turn our finances around. I was almost as frightened that my precious children would realize how afraid I was.

The next morning, a trip to the pawn shop temporarily solved the problem. We had put a Band-Aid on a major mess.

Immediately afterward, we created an action plan so that there never would be a moment of fear attached to finances again.

Step 1 — We decided to make gaining control of our finances a positive experience. We decided to control our future. The decision was not easy, but once the commitment was made we decided it would be a fun game.

Step 2—We made a list of financial liabilities. We had to get a clear grasp of exactly what our expenses were each month. We decided how every penny of a paycheck would be spent prior to receiving it. This made us less likely to run out of money before the essential bills were paid. It encouraged us as we watched our debts diminish.

Step 3—We looked for ways to save money. Non-essential spending was cut to a minimum, we used coupons, eating out was treated like a luxury, and we looked to see if competing companies might provide a way for us to reduce essential bills.

Step 4—We sought information that would turbo-charge our recovery process. We began to truly study money for the first time. Reading books on how to regain control of our finances and attending seminars became exciting. We took advantage of the immense amount of information available.

Our situation did not change overnight, but it was never again that dire.

Many of the new habits became a permanent part of our lifestyle. We had to reevaluate what was more important, living for the minute or a simplified lifestyle that radically reduced stress.

Kristin and Kara never understood that our camping adventure was traumatic to me. Now, when we camp, we do it outside as a family.

~Laura Harris

86

Then and Now

Still, I know of no higher fortitude than
stubbornness in the face of overwhelming odds.
~Louis Nizer

My husband and I were living the American Dream. The fifteen-year mortgage on our three-bedroom, two-bath brick home in the suburbs was cheaper than some people paid for rent. Life appeared to be going along smoothly.

Then hardships struck—one after another.

In February 1996, I had emergency surgery and was given a grim diagnosis of Stage III ovarian cancer with a poor survival rate. As if that weren't enough, in July 1997, my husband suffered life-changing back injuries in a work-related accident. With a heavy heart, he applied for disability. It took several months before the first check arrived.

We were forced to make drastic, difficult, and far-reaching changes in our lifestyle.

Instead of eating out, we scoured recipe books for nutritious, but inexpensive meals or simply invented our own. We spent evenings listening to CDs or watching movies checked out from the public library. Vacations? Forget it. Instead, we took long walks in area parks and observed the abundance of trees and wildlife, chatted with fellow walkers, and petted their four-legged companions. Visits with good friends were like warm blankets for our souls. We shared meals, discussed things of mutual interest, or simply let our guard down and laughed together. New books and name-brand coffee to go? Not a chance. We read the tomes already on our shelves and brewed store-brand coffee at home. Nothing transported our minds to another place and time like a good mystery.

Then, in September 2005, we made the painful decision to sell our home. The maintenance was simply too much for us to handle physically and financially. Moving from a large house into an apartment required downsizing in a big way. We sold some furnishings and donated the rest to a women's shelter.

The adjustment from a house to an apartment was tough. But that was offset by a much freer lifestyle where all the upkeep was taken care of by a maintenance crew. Instead of fixing something on the house or mowing the lawn, we swam in one of the pools or got a free massage. No more raking and bagging fall leaves. Instead, we'd sit in the hot tub on a cold day.

We started volunteering at a local food bank. We saw firsthand the effects the downward financial spiral had on people. Requests for food, clothing, and services escalated. Some of the clients were newly homeless, embarrassed, and distraught. We stocked the pantry shelves, sorted donated clothing, and tried to minister to people with far more problems than we had.

Together, my husband and I have been given the opportunity to see and appreciate what's most important in life—spending quality time with each other and our family and friends. We've both been called walking miracles: I've beaten the dismal odds I was quoted more than thirteen years ago and my husband has amazed doctors by not being paralyzed and confined to a wheelchair. Encouraging and helping others whenever and however we can is now one of our life goals.

~Ann Holbrook

87

Broke

Faith is a practical attitude of the will.
~John MacMurray

A few weeks after our daughter was born, I tried to write a family budget. My wife and I had taken a finance class at church a few years earlier, so I felt confident in my ability to write what our workbook called a "Bare Bones" budget—a plan that covers basic expenses like housing, food, clothing, and nothing else. There was little to no planning for the future or emergencies, like a flat tire, a stomach bug, or Christmas.

When I finished writing the plan, I estimated that we would be living above our means by more than one thousand dollars each month. Ten months later, we sold our home and moved our son and baby daughter into a two-bedroom apartment.

The move from the house to the apartment was a difficult adjustment. Our new home had fewer square feet, a smaller pantry, smaller cabinets, and fewer closets. The baby had grown into a toddler and now would have to share a room with her big brother.

Once we'd been in the apartment a few months, we settled into a regular spending routine and I attempted a new budget. Yet, despite our sacrifices, downsizing, and the second job I'd taken, I calculated we were still living above our income by several hundred dollars. To make matters worse, I couldn't figure out why.

I let this go on for months with the blind hope it would work itself out. One day, I got three automated e-mails from my bank with

"Overdrawn" in the subject line. I quickly logged onto my account and saw three separate "Not Sufficient Funds" charges adding up to more than one hundred dollars in fees. I grabbed the checkbook, and felt a rush of blood to my face when I saw one of the charges included the monthly rent check. The other two were from the debit card—each for a fast food restaurant and each less than $5.

After calming down from what must have been a panic attack, I called in sick to my second job and told my wife what had happened.

"How much do we owe?" she asked.

"I don't know."

"Who can we ask for help?"

"Someone who can help us make a long-term plan, because I can't do it. The only place I can think of that has the resources and the willingness to help is the church."

Together, we checked our church's website and found a ministry for financial planning. Prepared to beg for their services, we received our first bit of good news from a nice lady who put us in touch with their financial counselor, Jim, a retired businessman who offered financial counseling as a free service. Within a few hours, we had spoken to Jim on the phone and had a meeting set up. "Just bring your bills and a Bible," he told us.

Two days later, my wife and I met Jim at a coffee shop. "We can't figure out how to pay our bills and have money left over for the basics like food and clothes," I told him. "We just can't do the math."

"When money comes in, we either don't know or can't agree how to spend it the right way," my wife added.

Jim nodded. "Let me see your stuff." After studying our bills for a few minutes, he said, "Let me explain what I do. I teach from a workbook written by Crown Ministries that teaches the practical management of money and the spiritual attitude the Bible directs us to have toward money. If you get nothing else from our meetings, get this: that the latter is more important than the former. If you don't have the right mindset, then your behavior won't really change. You might be successful for a short time, but you'll ultimately fall back on doing what you've done in the past. However, if you listen to and follow God's Word, then He will bless that. Is that something you are interested in?" I didn't even have to think about it or check with my wife.

Over the next few months, we brought Jim our bills and completed the workbook. We memorized verses like, "The earth is the Lord's and all it contains" and "I have learned to be content in all circumstances." He helped us fill out a monthly expense worksheet which forecasted how much we spent each month in different categories, like food, savings, debt, etc. We also filled out an income allocation worksheet which had us divvy each paycheck forty-five days in advance.

While planning the budget was a lot of work, living by our new budget was even more difficult. The first few weeks had been exciting but, like a diet or a New Year's resolution, the initial enthusiasm wore off quickly. By the third day of the second month, my wife had to spend the entire clothing budget, which wasn't that much to begin with, on the baby. "I don't know what to do," she told me. "I still need to get our son new Sunday school shoes." A few months ago, she would have used a credit card and not bothered telling me.

"They'll have to wait until next month," I said.

"But he doesn't have anything to wear until then."

We started to fight. A few hours later, we cooled off and tried again to work it out. I changed a couple of things in the budget and came up with the money for shoes. Then I made a note for the following month to allocate more money for clothing.

God began to bless our efforts and, over time, we got the hang of it. We became more patient with each other and the monthly budget became easier and less time-consuming. The allocation and expense sheets became our salvation. When something unexpected came up, we learned to deal with it calmly and logically. My wife even commented that she felt like we had more money.

In the past few months, we've stuck diligently to our budget. The great thing is that it's better than the bare bones budget I wrote a year and a half ago. Each month we put cash in envelopes for food, gas, co-pays for the doctors, even Christmas.

Best of all, we've stopped using our credit cards and building up more debt. So far, we've paid $500 per month to creditors. By my calculations, at this rate we should be debt-free in about four years. This seems almost insurmountable at times, particularly when I remember that it took us less than two years to get into this mess. But considering our current standard of living, everything we've sacrificed and sold, and the blessings God has given us, we're doing far better now than we were two years ago.

~Billy Cuchens

Extraordinary Lessons from Extraordinary Debt

The willingness to accept responsibility for one's own life
is the source from which self-respect springs.
~Joan Didion

I vividly remember walking back to my house after collecting the afternoon mail, flipping through the envelopes in my hand. I saw a credit card statement, another credit card statement and our bank statements. It was in that moment that I felt a deep tension in the pit of my stomach.

I realized that even though I had married a man who I absolutely loved and adored, I really didn't have a clear sense of how he handled money and how the two of us were going to blend our different approaches to handling money in our marriage. I was more organized, detailed and frugal. He was more of a laid-back, free spirit type. I knew that getting on the same financial page was a key factor in creating a successful marriage and financial future.

I asked my husband if he would be willing to set up a time each week to talk about our finances and develop a plan for getting rid of our credit card debt (we had run up more than $43,300 in credit card debt over a three-year period). My husband said he would be willing to do this. Admittedly, he was skeptical — but willing.

We came to refer to our weekly meetings as our Financial Dates. We didn't really have a clue as to what we were doing. All we knew was that we needed to give our finances undivided attention. I remember the knot I would get in my neck several hours before our designated Date.

We had so far to go—how were we ever going to get rid of our debt? We basically made things up as we went along. At the beginning of each Date we would jot down a list of what we wanted to focus on and throughout the hour we progressed through the list until most of the items had been dealt with.

Some Dates were filled with tense conversations, accusations, and snide remarks. Other Dates were filled with laughter, joy and creativity. However, we kept showing up for our Dates and we never gave up. What started out as a means for survival became a powerful connecting thread in our relationship. Something shifted within us.

Instead of our finances becoming a source of divisive tension that pulled us apart, they became the glue that held us together as we became a unified team—creating electric synergy as we focused on the single goal of getting out of debt.

I still recall the day that we excitedly crossed off our last credit card payment on the chart we had created. We had finally arrived. We were free. We had been given wings to fly.

I gained several invaluable lessons from our debt struggles that will stay with me forever:

1.   We were committed to changing our situation. Even though we felt overwhelmed, uncertain and stressed about how we were going to turn things around, we were 110 percent fully committed to getting rid of our debt. I realize now how powerful a commitment can be.

2.   Opportunities presented themselves during our journey as a result of our commitment. Many people won't begin a journey or declare a goal because they can't see the means to achieving it—so they give up. More often than not you won't see the means of accomplishing a goal until you make a commitment and bravely begin your "hero's journey."

We had given ourselves four years to get out of debt—but we were able to do it in two and a half years. Creative ideas and opportunities presented themselves to us that we truly couldn't have envisioned at the beginning of our journey. We used extra money from Christmas and birthdays to put towards our debt.

And we even sold our beloved Eurovan because we realized that the deep peace and security of being out of debt meant more to us than having the van.

3.   We took full responsibility. Instead of blaming the economy or factors outside ourselves (although there were times when we got angry at each other), we were willing to accept full responsibility for creating our debt situation. Many times in the past I thought I was accepting full responsibility for my situation, when in reality, I wasn't.

Whenever I blamed anyone outside of myself (even if it seemed completely justified in my mind), I was giving away my power to change the situation. I ended up feeling like a victim and experienced a lot of waiting—waiting for the economy to change, waiting for my husband to change, or waiting for a friend to change—until I could be at peace.

Now, whenever I feel a twinge of stress or reactivity I ask myself, "how am I contributing to what is happening right now?" This gives me the ultimate power to change my situation.

Even though my husband and I don't have any guarantee against future challenges, I am left with something deep within that is unshakable and that can never ever be taken away—the memory of our past successes and the power to integrate these lessons in my day-to-day life.

~Leslie Cunningham

Blessed

Don't cry when the sun is gone, because the tears won't let you see the stars.
~Violeta Parra

"They can't do that—it's against the law!" cried family and friends at the news of our lost pension.

"Well, they did it," we told them, "but we're going to fight."

"How can they refuse to pay your pension? It was your money, wasn't it?"

"Yes, part of our paycheck was put into our pension fund every month for thirty years." My husband shook his head and continued. "We thought it was safe and protected and couldn't be touched. We were wrong."

Betrayed. We were completely caught off guard.

Fury, pain, fear. All these emotions raged within us. And we were incredulous when we learned that the company executives gave themselves bonuses that ran into the millions after declaring bankruptcy.

"It's not fair," I wailed. I was filled with feelings of revenge. And I cried a lot.

We fought in court and wrote to our senators, congressmen, and the President, outlining our situation and what we deemed to be an unlawful act. The few responses were cursory, at best.

Then the judge hearing our case ruled that the plundering

of retirement funds was "for the good of the company." We were crestfallen.

Depression set in. When he wasn't at the computer comparing notes with fellow co-workers and composing letters, my husband sat in his chair, unable to do anything other than stare at the television. I was no better. I cancelled social functions and dragged myself to meetings. I couldn't enjoy reading, TV, or even writing, my all-time standby in times of crisis. Only our children and grandchildren brought pleasure. We alternated between talking about the company's bankruptcy and the cost to us personally, to not saying anything at all for long stretches of time.

Retirement was going to be nothing like we'd expected. Gone were plans for trips to favorite places and a few unfamiliar exotic ones, our hopes of building our grandchildren's college funds, and dreams of remodeling, redecorating, and landscaping our home. We struggled to figure out ways to be able to remain in our house.

The fight continued in court as we wrote letters to the editors of major newspapers and magazines, but all to no avail.

One day my husband said, "Enough of this. It's not going to get any better so let's see what we can do."

Our retirement savings were stolen and we were going to have to alter our lifestyle. We went to work making lists, starting by writing down the unnecessary and often expensive things we enjoyed most, such as travel, eating out, and going to the theater. We even discussed the pros and cons of getting rid of one of our cars.

Our lives were disrupted but, gradually, we were able to adjust to a new lifestyle by cutting back—though not completely out—some of our favorite things. Instead of traveling to far-off places, we discovered the many attributes of our hometown community and surrounding areas. We waited for top-rated movies and plays to come to television, and sometimes swapped DVDs with friends, then popped our own corn in the microwave and had theater night at home. We decided not to sell one of our cars, but concentrated on savings gained by combining our errands when we left the house, zeroing in on low-cost items and avoiding gourmet favorites.

We've been joined by many others suffering from the drastic downturn of our nation's economy as well as those whose lives were destroyed by natural disasters. We learned that we're able to reach out to help those who were hit harder than we, including people right here close to home.

"You know," I said to my husband one day, "we are blessed."

"What?" He looked at me as if I was suffering some lapse of sanity. "What are you talking about?"

"We have family and health, shelter and transportation, friends, and our faith in God—all the important things. That's what I'm talking about."

He smiled and came over and gave me a hug. "And we have each other. You're right, we ARE blessed."

Life isn't easy. No one ever said it would be. Times are indeed tough right now. But we are tougher and now know that we can withstand anything together.

~Jean Stewart

Do It Yourself, or Do Without

Yea, let there be daily renovation.
~Confucius

Do it yourself, or do without. Ever since my husband and I bought our first home, eight years ago, that's been one of our favorite mottos.

The summer we entered the housing market, times were good for sellers, realtors, and builders, but bad for young families of new university graduates trying to finance home purchases for the first time. Instead of dangerously over-extending ourselves to buy the perfect house, we bought a small home with very modest finishes and an undeveloped concrete basement. Our plan was to gradually make our house into the perfect home by hiring contractors to carry out renovations as we saved enough money to afford them.

Unfortunately, the construction boom meant that home renovation services were in stratospherically high demand, and hiring a contractor was outlandishly expensive—if there were any available to hire at all. But as our family continued to grow, the possibility of my returning to paid work shrank and so did the budget we had available for developing enough bedrooms, bathrooms, and living space to keep us comfortable. There had to be some way to make our home suit our needs on a single, modest income.

While admiring the new improvements made to a friend's house,

I offered a compliment on her and her husband's prowess as do-it-yourself renovators. Surely her husband must have worked his way through his engineering degree as a construction worker of some kind. "You're lucky you guys know how to do all this," I said. My friend waved the praise away. "We just bought some books from the hardware store and figured it out ourselves," she explained.

I was amazed—and inspired.

Even though my husband and I had three university degrees between us, we had almost no knowledge or experience in construction. What we did have, however, were excellent reading comprehension skills. Armed with those, some building manuals, the Internet, and tips from the few, rare handymen in our family trees, we became our own contractors.

To start my amateur construction career I took on the scary and esoteric task of wiring our unfinished basement. Like any sensible person, I began the work completely terrified. A lifelong pattern of vigilantly keeping my fingers—and anything else I don't want burned black—away from electrical fixtures wasn't easy to overcome. A month after I began, I finally stood in my basement trying to act casually as a building inspector tested the circuits and questioned me about my methods. Somehow, I kept from squealing and dancing when he signed and certified the inspection.

Since that beginning, we've kept researching, kept saving, and kept expanding our repertoire of construction skills. We've learned everything from basic plumbing to delicate finishing carpentry. We learned little by little, season by season, spending money without going into debt. I do as much as I can during the day with my entourage of pre-school children. When my husband comes home from work, he slips out of his white collar and gets some real work done.

Some projects, like installing vinyl siding, are quick, easy, and gratifying. Others, like our never-to-be-repeated foray into the mucky, choking world of fireplace masonry, come with a more ambivalent sense of accomplishment. At the end of each project I raise my dirty, callused hand, slap my husband on the back, and say, "How do you like that, buddy? We just saved a fortune!"

Financial savings aren't the only benefits we find in building and caring for our own home. In an emergency, my husband and I now have the tools, background knowledge, and practical sense to take care of small problems without delay before they become disasters. We've been able to help friends and family with their own attempts to do for themselves. And I still relish the feeling I had the day I threw the switch on my family's household power supply and saw the whole basement light up. My sense of self-worth was boosted forever.

The recent cataclysms in the housing market mean contractors are far more abundant and affordable than they were eight years ago. But the uncertainty of today's economy means we're still just as reluctant to spend a lot of money on our home as we were during boom times.

No matter how the economy's performing, our family of five boys continues to grow. As our skinny little boys careen through the process of becoming 200-pound, six-foot-tall young men, our house endures hard wear. We are continually maintaining, re-finishing, and re-working our space. Thankfully, the solution to our household renovation crisis of eight years ago also happens to be the solution for our current renovation needs. The lessons of one hard time transfer easily to the circumstances of a different sort of hard time. As ever, we're pleased to do it ourselves... or do without.

~Jennifer Quist

Getting Up Again

Every day is an opportunity to make a new happy ending.
~Author Unknown

I am a firm believer that no one is given a burden they are not capable of handling. But there was a time in my life when the number of burdens that fell on my shoulders seemed so overwhelming that I didn't think I'd ever be able to get up again and recover from them.

My wife and I had been making a decent living working together at a private business school. It was Christmas, and we were looking forward to the yearly bonus we always got on the last working day of the year. When that day came and went and we received nothing, I began to get nervous. When I went down to find out what was going on, I found out things were even worse than I'd feared. The school's owner had disappeared with all the school funds, and left everyone holding the bag.

Not only did we not get a bonus, but we didn't get paid for the month. We couldn't collect unemployment because the owner couldn't be found. The bills began to mount quickly. We were suddenly in debt up to our ears, and were in danger of losing the house we were renting. I scrambled to find another job, but times were tough, and there were no teaching jobs to be found. I had to get three part-time jobs to make ends meet.

Around that time, I applied for a teaching job at a private school and was hired. Things began to look hopeful just as the last of our money was eaten up. Then the week before I was to start teaching I began getting sharp pains in my chest. I'd developed pneumonia from overwork and stress, and I thought that was the cause. But one night just before bed I felt a huge weight slam down on my chest. I was rushed to the hospital where the doctors told my wife my aorta had ruptured and my chances of survival were very, very slim. I slipped into a coma. My family began to prepare for my death.

But I didn't die. Somehow, through endless prayer, I came out of the coma, and though the doctors said they couldn't operate because of my condition, I survived. I left the hospital two weeks later with all the experts telling me I would be disabled for the rest of my life. Lying at home on the sofa, wracked with intense pain, through the haze of dozens of pills, I pondered what to do.

I'd always been taught that when life knocks you down, you gather your strength and get back up. That's what I did. My wife and I worked every day to help make me stronger. I was under orders not to strain myself at all, but life is a great motivator, and I had a family to take care of. I got back on my feet and went looking for a job.

By that time I'd lost the teaching job I'd originally been offered, and had to start over. We were broke, I was sick, and we'd used up all the resources we had. Family and friends offered what they could.

My wife worked part time from home while I began work as a substitute teacher. I went back to college to get my public school teaching certification. Each day I crawled home and fell into bed, exhausted, in pain, and praying I'd make it through another day. The process seemed to go on forever, and we barely got by. We put off creditors, worked with our landlord, and found every odd job we could. I put one foot in front of the other and kept going.

Finally, two years after my visit to the hospital, I walked across the stage at my graduation and got my teaching certificate. I was stronger, and more determined than ever to make it. I got a job teaching at an elementary school and prayed that I would be well enough to keep it. The first year was rough, but our prayers were answered and I found myself able to handle the load. I decided that if some education was good, then more was even better. I kept on going to college in the evenings.

Now, years later, I am still teaching. I also write, having pursued that dream for a long time and finally seeing some success. I am in a Ph.D program and we are working to recover from all the debt we accrued from school and my illness. My wife and I have faced other challenges since then, but together we know we'll be able to handle anything life brings us, because we'll face it together, in faith and love, and with the knowledge that as long as we can get up again, we'll always be able to find a way to make things better.

~John P. Buentello

The Legacy

The only thing you take with you when you're gone is what you leave behind.
~John Allston

The oil painting is still in the back of my husband's SUV. I steal glances at it and reflect on how well the painter captured Ken's bright smile. Soon, Ken will have it framed. It will be my birthday gift. Perhaps the last.

"I won't make it to Christmas," Ken said last Halloween as we waited for the first of the trick-or-treaters. We had squabbled about where to position the jack-o'-lantern, if we should put the dogs in their outdoor cage or let them howl when the doorbell rang, if we should watch *Jeopardy!* or an *NCIS* rerun. Then Ken blurted out this news.

A diabetic, Ken's kidney functioning had fallen dramatically since he had quadruple bypass surgery. But he had been holding steady for over a year on his GFR and creatinine levels, hovering slightly above what is termed end-stage renal failure.

I stared at him. "What do you mean?"

"I asked the doctor how much time I have left," he said. "Since I've decided not to do the dialysis, it might be two months or two years. I'm so tired I think it's probably the former."

Earlier, we had visited a renal center in Spokane to watch videos where kidney patients discussed their experiences with the various forms of treatment. We had identified an upstairs bedroom that could serve as a sanitary refuge for home peritoneal dialysis. Until now, Ken hadn't revealed that he'd changed his mind.

"I just don't want to do it," he explained. "I don't want to have the procedure for the connecting tubes, and I don't want to be tied down to sitting still for half an hour four times a day to do the exchanges. I want to go gracefully."

Stunned, I handed out chocolate the rest of the evening to the Spidermen, princesses, and Hannah Montana look-alikes who thronged to the door, as Ken slouched in his recliner watching his rerun. I read a travel brochure. I didn't want to see anything involving hospitals, death, or autopsies.

The next day, I reminded Ken of the advantages of the home dialysis as they had been explained to us. The supplies would be delivered to the home. We wouldn't have to drive seventy miles three times a week on icy roads. We could take car trips to visit friends and relatives. He just shook his head. "I've made my decision."

Though well past middle age, we had been married only seven years. I felt sorry for myself. It wasn't fair. Ken had convinced me to retire three years earlier and move to a home in the country. We had acquired two dogs, three cats, pastures to mow, gardens to weed. I couldn't handle it all on my own.

Then I felt sorry for Ken. It wasn't as if he had been fading mentally. He still played chess and checkers online with a longtime friend. He still vied with me guessing answers on *Jeopardy!* each weeknight. He still presented himself as the snappiest dresser at the WSU Agriculture Extension harvest dinners or the Habitat for Humanity Valentine banquets.

By Thanksgiving, Ken had rallied in spirit, if not in strength. Though he still dozed off several times a day, he had more energy. We dined at our favorite bistro on the Columbia River where he treated himself to a rare martini. His son and daughter-in-law shared Christmas with us, just as they had the previous three years.

Through the bitter winter, new symptoms appeared. Ken couldn't get warm, despite extra layers of sweatshirts and swaddling in thermal blankets. Often he fell asleep on the sofa, too lethargic to climb the stairs. He complained that our firm mattress no longer gave his hips and legs proper support.

Often he couldn't find his glasses. Or the remote. Or car keys or wallet. Sometimes he would run errands and come back without the very item he had set out to buy. I read that such short-term memory loss is typical with kidney failure, as is irritability. Once or twice I overheard him telling people how irritating I had become. I knew I hadn't changed. Perhaps I always have been irritating and Ken just hadn't noticed until his health started to fail.

I watched him experiment. His GFR had gone up after a trip to England where he downed a pint in a pub each day; he tried drinking a beer each evening. He decided that the carbonation in his diet sodas had some negative impact; for months he substituted green tea. He purchased an over-the-counter kidney pill, stopped eating bananas, and finally eliminated most sugar.

Every six weeks he gets his blood test. I hover by the mailbox for days, waiting for the results. I hand him the envelope and letter opener and hold my breath. He scans the results and usually smiles. He's holding steady.

Our birthdays passed, and our eighth anniversary. Soon we'll be making plans for the fall and winter. Will we have another Halloween? Another Thanksgiving?

Another two months or two years? Two weeks? I sometimes sidle into a silent living room and edge towards his chair where he sleeps. I watch to see if his chest moves with his breath. When he snores, I'm relieved.

In the meantime, Ken handles each day with courage. He's sorted through his jewelry and given his valuable tie tacks to his three sons. He's mentioned who should get his John Lennon lithograph, the 19th century *Vanity Fair* Spy prints, the wooden masks, and oils.

He's contracted with handymen, fence builders, and painters to get the house up to snuff. He's worked with a gardener to plant the proper shrubs, honeysuckle, roses, and grape vines.

He still barbecues rib eyes and beats me at gin. And his portrait still dries in the back of his van. He's ensured that I'll still have his smile to brighten my days, whether or not he's here for *Jeopardy!* He's said it's his legacy.

~Terri Elders

Going Back

There are people who have money and people who are rich.
~Coco Chanel

Funny how something as simple as a grocery store can cause pain. Armed with a grocery list, calculator and coupons, I cross the threshold and enter a vast display of options and delights that tempt my eyes and stomach. I walk the aisles dropping items into my cart, entering the amount in my calculator and crossing those items off my list. About three-fourths of the way through my list, the calculator shows I am close to the limit of what I have in my wallet for this shopping trip. I look at my list to see what is left and I look in my cart and ask myself, "What should I put back?" There are things still not crossed off that I must get. Going back down the aisles I have already walked, I put items back on the shelves and recalculate my spending, as the tears begin to fall and my lips taste salt.

Will I ever walk into a grocery store without my calculator and fill my cart with anything I want? Will I ever be able to buy my children all new clothes instead of garage sale finds? My wallet is empty, with not even enough change to drive through McDonald's for a Coke. More tears.

That was in the late 1970s. Life did get better. I was able to put away my calculator and could afford a Coke; even better than that, I could afford Starbucks several times a week. I could go out to eat with friends and pay for their lunch. I got my nails done once a month so my hands would look pretty and people would notice my nails and not the age spots on my hands. On birthdays and Christmas my husband and I lavished gifts on our three children and their spouses and our granddaughter. My husband and I went out to eat once a week; the long hours I worked made this a special treat. How good it felt to not be weighted down with money worries.

We tend to think that once we have a breakthrough, we will always be there, no "going back." 2008 was a "going back" year for us. My husband, Bob, and I both lost our good jobs. My husband sent out resumés and started receiving calls right away for interviews, so we thought it wouldn't be more than a couple of months before he was employed again. That couple of months has stretched into almost a year.

At the start of our backward walk we looked at our expenses and began to cut back. We don't drink or smoke, so we never had those expenses to cut. Dinners out—well those were now "out." I miss the lunches with my friends, and my nails are looking pretty ragged. Birthday and Christmas gifts are minimal and Starbucks—well that's not happening either. Bob gave up his monthly massages, we dropped our dental insurance, and we dropped long distance service from our home phone. Angel Food Ministries is helping us keep our food budget in check. We cut back spending wherever we could.

I know that things wear out, but the timing of those happenings always seems to be the worst. Our hot water heater began leaking and we finally had to replace it. The tires on my car were so bald that when I braked it took a while for my car to finish sliding and come to a stop, a fun sensation if I wasn't too close to the car in front of me. Winter was coming and there was no way I could continue to drive on those tires, so four new tires and an alignment later, I was safely on the road again but with a drained checkbook. Heavy vet bills for a sick dog pressed in more. Our savings are dwindling.

Every day we wake with the hope that our breakthrough will be this day.

My husband is working right now on a temporary project. We are told it will only last two months but we are praying it will be longer.

Truthfully I don't like the "going back" but the tears are not there like before. I have something I didn't have in the 1970s. I have peace, strength, joy and hope that comes from Jesus. We will get to the other side again. The things we have given up are not really important things and we may have more yet to give up, but that's okay too.

There is a saying, "I've been rich and I've been poor. Believe me, rich is better." That's true. Rich is better, but rich doesn't always mean having money. Richness comes in relationships and from having peace, which is something money can't buy.

There have been high points in this last year. Our children gave us a surprise fortieth wedding anniversary party—children and friends came from out of state and friends from church joined us to celebrate. It was such a fountain of refreshment in a dry place. We even got gift cards for restaurants—yeah! Church friends gave us a new dog when we had to put our old dog to sleep. Walks with our new dog, Sammy, are getting me the exercise I very much need. My husband and I share home-cooked meals every night and I enjoy spending time looking at cookbooks for new dishes to try. We take one day at a time. Worrying about what "may" happen tomorrow only takes away peace.

~Diane Shaw

Tough Times, Tough People

Grief and Healing

*There are things that we don't want to happen but have to accept,
things we don't want to know but have to learn, and people we can't
live without but have to let go.*

~Author Unknown

Losing a Wife, Mother, and Daughter

To live in hearts we leave behind
Is not to die.
~Thomas Campbell

When someone you love is dying, it knocks you off balance and shakes you to the core. Roles shift and relationships change. Life becomes painful beyond words.

For fifteen months, my wife, Linda, battled a rare form of cancer called Primary Central Nervous System (CNS) Lymphoma. She underwent countless sessions of radiation therapy and chemotherapy. Treatment after treatment was the same. She was hit hard, knocked off her feet. The only difference was that each treatment was more powerful than the last. The previous exhaustion was nothing compared to the next wave. Each time Linda thought that she had turned the corner, that the worst was behind her, and that her body was growing stronger despite the chemical and radioactive bombardment, she was actually growing weaker.

As the end grew near, I wasn't sure what to expect. Neither were our children, Emily and Tyler, or Linda's parents who had come to stay with us. The curative treatment was over, and now a new challenge was about to begin. I knew there would be grief, but I had no idea how much confusion, disorientation, fear, anger, and guilt our family would go through.

During the final weeks we lived day to day, moment to moment, in a kind of poised-to-flight tension. And with each passing day, a terrible agony pushed all of us closer and closer to the edge.

Linda's parents were, understandably, at wits' end. They were losing their daughter, watching her die before their eyes, and there was nothing they could do.

My job was to maintain stability in the house. Emily and Tyler still had to get to school. Meals had to be cooked, laundry done. There were Linda's care and medical needs to attend to, as well as friends coming and going at all hours. At times, the tears and sorrow became almost unbearable.

One morning, my mother-in-law came in and found my blankets on the floor, next to Linda's bed.

"Why are you sleeping here?" she asked.

I told her that I wanted to be close to Linda in case she needed anything during the night.

"What are you trying to be?" she said. "A martyr?"

There were other shots fired, lots of them. We argued over estate issues, religious issues, and who would be allowed to visit Linda during her final days. Finally something inside me snapped. I raged back at her parents, letting it all go. They met me head on. We stood in the kitchen, shouting back and forth at the top of our lungs, hurling threats and accusations at each other like steak knives.

In the other room, Linda lay dying.

How does one normalize the death of a loved one, the roller coaster of emotion with highs and lows coming at every turn, at every moment? How do you make sense of the anger, sorrow, and tears?

For our family, hospice was a great help. They were instrumental in keeping everyone sane amid a cacophony of confusion and sorrow, as well as keeping Linda comfortable and pain-free. In the weeks leading up to her death, they helped us immeasurably. They taught us how to confront death without fear and to find meaning in the midst of chaos. I'm not sure if we would have survived without them.

Hospice taught me another important lesson: in the midst of sorrow, one can often find beauty. I witnessed this in a letter my oldest son, Micah, wrote to Linda in the weeks before her death. In his letter he said:

I am who I am today because of you, my stepmother. You came into my life and colored my future with your love. I am creative because you nurtured my imagination. I am sensitive because I knew it was okay to cry around you.

I know that I am worth love, because I was raised in love. I know it's okay to be different because you always accepted me, and when I faltered you never gave up on me.

When I was seven, and running a race, you cheered for me like I was your hero. I felt so important. When I was afraid at night, you came into my room. You rubbed my back and ran your fingers through my hair. Then you would say, "It's okay." I never felt alone or afraid after that. You hugged me like I was your own son and told me that you loved me. I knew it was true because it was real.

I love the way you show your love with a warm smile. I love the way you never yelled at me. I love the way you treat animals and respect nature. I love the way you see beauty in everything. You taught me to do the same. I love you, Linda. You mean the world to me.

I was with Linda the night she died. The hour was late and everyone was asleep. I sat beside her bed, holding her hand. Her breathing became irregular, and I could see the end was near. I felt a sorrow unlike any I had ever known, as if my own body was closing down along with hers.

But as something shut inside me, something else opened. I apologized to her for the way I had spoken to her parents. I told her it was okay to let go. I assured her that Emily and Tyler would always be safe, and they would grow up to be kind and compassionate people, just like their mother. As Linda took her final breath, I told her that we would never stop loving her.

Is life long enough to recover from the death of someone you love? I'm not sure. But when I think back on those final days, on the anger and sadness that surged through our family, I realize the healing had already begun.

Six months after Linda's death, her parents returned for Emily's eighth grade graduation. When the ceremony was over, I thanked them for taking the time to be there, and told them they were wonderful grandparents.

As we said our goodbyes, Linda's father shook my hand and said, "Tim, I hope you understand the reason we acted the way we did when Linda was dying. We were losing a daughter. Imagine if you were losing Emily."

His words explained everything. Over the next months we shored up our differences and became friends again.

Linda returns from time to time, not only in memory but in real life. She is here, of course, to watch over Emily and Tyler. She remains with us, absolute and unchanging, and is a guiding light for our family.

She returned not long ago on a clear summer day. I was in the backyard when I glanced up and saw a cloud overhead, one solitary cloud in an otherwise flawlessly blue sky. That cloud was in the perfect shape of a heart. It was a gift from Linda, of that I have no doubt.

It was her way of saying, "Thank you for understanding."

~Timothy Martin

Dear Danielle

She was no longer wrestling with the grief, but could sit down with it as a
lasting companion and make it a sharer in her thoughts.
~George Eliot

Abottle of perfume, a pallet of eye shadow, and a can of hair spray sit on my bathroom vanity. Other than a daily dusting, they remain untouched. Her beautiful smile and flashing brown eyes continue to whirl around the misty corners of my brain to haunt my dreams each night. The memory of her tinkling laugh makes me smile wistfully each time it glides across the silence of my empty house to tickle my ears. My daughter Danielle may no longer reside in my house, but her spirit remains eternally young and beautiful in my heart.

Losing my mother in 2007 knocked the wind out of me, but the loss of my daughter in 2008 brought me to my knees. As I scramble for a way to cope, familiar passages from The Holy Bible have become my best friend. Each word is like a rainbow from above, a sign of his eternal promise of comfort and hope. The reading of his sweet, familiar word offers so much encouragement in those dark, early morning hours when sleep evades me. Clinging to the hope of eternal life strengthens me. Faith in my redeemer brings me peace. Acting like a lifeline, it encourages me to get up each morning to go on. In all honesty, my faith in Christ is the only thing preventing me from slipping into the black hole of depression and misery.

Writing has become a great catalyst to rid my soul of anger and resentment. Cataloging my thoughts helps ease the pain. As I channel my loss into a poem, I can feel Danielle's presence in my life. Precious memories deserve their place of honor. A daily journal of my inner feelings encourages me. It is the one place where I can write down my feelings without feeling any shame. Daily, I spill out my innermost thoughts, the good, bad, and ugly.

On New Year's Eve when the stars twinkled brightly in the sky, I inhaled the scent of my Irish Cream coffee and wondered about the year ahead. Did I have anything to live for in the year ahead? Then I thought of my other two children, my husband, and my seventy-five-year-old father. Praying for strength, I somehow made it through the night. It's funny but I remember wondering how many in the world were wearing silly hats as they tooted paper horns and toasted each other with a glass of champagne.

As the long months of spring and summer loom ahead, I continue to struggle to regain my footing. When the spring flowers began to unfurl with a prism of bright color, how will I be able to feel any joy? Spending time with my earthly father helps. Reminiscing about the past, somehow bridges the pain I feel. I hope by spending more time with him, the gaping hole in my heart will eventually heal. He is my rock, solid and strong. He has suffered the loss of mother, father, brothers, a sister, wife, daughter, and now a granddaughter. Yet through it, all, his faith has remained steadfast and sure. He continues to talk about the goodness and love of the Lord. Through his faith, I find peace.

Death is one of the hardest lessons life can hand us. We have all faced the long dreaded trip to a funeral home. Yet nothing prepares us for the scars these visits leave on our heart and soul. All loss is painful, sad, and in some ways eye-opening. Each trip drives home the reality that life on earth will not last forever. I struggle for answers. Why did my daughter die so young? If I had done things differently, would she be here with me today? How could the Lord see fit to remove a twenty-seven-year-old from this world? Yet through it all, I know it is not my place to question. In his infinite wisdom, God knows all. He has a master plan, and we each have a tiny spot where we fit in. Many things happen that leave us wondering why. A mere human can never understand it all.

Through the years, people always told me a mother's intuition is greater than radar. That statement is no longer questionable to me. As I sit here writing this, I know beyond a doubt my daughter is in Heaven with the Lord. I am assured she is happy and at peace. Now as I continue my daily struggle in this cold, cruel world I must look up in order to survive. He never promised the journey would be easy. Never guaranteed we would live each day in comfort. Struggling to overcome the death of my daughter is the hardest thing I have ever done. Yet in my heart, I know with the help of the Lord I will endure.

Each morning I get up to follow my familiar routine. As I go about my daily life, I cling to my memories of my daughter. Spending time with my husband and my two other children encourages and inspires me. Then late in the evening, after things have settled down, I sit at my computer to write. As my daily journal flashes onto the screen, I type in the familiar words, "Dear Danielle."

~Sharon Rosenbaum-Earls

To Forgive Is to Receive

To forgive is to set a prisoner free and discover that the prisoner was you.
~Lewis B. Smedes

I don't know if it's really possible to get over the effects of childhood sexual abuse, but I've spent the past fifty-eight years trying.

In those years, I've learned a lot about the healing process. For example, I've learned that the more you say it out loud, the easier it becomes to talk about. Saying it out loud to other people, now that is a whole different ball game. The response they give you is never the one you wanted or needed.

The very first response was from my mother. "My God, he's ruined you for life!" was NOT what I had hoped to hear. It is emblazoned on my mind like a brand, identifying me as one of the "soiled" ones who must fight a lifetime fight to believe we are worthy of respect, love and intimacy.

Other responses—pity, shock, anger, and attempts at relating to our pain—just magnify our shame. Although the shame is not rightfully ours, we clutch it close like an old familiar friend. Then there are those "pull up your bootstraps" people, the ones who tell you to just get over it and move on. They go on to give you advice like, "Forget about it. It happened a long time ago." Or, "The trials and turmoil in our lives make us stronger." Perhaps they're right and maybe that's how they would handle that kind of trauma... but I doubt it.

Through all the therapy sessions, support groups, survival workbooks, looking for my "inner child," and countless recommendations from the well-intentioned "novices," there was one piece of advice that angered me more than any other. It was one simple, yet very powerful word: "Forgive." Someone told me that in forgiving, I would find healing.

Forgive? You've GOT to be kidding! Forgive him for betraying me, for hurting me like no one else ever could, for elevating his evilness to even higher levels with my little sister? Forgive myself for letting it happen... to me and to her? Forgiving means excusing the transgression and saying to the person who wronged you that you are okay with what they did, right? Forgiveness was simply not an option.

I spent many, many years hating him, avoiding him, punishing him in as many subtle ways as I could, and telling myself that being related to him by blood did not make him my father. As he aged, I imagined his death, and the freedom from fear and shame it would surely bring me. I even wondered if I would attend his funeral and whether I would cry with relief or find pleasure in silently saying to him, "Now you can't hurt me or anyone else ever again."

Almost five years ago, we got the news. Dad was diagnosed with lung cancer. It had metastasized, spreading to nearly all his vital organs, brain, and bones. There were no treatment options. He was dying and he was alone. I confess that at the time, I felt a twinge of satisfaction at the thought that his ultimate punishment would be intense suffering and isolation. How appropriate that seemed.

I had intended from the beginning to remain detached. I didn't visit or call him while he was still living in his apartment. The youngest brother and sister of the six of us took on all the responsibilities of his affairs and health care. It was for them that I offered financial assistance to help cover their travel and lost work time. It was for them I went to help clean out his apartment when he was moved to a nursing home. I had still not decided whether to visit him at the nursing home when I pulled into the apartment complex and parked my car.

As we sorted through his personal effects, something happened to all of us. The man we thought had turned his back on us had pictures of all his children in their younger days on his walls. Photos of his fondest childhood memories were tucked away in treasure boxes. The man we thought did not believe in God had religious artifacts displayed throughout his home. And, the man we thought didn't have a heart had saved mementos of special life events and the people he cherished. It was only during those moments that I could look past the "monster" to see the "daddy" I had once adored. When we finished cleaning the apartment, I followed my brothers and youngest sister to the nursing home.

He couldn't disguise his surprise at seeing me. His drawn and tired face lit up and a smile broke as he said, "Hi, Sis." He was never a very pleasant man and the cancer in his brain had made him erupt into yelling fits that brought both his younger children to tears. On this day, however, it was obvious he was trying very hard to be on his best behavior. My brother said it was because I was there.

Being true to myself, I kept my distance from him. At one point he said to us, "I know I wasn't a very good father." I couldn't disagree with that revelation, so I said nothing to dispute it or to make him feel better. On the drive home, it suddenly hit me... those words were the closest he could come to an apology, something I never expected to hear. As insufficient as they seemed when he said them, those words had opened—just a tiny bit—a door I thought had been closed forever.

When the call came that he was expected to pass at any time, I wasn't sure how to approach my middle sister who had suffered the most at his hand. Although she too had been helping our younger siblings from a distance, she was unable to bear the pain of facing him. I think it was her sense of responsibility to us that made her agree to go with me to be at his deathbed.

She and I had talked in the past about the traumas we shared, but I don't think I really heard her when she said the only memories she had of him were as the monster, not as a dad. For the first time, I shared with her the good memories I had of a man who got down on the floor with his sons to assemble the Christmas train set, who took his kids fishing on weekends, who taught them how to build things, who made a beautiful rocking swan for her when she was a toddler, and who doted over each child when they were born. We talked and talked... and cried.

When we arrived, the nurses told us it seemed he was waiting for something or someone. My sister and I looked at each other with a mutual knowledge of what he was waiting for. As we stood on either side of him, each holding a hand, we saw how vulnerable and small and scared he was... just like we had been. It was in that moment we had to choose whether to hurt him as he had hurt us or to prove ourselves to be decent and worthwhile human beings. Neither of us could tell him what he needed to hear—that would be a lie—but we both told him to go in peace, and we meant it. He quietly took a last breath and slipped away.

In freeing him, we had begun to free ourselves. In opening the door to forgiveness, we had finally and honestly begun to heal.

~Sis

Healing Connections

It is some relief to weep; grief is satisfied and carried off by tears.
~Ovid

A dusting of snow fell that late October morning in Colorado. By lunchtime brilliant sunshine was melting most of it, but that evening, as I drove through an older neighborhood of Colorado Springs, streetlamps glittered on small white patches that had been shaded during the afternoon.

I parked my car and walked carefully up steps to the front porch of a frame house that would have been new when my grandparents moved to Colorado Springs in 1908. I was not sure what had drawn me to this city but I felt a strong pull when an acquaintance there had asked me to house- and dog-sit for her for a month while she was abroad. I looked forward to exploring this area, as I remembered my grandparents' stories about their year in Colorado. And so I had come from Texas for a month in the mountains.

As I prowled historic Manitou Springs, I recognized why I had come to the region for the first time: connecting. For this is where my grandfather brought Grandma after the death of their oldest child, my mother's "big sister" and my aunt. And I, too, was moving through the grief process following the sudden death of my younger son.

Little Kathryn died at age six of complications of diphtheria and whooping cough. My grandmother had to cope with both her grief and the pregnancy that resulted in my mother's birth a few months later. Their five-year-old son who was inconsolable at his sister's death added to the trauma, and Grandma's health suffered. Doctors recommended a change of scene. Grandfather moved the family from Oklahoma to Manitou Springs.

My grandparents would have understood my grief. I had spent most of my childhood in their home during the Great Depression of the 1930s. We had been exceptionally close. As I walked the streets of Manitou Springs, I could easily imagine them as the young couple they had been when Kathryn died. I felt them with me in spirit now as I coped with the loss of my son at age twenty-seven.

At least my grandparents had each other. I was widowed, with one loving son now, far away in graduate school and working. I did not want to burden him further as he, too, was grieving for his lost brother. With no other close family, I had to find my own way. And I reached for whatever comfort and help I could find, even from strangers.

I had been in Colorado Springs a week when I read in the newspaper of a meeting of parents who had lost children. And that is what brought me to a house I did not know on this cold night.

A small woman answered my knock and drew me into a warm living room.

"Please come in and join us," she said. "Let me take your coat."

Eight people in a semi-circle of chairs around a couch seemed to fill the room. I was offered space on the couch. As I sat down, I saw that a woman was crying. Another woman's arm was around her shoulder. The weeping woman had been telling her story and resumed as soon as I was seated. When she finished, each person introduced himself or herself with not only a name but why they were present. The stories were heart-rending, starting with that of a stillborn whose parents had known only a brief moment of holding her, yet such an important moment to them. That young couple was grieving for what they had not known of their child. I grieved for what I did know as well as for what would never be.

I do not recall all the details of that evening. I know there were some stories I did not want to hear. I gritted my mental teeth and reminded myself, "They need to talk and we must offer ears and hearts to listen. We do not have to absorb each tragic word. We need only allow them to talk, so they do not have to scream to an empty room. And after a while, they will listen to me, too."

We touched one another with compassion. Arms went quickly around a man whose son had shot himself. Hands held tightly to a woman whose son had died while sending messages to buddies on his computer. Hands held mine as we prayed together for courage and faith in a humane world.

I left that meeting feeling drained and terribly sad. For the woman who had been crying when I entered the house and who was obviously in shock. I thought of the middle-aged man who had made room for me on the couch. He had said very little, still not understanding his loss. I remembered the young couple who held hands when they spoke of losing their baby. And of the woman who had offered us hospitality, whose daughter had died because of a mistake in a hospital.

There had been much pain in that living room, but also much loving understanding. I saw from the other faces as we left that the hour we spent sharing our pain had helped us all. We had given each other strength in this toughest of times. It was an important step in healing our raw wounds. My gratitude ran deep.

As I got into my car, I looked up at the dark autumn sky, with its brilliant points of starlight. I took a deep breath of ice-tinged mountain air. How small we are in the universe, I thought. Yet I felt connected to the whole of life and all its drama, good and bad.

Back at my temporary house, I took the dogs for a last quick walk. Then we hurried inside to warmth and bed, mine under a great down comforter and theirs companionably nearby in a large lined basket. Before falling asleep, I thought again of my grandparents during their time in these mountains. I felt a closeness to them that spanned time and generations. That, too, was a comfort I took to myself and I slept blessedly without sad dreams.

~Marcia E. Brown

98

Memories of Sarah

A photograph is memory in the raw.
~Carrie Latet

One evening I get a call from the hospital about a photo session. My evening plans are forgotten as I collect details from the nurse. I discover baby Sarah will be delivered by C-section, but she has not moved in her mother's belly since yesterday. At the hospital, I carry my photographic equipment with me through the sterile, white halls. I check in with the head nurse, and sit in the waiting room, waiting for her to tell me when they are ready. The C-section is underway. Silence permeates the empty waiting room, and I see baby Sarah's extended family waiting; waiting for a miracle.

As a professional photographer, I'm no stranger to capturing smiles and exciting, happy times in peoples' lives. Most of my clients want me to document joyous events—those moments you will remember forever. But, occasionally my calling as a photographer requires capturing a different kind of memory. You see, I volunteer for an organization called Now I Lay Me Down to Sleep, which provides compassionate portraiture for families facing the loss of their newborn (or unborn) child. The parents often have only a few hours, or even minutes, as their child clings precariously to life. They do not get to welcome their child home, and have to say goodbye forever.

The staff leads me into the recovery room so I can assemble my equipment. After what seems like forever, a nurse tells me the delivery is complete—but baby Sarah is stillborn. My heart sinks. The recovery room doors open, and a hospital bed rolls through the door. I see baby Sarah, in her mother's arms. Both parents' eyes are red and glistening. Grief floods the room, filling every nook and cranny. I am sorrowful but focus on the task ahead. My soul aches for the parents as I tell them I am their photographer.

Baby Sarah is put into my arms. She is beautiful: her skin is unmarred, curly wisps of hair grace her head; it is almost as if she is sleeping. I tell her parents how beautiful she is, and then begin photographing. With her little hat on, Sarah appears to be simply asleep. I gently unwrap the blanket, revealing Sarah's tiny hands and feet—which I photograph as well. Once I am finished, I ask her parents if they would like to be photographed with Sarah. I position Sarah in their arms so she appears to be sleeping. Through their grief, her parents caress Sarah's petite fingers. I do my best to capture these poignant moments. Their faces are exhausted from the long ordeal. I see it is time to wrap up the session.

I have not been in the shoes of these parents. I sense their pain and witness their grief, but know that I cannot fully comprehend their anguish. No words will ease their heartache, yet I say, "I am so sorry for your loss. Your daughter is beautiful." Gratitude fills their eyes. Each of these sessions changes my perspective, reminding me how precious life really is. I am honored to be a part of Now I Lay Me Down to Sleep. It takes my photography calling to a deeper level. I am still creating memories. Baby Sarah's portraits memorialize her brief existence. Sarah really was here.

~Betsy Finn

Patchwork Memories

Memory is a way of holding on to the things you love,
the things you are, the things you never want to lose.
~from The Wonder Years

little blond-haired boy, freshly bathed with neatly combed hair and clean pajamas, runs to the sofa and waits, sitting on a patchwork quilt, for his favorite movie to start.

He asks Mommy to bring him "Daddy's Blanket." His young mother brings him the blanket, much like the one he is sitting on. He sees her reach for her camera and Liam's blue eyes sparkle as he smiles at his mom, who captures a smile and a moment she will treasure always. The smile of her handsome son, with its hint of mischief, so like his daddy's.

It's a familiar scene, played out in homes where children are loved, adored, cared for, and feel secure. But there is something different about Liam's life. Somebody is missing, and can never be replaced. His daddy, Mitchell Glavine, has died.

He was a victim of carbon monoxide poisoning in a cabin, a year before this photo of Liam was taken. It has been a year of pain, sorrow, and heartache.

How could life be so cruel to let this happen to such a promising young life? A young man who graduated from St. Francis Xavier University, liked his work in technology, and loved Liam and his mom more than life itself.

Liam's mother, Vanessa, is young, but she has had to face

incredible gut-wrenching heartbreak in the year since Mitch's death, and she has had to do it while caring for Liam and making a life for him. Never in her wildest dreams did she imagine living her life without Mitch.

In the weeks following Mitch's death, well-meaning people advised Vanessa—a young mother awash in grief, bewilderment, and pain—to "get rid" of Mitch's clothes "right away." Others advised her to "wait a year" before doing anything.

Through the fog of pain and shock, living in a daze, Vanessa could not make a decision. She couldn't let Mitch's clothes go, and she could not keep them. Decision-making was impossible.

As often happens, the answer came to her very unexpectedly, maybe with the help of a guardian angel, and the answer was indeed an innovative idea. The glimpse of a solution came to her during a conversation with her friend, Jo. As young women often do, they shared each others' lives, hopes, dreams, and hurts, gaining strength from each other.

Jo spoke of having a quilt made for her daughter's graduation. She told Vanessa about a lady named Shirley Zillman who both Mitch and Vanessa knew, who lived in the community of Port aux Basques, NL. Jo spoke of how extraordinarily beautiful Mrs. Zillman's quilts were, and she planned to ask her if she would do one for her daughter.

Vanessa shivered! Would it be possible to have a quilt made from Mitch's clothes, and in so doing let them go, but yet keep them?

She still has no idea where the thought came from—she had never heard of such an undertaking, nor did she know if it was possible to do.

She visited Mrs. Shirley Zillman, a lady with a kind heart, who showed Vanessa some of her magnificent quilts. Hours and hours of work were required to make each one, and it showed. She had some portraying Newfoundland scenes, support for breast cancer victims, and various others—each one a work of art in itself.

Vanessa told Mrs. Zillman of her idea, and how honored she

would be if she would at least attempt to make a quilt from Mitch's clothing.

"I'll do it Vanessa," she told the grieving young woman, "and the only payment I want is a photograph of you, me and the quilt!" It was a remarkable act of kindness from an extraordinary lady.

Later that week, with a heavy heart, Vanessa delivered Mitch's belongings to Mrs. Zillman. Time passed, and with each day she doubted her decision more and more. What if it didn't work? What if it was the wrong decision? Her anxiety and self-doubt grew.

Then the call came. The quilt was ready.

Vanessa was ecstatic, terrified, grief-stricken, so much so that she asked her friend Jo to go with her to pick it up. She needed support and somebody who understood her anguish. She was a twenty-nine-year-old woman with a two-year-old, having her husband's clothes made into a quilt! Nothing was fair.

Then Mrs. Zillman brought forward the most precious thing Vanessa had ever seen. The patchwork quilt was absolutely beautiful. Vanessa burst into tears of grief for what was never to be.

As promised, the photograph was taken of Shirley and Vanessa holding the beautiful quilt. Shirley Zillman then shared a secret, she was working on a smaller quilt for little Liam. More tears flowed as Vanessa was overwhelmed by the generosity being shown to her and her small son.

Now was time to share the well-kept secret. Vanessa casually asked her sister, Jesse, to come and see something she had, just for an opinion.

When Jesse arrived, Vanessa produced the comforter saying only, "Shirley made it for me!"

"Oh, nice," Jesse said, as she closely examined the handiwork.

Then she recognized a patch of one of Mitch's shirts, realized what it was, and cried as if her heart would break. Two sisters, brokenhearted, holding a precious work of art, done by a gifted lady, is something they will never forget.

Liam soon had his own "Daddy's Blanket" as he calls it. Already he has identified a few pieces in it. And with the help of time and a loving mom, he will learn more about his dad, and about his special "Daddy's Blanket."

Vanessa finds comfort in her special possession, as Liam does in his. They wrap themselves in their "Comfort Quilts" as if they were being wrapped in the arms of their cherished husband and dad.

The problem was solved, the clothes were gone, but they were back in another form. Vanessa and Liam have their beautiful quilts of "Patchwork Memories" that will give them consolation and they will hold close to their hearts forever.

~Bonnie Jarvis-Lowe

He Can't Hide from God... or His Mother

Love builds bridges where there are none.
~R.H. Delaney

Every mother knows the day will come when she must let go of her children, but I never expected that my letting go of our son would have to be so total, so complete.

When our twenty-two-year-old son, Lorne, became a missing person statistic in January of 1986, I kept asking, "Why me?" Missing person stories only happen on television melodramas, not to loving families like ours. After all, we didn't have problems of divorce, poverty, abuse, alcohol, or drugs. My husband and I had been involved with our four children and their many activities. How could this happen to us?

The first month after Lorne's disappearance was a frantic blur. Our son changed from a University of Arizona student to a Tucson Police Department case number.

First it was thought that since Lorne was a long-distance runner, he could have fallen into a ravine in the Catalina Mountains behind his old high school. Soon, Search and Rescue, tracking dogs, the Sheriff's Department, and police helicopters became involved. People on horseback and on foot, along with Lorne's former high school cross-country coach and team, thoroughly combed the trails. There were no leads.

Meanwhile, I felt overwhelmed. I became consumed with, "What if?" What if I hadn't shown long, lanky Lorne how much I loved him? What if I hadn't understood this quiet, good-natured young man who kept his successes and worries to himself?

I shed numerous tears, took ulcer medication, and quickly descended into an "I can't" phase. I convinced myself I could cope no longer. I felt hopeless. There was nothing I could do.

But slowly, as the weeks passed, I got back into a daily routine. I returned to my teaching job. I quit looking at time as a huge block, and worked on getting through each day.

One day I had a serious talk with myself. Lorne's disappearance wasn't my fault! I'd been the best mother I knew how to be to him — to all our four children. What was it about Lorne that I'd missed?

Thinking back, I tried to understand what had happened. Lorne had always shown a strong desire to please everyone else... but maybe not himself. His boss, the head athletic trainer at the university, described him as "reliable and responsible," and his friends said, "He's one of those people everyone likes."

Leaving so abruptly was out of character for Lorne. Had he grown tired of pleasing other people?

No one, including me, ever dreamed that the guy everyone liked might have problems. But if I could have done anything differently, it was too late now. Lorne was a grown young man and could legally choose to be gone.

One day while lunching with friends at a Chinese restaurant, I opened a fortune cookie. The little slip of paper said, "Your sense of humor allows you to glide through difficult times." It was true. I'd always laughed easily and had a healthy sense of humor. It was my strong point!

I resolved to get that laugh back in working order again. I pinned that fortune cookie to my bulletin board, where it remains to this day. I was ready. But where was Lorne hiding?

The man in charge of the Salvation Army Missing Persons Bureau patted my hand. "He can't hide from God," he said.

"Or his mother!" I replied, standing straighter.

At homeless feeding stations, I held up a poster with Lorne's picture and the words, "Have you seen me?" The posters were also displayed in various shelters and blood donation centers in the Southwest. Lorne's extreme vision correction prescription went to optometrists in the western states, and his dental records to the national computer system. My husband and I engaged two different private investigators.

My attempt to get Lorne's case on the television program, *Unsolved Mysteries*, proved unsuccessful. The producer said that it "didn't have a strong story line." It was a strong story line to me! I did prevail, however, in getting his case on a syndicated show called *Reunion*. I felt that someone somewhere had seen Lorne. Yet despite all our efforts, Lorne remained "missing."

And twenty-three years later, Lorne is still gone without a trace. Meanwhile, I have had to go on with my life—coping with being a widow, helping my grandchildren, being there for our other grown kids when they need me. But most importantly, I've worked on keeping laughter in my life.

I've never stopped looking for Lorne in crowds, but now I remind myself that I'm looking for a middle-aged man. And since time has marched on, what if we wouldn't recognize each other?

If I'm ever lucky enough to see Lorne again, I have a mental list of things I want to remember to tell him. I want him to know his friends liked him so much that they began a scholarship at the university in his name. I want to laugh with him at the humorous antics of his older sister's children. I want to sit next to him and talk with him about his hopes and dreams.

I have never stopped loving Lorne and never will, but I like to think the love I send him now is somehow stronger. Loving Lorne without knowing where he is feels like a ribbon flowing from my heart. It travels across time and forever. We never totally let go of our children.

I believe what the man at the Salvation Army told me so many years ago is true. My son can't hide from God... or his mother's love.

~Sharon Landeen

Rows of Grief

All the art of living lies in a fine mingling of letting go and holding on.
~Havelock Ellis

There was no wake, no funeral, no graveside service, but I lost my son today.

In reality, I lost him long ago; today is the day I accepted that reality. What happened to the infant I consecrated to God at his Baptism? What happened to the adventurous toddler I had to rescue from our maple tree? The curious youngster who took apart a radio and put it back together... at age four? The adolescent whose humor defused so much stress when there were five teens in the house? The sensitive youth who knew when Mommy didn't feel well, and urged his siblings to be quiet? The man whose wedding I witnessed and at whose reception I danced? The man who drove me through three states to fetch tangible memories when my mother died, and who extolled his love for his wife and children all the way?

What happened? Drugs happened.

Parental neglect. Fiscal irresponsibility. Criminal behavior. A twelve-year prison sentence. That's what happened.

A mental health care professional whom I trust helped me to see that today. I read her his latest letter. She pointed out the blaming, abusive, hedonistic attitudes common to addicts. I know in my knower that she is right; I appreciate her directness in getting through to my heart. There's such a fine line between encouraging and enabling. Repeatedly crossing it does no good for him. Or for me. I must detach, for both our sakes.

My heart is so heavy I can hardly pick up my knitting to pray my grief in inches. I make it through one row. This shawl is cocoa brown, with a wide ribbing pattern. The ribs remind me of prison bars. I put it down.

Next, I turn to the shawl of variegated shades of fig, chocolate, and orange. My son asked for those colors—the grape and orange. I don't know why. I can't give it to him while he's incarcerated and I'll probably be dead before he's released. I usually pray for him while I work on this one, but not today. This is the shawl I'll use to process my pain. I will finish it, of course, and pass it along, like all the others, to the sick and dying in our congregation. And I will pray that my pain and grief will assuage someone else's.

Finally, I reach for the soft burnt orange worsted. There is no right side or wrong side to its basket weave pattern; it is reversible, each side a mirror of the other. The color, too, seems to symbolize different ways of looking at the same thing: it glows like embers of a dying fire and it blushes like a summer sunrise.

Tears blur my vision. Mechanically, I knit three, purl three for three rows. Then I purl three, knit three for three rows. Repeat. The checkerboard squares climb under and over each other, intertwined. "Comfort, Lord," I pray, "for me as well as the recipient... Healing... Forgiveness... Detachment. I release my son to you, O Lord."

I knit until my arms are sore. One hour? Two hours? Three?

I fondle this shawl as it shrouds my lap, my knees. The tears continue. I have forgiven this child many, many times. I pray that my emotions will catch up with those acts of will. Soon. But I know it will take a long time. Long after his family and I emerge from the financial crises his addiction created. Long after his children get the therapy they'll need because of what his lifestyle exposed them to. Long after his wife, whom I love like my own daughters, finishes school, finds a job, and addresses reality. I already hurt for her in that process. My God walks with me in my sorrow. He'll walk with her in hers.

He is my son; I will always love him. I will cry until I don't need to cry anymore. With God's grace, these floods will lessen; the triggers will be less frequent.

I will pray by inches for his salvation. He rejects God now, but I believe that the God who created him is always reaching for him. Where there is life, there is hope. I will pray for my son to be open to God's love all the days of my life. Then, I will wait expectantly in Heaven for him to come home.

In the meantime, I know I can face this the way I've faced previous trauma—with hope and humor. There's a bumper sticker that proclaims: "Sh__ Happens." Well, "sh__" is manure and manure is fertilizer and fertilizer helps things grow. When this latest excrement recycles, my family and I will bloom large!

~Diane C. Perrone

Tough Times, Tough People

Ten Bonus Stories of Faith

*As your faith is strengthened you will find that there is no longer the
need to have a sense of control, that things will flow as they will,
and that you will flow with them, to your great delight and benefit.*

~Emmanuel

Why Not?

Rejoice always, pray constantly, and in all circumstances give thanks.
~The Desert Fathers

Growing up in a small town in Mississippi, church was a major part of everyday life. Everything revolved around it, even social activities.

Due to illness, my mother couldn't take me to church much, but my Grandmother Wilmer made sure I was there every Wednesday night and most of the day Sunday. As a child, I was mesmerized by the congregation. During altar prayer, everyone would be thanking God, clapping their hands and working themselves into a frenzy with every word the pastor said.

"Thank you, God for all you have done for us and what you have brought us through!"

Amens and Hallelujahs could be heard all around. The pastor would step out of the pulpit, wiping sweat from his forehead, headed straight for my grandmother who was set to send up her portion of loud praises. As he got closer to her, the spirit seemed to engulf the whole congregation — praises were all through the church.

"Lord, you didn't have to do it, but you did and for that we thank you! Can I get an Amen, sister?" he said, grabbing my grandma's hand and shaking it.

"Amen, Amen. Yes Lord!" she shouted, running up and down the aisle until finally falling to the floor. I don't know if she fell from the Holy Spirit or if she just wore herself out. But I could certainly understand her praises.

For as long as I could remember, she was always considered blessed and highly favored in the Lord by her church members and friends. She was the first African American on her street to move, and bought her house with cash. Well respected in the neighborhood, she was always the leader of neighborhood watches and summer bake sales.

As a young girl, I decided that I, too, wanted to be a church lady like Grandma, shouting and thanking the Lord the way she did. From then on, I became very active in church, trying to emulate my grand-mother. But things just didn't seem to go right for me. God didn't seem to want to answer any of my prayers. I would sit on the same pew every Sunday, and feel nothing spiritually. What had I done so wrong that the Holy Spirit, which seemed to fill my grandma's soul, would elude me all together?

I finally gave up. I stopped going to church and moved six hours away.

Things only got worse. My mother had finally succumbed to her illness. And at twenty-six, I was a divorced mother with two toddlers, working a minimum wage job.

I was so angry with God, I got into my own personal shouting match, shaking my fist, asking how could he forget me when I tried so hard all my life to serve him and do right? How could everything I did turn out so wrong?

I exhausted myself shouting, and went to lie down. I tried to remember the happiness I felt as a child going to church, but it seemed far away.

The phone rang.

"Hello?" I said in a whisper, hoping it was not someone I owed money.

"Joyce?" It was Grandma. "Is that you? What's wrong, baby?"

The tears started. "Life, Grandma. I am a failure. I just can't do this. Why can't I keep it together like you?" For the next thirty min-utes, I went on and on about how bad things were.

"What in the world can be so wrong that it's causing you to give up?" she asked.

"Grandma, you wouldn't understand. You have your own house so you don't have to worry about rent. Your monthly pension is more than enough so you don't have to worry about money. Auntie gets her own money. (My grandmother's oldest daughter was born with Down syndrome.) You worry about nothing. It seems if God threw all the blessings at you and walked away when it came to me."

She listened, but she was still old school. "You quit your blaspheming, Joyce White. If you quit, not only are you disappointing yourself, you will instill quitting into your children. It's not written anywhere life is going to be easy. I should know. I had some tough times when I was young, but God saw me through."

"Tough times when, Grandma?" I asked. "I know for the last forty years you haven't paid rent to anyone."

"Do you think I've always had this house? You think my life has always been this way?"

"Yes ma'am," I said truthfully.

"But you don't know how I got this house."

"No ma'am. I guess I never thought about it."

"My nineteen-year-old son was killed in Vietnam. I got this house with the money the Army gave me. I had to lose a child to get a decent home. And before I got this house, I raised four children in a three-room house so run down they put a condemned sign on it. I felt despair just like you, but I had no place to go. You know what we did? We took the sign down and lived there until I could do better."

I was stunned.

"I have lost three of my four children, your mother included. They were supposed to help me take care of your Auntie. It was easy for me at first, but, at eighty, it gets harder every day.

"As far as my monthly pension, that's not something that was given to me. I put in forty years at a processing plant, working my fingers to the bone to earn that."

Now I felt ashamed. I never knew she had been through so much. When my mom died, and my aunt six months later, I guess

I was caught up in my own pain. I didn't realize she had lost her children.

"Grandma, with all that's happened to you, why are you always so happy in church?" I asked.

"Why not?" she said. "Baby, sometimes, you have to 'why not' yourself to happiness. Why not praise God? It's not doing any good to be mad at him. Why not shout praises? It keeps you from crying. Why not say Hallelujah? It keeps your spirit happy. Even when you don't feel like it, say, 'Thank you Jesus.' Just try it. I will send you a little something to tide you over until you can do better."

"Thank you so much, Grandma. I needed that."

"I know you did. Talk to you later." She hung up without another word.

"Just thank him anyway," I said, repeating my grandmother's words aloud. "Even if you don't feel like it."

I closed my eyes. "Thank you, Jesus," I whispered. "Thank you, Lord." The more I said it, the more I meant it. "Thank you, Lord." I stood up and walked from room to room. "Thank you, Lord!"

Grandma was right. Tears welled up in my eyes. God hadn't eluded me. I had eluded him because I was mad at my own failures and losses. All this time, the blessing was in thanking him anyway. Now I understood the people at my childhood church. They were not praising God because things were good. They were praising God until things got better.

The following Sunday, I decided to go to church. I made the six-hour drive to my hometown to attend church with my grandma. When the pastor called for altar prayer, I followed my grandmother to the front of the pulpit, along with others.

"I just want to say, thank you Lord for all you've done!" pastor shouted, with a loud response from the members.

I looked around to see some with their eyes closed but mouths full of praise. Others with their hands in the air, and barely audible. *Why not?*

"Thank you Lord!" I said as loud as I could.

Then it happened. As I continued my praise, I felt what I had been looking for all this time. The Holy Spirit. Now I knew just how everyone else felt when they found their own personal peace with God, and it was wonderful.

My grandmother looked at me and smiled. She knew I was having a "why not?" moment.

~Joyce Terrell

Free Faith for Sale

Faith makes things possible, not easy.
~Author Unknown

After I was laid off last winter, I didn't know what to do. Having worked in television as a writers' assistant on several different shows, I was used to them being cancelled; such is the life of a freelancer in entertainment. But I wasn't used to not having another TV show to go to. I had bounced from show to show for nearly ten years straight. And now... nothing?

Unfortunately, I wasn't eligible to get unemployment (that's what happens when you default on your student loans enough times). And my temp agencies were all on a hiring freeze until January; it was only November.

I made a list of everything I could do for money (everything that was legal, anyway): baby-sit, dog-sit, plant-sit (don't ask), return unworn new clothes, brew coffee at home versus buy it out, and so on. But it still wasn't enough money to live on.

My family in Chicago had none to spare, nor did my friends, for many of them were unemployed too. Maybe they couldn't lend me money, but could they help me out with other basic needs? I decided to put my requests on Facebook. After all, God had said, "Ask, and ye shall receive," right? I couldn't afford to pay for heat in my apartment; a friend loaned me her space heater. My cabinets were bare; friends gave me food. (I would also go to the grocery stores for free samples; I had each store's free sample days memorized.) My laptop died (not good for a writer); a friend loaned me one for "however long you need." I got a flat tire; a stranger fixed it for free. I couldn't afford to go home for Christmas for the first time in ten years; my L.A. friends hosted a dinner for me. My cell phone broke; Verizon discovered that my plan was up and I could get a new phone for just thirty dollars. The list goes on and on, all in the same few weeks.

I kept job-hunting, but to no avail. Finally, I remembered my roommate was up in Mammoth, snowboarding. That was it—ski resorts were probably hiring! I immediately applied and got hired.

Everything L.A. is, Mammoth is not. In L.A., my life is all about working sixty to eighty hours per week, networking, trying to get hired as a writer... which leaves very little time for the key component to being a writer: writing. In Mammoth, I only had to work around twenty hours a week, didn't have any entertainment people to network with, and had all the writing time in the world. In L.A., "the industry" is entertainment. In Mammoth, "the industry" is snowboarding (or "riding," as they call it, which I kept mishearing as "writing"). In L.A., I see the beach from my apartment. In Mammoth, I'd see mounds of snow. In L.A., I drove everywhere. In Mammoth, I didn't (my MINI Cooper didn't like the snow). In L.A., my roommates and I had Wi-Fi. In Mammoth, we didn't. I learned to rely on face-to-face interaction, something we tend to forget about in big cities, where e-mailing or texting someone is easier, even if the person is just in the next cubicle.

Soon, I learned to enjoy the simple life, to take in and appreciate the beauty of the mountains around me. I started to not fret over things I did in L.A.—mainly work and guys; I just focused on the thing I love most: writing. I spent every free moment working on a book, and finished it by the time I left seven weeks later.

All was going well, until there was a snow and economic drought; everyone's work hours were reduced. Just my luck. I went from working twenty-eight hours a week to eight. So much for the idea of going to work at a ski resort. Now how would I pay my rent?

I realized the only thing I could do to save money was give up the apartment I so loved by the beach. All day, I prepared my "Sorry, but I have to move out" speech for my roommates.

I decided it was time for some inspiration, to finally read *The Secret*. I would read a chapter every night. Tonight, I was on the money chapter, which encouraged you to think positively about wealth, even when you don't seem to be making any money. To pretend you have money, even when you don't. To pretend your bills are paychecks written out to you, and so forth.

I drove back to L.A. that night and found a stack of mail—all bills. Except for a greeting card-looking envelope. I went into my room, to rehearse my moving out speech once more, and looked at the card's return address. It was from a writer I knew, David, who was like the father I never knew growing up. Also one who had tried to kill himself a year prior. At that time, he had been obsessed with Starbucks CDs; he said he couldn't believe that his morning cup of coffee always ended up costing him twenty dollars instead of two. And what do you say to someone who tries to commit suicide, anyway? So I made him a card, telling him how happy I was that he was alive, bought him the latest Starbucks CD, and popped it into the mail. A few weeks later, he thanked me, and we have sent e-mails to each other about once a month since.

Now, I opened up David's card immediately, hoping he was all right, for he was not particularly a letter-writing type. I read the card, "Merry Christmas, sweet girl. I hope you had a good holiday. I miss you! Love, David." I was touched. As I reread the card, a check fluttered out of the envelope. I got tears in my eyes: it was the exact amount of my rent. I wouldn't have to give my moving out speech, after all. I didn't know if the note from David was karma, faith, God, *The Secret*, a guardian angel, my biological father in heaven...? Whoever it was, I thank you. I immediately had renewed faith that all would be okay. The odd thing was, as I looked at the postmark, I noticed that David had mailed the check weeks before; it had gone to my previous apartment first. And, now, I received it the same day I needed it most. I hoped the same would happen with a new job.

The next day, I got a phone call from a friend who had seen my status on Facebook, which read: "Natalia will be sleeping on your couch soon if she doesn't find a job." My friend said to call her friend right away about a new TV show. I interviewed, and got the job.

Being unemployed was not fun, but it did re-instill my faith in the goodness of people. It also reminded me to continue to have faith in myself, even when it seems like all is lost (like a ski resort without snow). And the good news is, faith is free.

~Natalia K. Lusinski

104

Miracle on Michigan Avenue

Prayer does not change God, but it changes him who prays.
~Søren Kierkegaard

I am paralyzed, too terrified to move. As he screams horrible obscenities, he rockets around the room. Hopeful, my eyes seek the telephone, but he grabs it and rips the cord from the wall. My poor baby, fastened in her stroller, shrieks in terror—scared by the noise. I have to protect her. In his fury, he kicks the desk chair, hurtling it against the wall. What if our assailant kicks my seven-month-old baby? I can't escape. Poor Mary and her stroller are between him and me. How can I get both of us out of here? Like cornered rats, my thoughts keep climbing on top of each other.

I should scream. But no one would hear me in this high-rise Chicago hotel. The windows are sealed. Since it is mid-afternoon, the housekeeper, businessmen and other guests have left the floor. I scold myself for being so naïve as to answer and unlock the door. I thought my relatives were arriving early. Instead, this drug-crazed mugger shoved his way in. Who can protect us? I feel totally helpless.

Earlier, I'd been visiting my mother, a patient at Northwestern Memorial Hospital, a few blocks from our Michigan Avenue hotel. Pushing my baby in her stroller back to the hotel, I struggled to steer it against Lake Michigan's strong, wintery winds. Focusing on the weaving stroller, I didn't notice someone following us.

But then we arrived in our room, and he appeared from nowhere, smelling of a sweaty, desperate rage. Now, I wonder if we'll die.

I pray, "Dear Lord, you gave me this gorgeous baby when the doctor thought I would miscarry. Please protect her now. Tell me what to do." Almost immediately, I feel less frightened.

What I hear is a strong, reassuring voice saying, "Talk—tell him why you're here." Although the answer seems strange, I begin talking in a high voice.

Ignoring my words, my assailant grabs at me, ripping my blouse, as he yells above my baby's cries. All I can see is his pock-marked face leering at me while his foul breath makes me want to vomit. Still, I'm grateful he is concentrating on me and not my poor child. As long as he doesn't hurt her, I don't care what happens to me. Again I hear the voice, "I'm here to protect you. You do matter. Keep talking."

I talk, but my attacker doesn't seem to hear anything I say, as he keeps bellowing. I want to grab my baby and run. I want to escape to our Oregon home where my strong husband and wonderful teenage daughters wait for us, but we can't leave. He has us trapped.

"Please, please listen. We're here because my mother is in the hospital. She's very sick. She needs an operation, but they don't know if they can operate. Her heart is so bad." I keep repeating the same words. My head is pounding, and I gasp for breath as the words gush out. Words I can't hear because of his wild ranting. I keep praying for help. Even though I'm terrified, I feel a calm stillness separating me from his craziness.

He stops yelling. His thin, dark body ceases gyrating in its drug-induced state. Late afternoon sunlight, filtered by heavy hotel curtains, catches in his single earring. Then, for a brief instant, his yellow, bloodshot eyes stop darting and see mine. The tiny contact gives me hope.

"Please," I beg. "Don't hurt my baby. She is so scared." I keep pleading with him, trying to calm his rage.

Finally, whirling away from me, he suddenly, angrily demands money. I am struck by the coherence of his words, his first intelligible sounds.

"Sure, anything." I grab my billfold on the dresser and give him all I have — forty dollars.

Before he leaves, he says, "If you open the door, I'll kill you." Then, he slams the door. Quickly, I lock it and open the door to my father's adjacent room. Even though my father is still at the hospital, I can use his phone, calling the front desk and asking them to notify the police. While I wait, hugging and soothing my baby, I thank God for His strength and guidance. Without His wise advice, something awful could have happened.

The following day, I identify my attacker by his unusual earring at a Chicago police station line-up. I'm told he has been stalking and raping out-of-town visitors (believing they would soon leave the city and be unavailable to identify him). The police had been staking out my hotel, which was why they caught him so quickly. When the concerned detective asked how I escaped being raped, I told him I just prayed and was told to talk to my attacker. Further, I explain I was afraid to fight for fear my baby would be hurt. He tells me I did the right thing by making a connection with the perpetrator — helping him see us as human beings and not as objects.

Since I don't want my assailant to hurt other women, I testify at a judge's preliminary hearing. When I call my worried husband in Oregon, his reassuring support comforts me. Fortunately, I don't have to return for my attacker's trial. Other witnesses provide convincing evidence, and he is convicted.

When I return home to Oregon and my Christian Family Class, I tell Sister about our miracle. "God calmed my fears, instilled courage and helped me concentrate on what to do. The same day, police just happened to be staking out our hotel and were able to capture my would-be rapist." Sister nods wisely, as she hugs my precious baby, whose beautiful, almond eyes smile at us. Then, Sister whispers, almost like a benediction, "God will always protect us, if we just ask Him."

~Carol Strazer

105

In the Hands of the Chief of Surgery

Adversity introduces a man to himself.
~Author Unknown

W hy did I feel so lousy? I never considered myself the epitome of strength and health, but, in 2002, at age thirty-five, the five-mile bike ride I took the night before shouldn't have whipped me nearly as much as it did. I felt like an elephant was sitting on my chest. Like many males faced with health issues, I denied I had a problem. I went to my job as a video producer and whimpered throughout my day.

When I returned home, and lay down, my chest pain felt even worse. Something was seriously wrong. I drove to one of those quick care centers, and after a series of tests, the doctors and nurses there felt I needed a one-way, do-not-pass-go, direct trip to the emergency room.

One week and a myriad of tests later, the lead cardiologist at the hospital determined I had a rare artery disease called Takayasus Arteritis. Named after a Japanese doctor who first described the condition in 1908, the disease is an inflammation, narrowing and scarring of the aorta and the other great vessels attached to the aorta. Left untreated, it could be fatal, and even with treatment, most victims of the disease succumb to some sort of disability, facing limitations to normal, everyday activities.

The doctors said I was medically "interesting." I didn't want to be "interesting." I wanted to be boring, and have few or no health issues. But for the next two years, I had four heart catheter interventions, three involving angioplasty and stenting to hold my at-risk coronary arteries open, so that I didn't have a heart attack.

In April 2004, while I was at work, I found what looked like a speck in my eye, a little dot that I couldn't wash or wipe away. Throughout the day, the dot became larger, and by the end of the day, I realized I had a serious vision problem. Ophthalmologists told me I had an ischemic optic neuropathy. I called it an eye stroke. The bottom line is that my disease had restricted the blood flow to my head, and the vessel serving my left optic nerve shut down, causing irreparable damage. I was legally blind in my left eye. Something radical had to be done.

Not long after that, I was scheduled for vessel replacement surgery at the University of Michigan hospital, with Dr. Deeb, one of Michigan's finest cardiac surgeons. He had performed surgery on some of Michigan's most respected citizens. The goal was to remove my aorta, both my subclavian arteries, and one of my carotid (neck) arteries and replace them with artificial arteries. The procedure would be long and very dangerous. There was a serious risk that I would stroke or die on the table. If I didn't have the surgery, my prognosis was even grimmer.

This set of circumstances would emotionally cripple most people. Few could stand tall above the dire reality of my situation. So, being made of flesh and blood, I began my own descent into despair. Thankfully, three surprises kept me from sinking into utter darkness.

First, I came across an unusual postcard that I eventually carried with me everywhere I went. The postcard was of a painting by Nathan Greene entitled "Chief of the Medical Staff." The painting shows Christ standing in a high-tech operating room, guiding the hand of the surgeon cutting into the body of a patient. I studied and meditated on that painting for weeks leading up to my own surgery. And when I became afraid of what might happen to me, I pulled it out and looked at it again. I realized that whether I lived or died on that operating table, I was in good hands: the hands of the Chief of the Medical Staff.

Secondly, I strengthened my friendship with a man who lived through an even grimmer medical diagnosis. Sean's job, weight, and family relationships had already taken an extreme nosedive when he learned that he had a grapefruit-sized tumor growing in his brain. But Sean had undergone extensive surgery and months of rehab, and emerged from the other side a more grateful human and a better husband, father, and worker. He was a living medical success story, and he, during my darkest hours, gave me the time, support, guidance and hope that I so desperately needed.

About a week before my surgery, I went out to eat with a group of my closest friends. We ate at one of our city's oldest privately-owned restaurants—the kind with stuffed animal heads all over, tin ceilings, and an enormous bar carved from a single tree. Laughter and good times lasted late into the evening, and then we went back to the home of one of the diners to pray.

One by one, my friends prayed a blessing over me, the doctor, the nurses, the hospital, and my family. I told my friends afterwards that I felt like Moses who had his hands raised in battle. As long as his hands were raised, the Israelites were winning the battle. When Moses tired, his friends came to him and held up his arms, so that he and the Israelites would continue in victory. The prayers of my friends were like hands holding me up. I couldn't descend. I could only go up. My friends wouldn't let me fall. The battle belonged to God.

The night before surgery, I slept peacefully. Strangely, I didn't care what happened to me on the operating table. If the surgery was a success, than I would be grateful. If it was not, then I was going to a better place. Eight hours later, the surgery was a success. Old arteries were taken out. Replacement arteries were put in place. I hadn't stroked. And in time, I'd have a complete recovery. My left eye is still blind, and I still cannot be as active as I'd like to be. However, my life is very close to normal. Plus, I have an enthusiasm for life that's greater than ever. I savor all of life's moments, knowing that life is fragile and precious. Chronic disease is something I wish all people could avoid, but I know that it is not necessarily a complete liability. Every challenge carries with it a lesson of hope and triumph.

~Matthew P. Kinne

A Job for Roy

We must accept finite disappointment, but never lose infinite hope.
~Dr. Martin Luther King, Jr.

Times right now are hard for many people. Layoffs, foreclosures, poor health, and family breakups plague people of all ages and cause many to feel utter despair, while others exude genuine joy and peace in spite of these adversities. My friend Roy is such a person. Even though the vicissitudes of life have kicked him a lot lately he carries a smile on his face and speaks a peaceful word to everyone.

We met last summer at the local employment office. While searching online for work I heard a melodious baritone voice make the following inquiry from a nearby computer, "Do you have a pencil I may use?"

Looking up from my computer monitor, I surveyed the room for the source of this wondrously resonant voice. Directly across from where I was seated was Roy, a slender, modestly-dressed gentleman who, like me, was out of work. This gentleman appeared to be someone well-acquainted with hard physical labor, yet he spoke as a genteel scholar with flawless grammar.

Curious, I inquired as to the type of work he was seeking. He informed me that he was searching for ministerial jobs across the southeastern U.S. Roy is a minister now, but in his former life he was a university professor and an assistant to the Governor of the State of Florida. Previously married with a fine house and furnishings, Roy now lives a simple life unfettered by most of the stuff that the rest of us have, want to have, or used to have. The uninformed observer would say that Roy was down on his luck, but Roy would never say that.

Throughout our entire conversation, a radiant smile graced his face. Roy had recently returned to his hometown after years of living elsewhere. His car had broken down somewhere across town, and he had it towed to his home. He told me that as he walked to the auto parts store to get the parts he needed to make the repairs, someone stole the car from his yard.

After his car disappeared, he learned that it had been taken to the local recycling place. In dismay, Roy investigated the matter and discovered that his car had become part of a large wad of mangled metal along with several other demolished vehicles. The recycling center had purchased his vehicle as scrap. The thief had the money. Roy had no car.

When the offender was identified, Roy asked the police whether they would pursue the matter. Both the police and the state prosecutor told Roy he had no case. Now wheel-less but not hopeless, this major setback did not stop Roy. He said, "Well, that's just how life is."

A few days later, Roy was given a bicycle. He would bike to job interviews and to perform the few temporary jobs he would get here and there. One day, he pedaled to the employment office. As was his practice, Roy locked his bike with a chain and padlock, while searching online for work. When he was ready to leave, he mounted his bike to ride off, but remembered that he had left his hat at the computer. In the few moments that it took Roy to retrieve his hat, his bike was stolen.

Once again Roy was the victim of a transportation thief. Did Roy get angry? No, he decided that the thief must have needed the wheels more than he. Roy commented, "I still have two good legs and feet to match. I can walk."

A few weeks went by before I returned to the employment office. When I arrived, a mutual acquaintance asked me if I had heard the latest about Roy. She told me that Roy was given a new motor scooter.

The day after he received the motor scooter, he decided to ride it to a job interview. Unfortunately, the scooter was electric and had lost its charge.

Amazingly, as Roy began pushing the motor scooter down the road, a "Good Samaritan" drove by and offered him a ride. Placing the scooter on the back of the Samaritan's pickup the two men proceeded on their journey. At the very first red light the truck had to slam on its brakes, which caused the truck's tailgate to fly open. Roy's motor scooter landed hard on the pavement and was irreparably damaged. Poor Roy, once again he had to rely on his own two feet to get wherever he wanted to go.

After hearing of Roy's misfortune, I asked the preacher why he was the victim of these events. He then reminded me of Job's friends who wanted to know why all those terrible things plagued only Job. My response to him was, "Your name's Roy, not Job!" His response: "God in all ages has men who are righteous that are persecuted. Their life stories are a testimony to the goodness that is God despite the misfortune of their circumstances. We are reminded that bad things can and do happen to good people. We all should be prepared for what may happen to anyone of us."

Upon hearing that, I told Roy that I just had to share his story.

~Marya R. Latson

The Ultimate Landlord

Faith sees the invisible, believes the incredible and receives the impossible.
~Author Unknown

Another beautiful day in paradise, I thought, as I sipped my morning cup of coffee. It felt so good to be back. I had missed living in the warmth of the Florida sun and was anxious to sink my toes into the sugar white sands of the beach and never leave again. As I took the last sip of my coffee, the doorbell rang. My husband, David, stood at the front door cradling a large box in his arms. Where was his company car?

"Just let me in, Karen. It's okay." What was he talking about? What's okay? As he put the box on the floor, overflowing with everything from his office, I heard him say, "I've been fired... and they let go four others on my staff as well."

I was stunned! We had just moved from Michigan to Sarasota, Florida, three months before, when David had been recruited to be Vice President of Franchising. Now he and most of his staff had been terminated.

Four months went by without a promise of a new job. No matter how many resumés David mailed out, no one seemed to need a vice president. The reserve in our savings account was quickly dwindling. "Don't worry, we'll manage," David kept saying, trying to reassure me. When the pastor of our church came to extend a helping hand, David continued to say, "We'll manage — there are things we can sell to meet our obligations."

Sensing the pride in David's voice, the pastor gently responded, "When you get to Aunt Tillie's antiques, stop. God does not intend for you to sell everything you have. Our Benevolence Fund is there to help you." I knew it was hard for David to accept help from anyone. He had always been the one to give it. Now he had to learn what it meant to receive it.

When our son, Michael, emptied his bank account to cover a month's rent, we realized we could no longer postpone telling our landlords. We had leased their home for one year until they retired the following summer. Where would we go—what would we do? David dialed their number.

"Don't even think about moving out. We know David will get another job and when he does, you can pay us." Were we hearing right? This couple hardly knew us, meeting us for the first time when we signed the lease. As they continued to reassure us, we began to feel God's reassurance. He had obviously hand-picked this place of refuge for us months before.

Long walks on the beach continued to help us keep God's perspective. The waves softly lapping at our feet seemed to whisper "don't worry, don't worry." The display of His brilliant sunsets sinking into the tranquil waters of the Gulf constantly reminded us of His glory and power. Just as He controlled the ebb and flow of the tides, we knew everything in our lives was under His control.

More months went by—still no promise of a job for David. My job at the real estate office helped to put food on the table and gas in the car, but could not begin to meet our major obligations.

My heart ached for David. I knew he so badly wanted to be the good provider he had always been, and I became so acutely aware of how delicate the male ego can be. I prayed, "Dear God, help me to be sensitive to David's feelings and his emotional needs." I knew David was drawing his strength from God—I wanted to be a positive influence for him as well. Our devotion to each other was deeper than ever before.

One morning we woke to the sounds of a storm hurling the waves against the nearby beach. When it was over, we decided to take a walk to view the damage. As we strolled the beach hand in hand, we noticed another couple coming toward us. Squeezing my hand, David said, "They look like our landlords from Chicago!" As they caught up to us, we exclaimed, "What a surprise to see you! Are you on vacation?"

Somewhat embarrassed, they said, "No, we're renting a condo for a couple of months on the beach. Then, for the summer we are going to house sit for friends." When we began to protest, they continued to say, "We changed our moving plans and didn't want you to think you had to move before the lease is up in August. That's why we didn't tell you we were here." As we said our goodbyes and walked away, once again we were overwhelmed by their generosity. How could such kindness be extended to us from people we hardly knew?

David had now been out of work for ten months and our lease would soon be terminating. We were facing the reality of once again not having a place to live.

One morning as I prayed, it occurred to me that I could check on rentals through the real estate office. Out of curiosity, I began to look at two-bedroom condos, knowing we could manage with a smaller living space. A listing for a condo facing the Gulf of Mexico caught my eye. Could we really have a view of the Gulf? I was so drawn to the beauty and tranquility of those sparkling turquoise waters. They seemed to be a visual manifestation of God's promise of peace. A verse from the book of Psalms—"Take your delight in the Lord and He will give you the desires of your heart"—gave me courage. It wouldn't hurt to try.

Not knowing how we could put this together, we went to see the condo. Shades of royal blue, lime green and shocking pink carpeting, outdated wallpaper, and worn printed drapes greeted us as we walked through the door. My perfectionist nature and eye for decorating made me flinch as I took in my surroundings. Yet, I realized the floor plan would accommodate our furniture and the view—the view of the Gulf was beautiful! Could we live here like it was? It really needed to be redecorated. What if! What if the landlord would let us replace the carpeting, drapes, and wallpaper in lieu of six months rent and no deposit?

The realtor had never heard of such a thing. How could she present that kind of offer to the out-of-town landlord?

Time was running out—just a few short weeks before we needed to move. Then God's answer came. First, David was offered a job with a franchise company based in Atlanta. Because they needed him to represent them in the field, we could stay in Florida. Then, the frustrated realtor gave David the opportunity to negotiate with the landlord. We got a three-year lease with no increase, no deposit, and six months free rent in exchange for decorating the condo just the way we wanted it.

As we settled in to enjoy the magnificent view of the Gulf, our hearts overflowed with thanksgiving and gratitude. Not only did God meet our needs, He gave us our heart's desire. He was our Provider—the Ultimate Landlord!

~Karen R. Kilby

Demon

Faith assuages, guides, restores.
~Arthur Rimbaud

lived with Glen for ten years before we amicably separated. During those ten years, he raised my daughter, Meara, as his own child. We also had a son together.

During our time together, he had a project car, a 1972 Dodge Demon. He poured blood, sweat, and tears into that car, and I helped as much as I possibly could. After it was completed, it was beautiful; and I loved it so much, he gave it to me. A year after driving this gorgeous car, I had to swap it for a more fuel efficient vehicle and it was sold to someone from out of town. I missed my Demon, but I just could not afford it. I tried to keep track of it for awhile, but it changed hands too many times. Now all I have are pictures and memories of it.

After our split, Glen and I remained close. I had always counted on him to be a good judge of character during our years together. I rarely have the good sense to choose friends who will be "true" friends—mostly, I attract hangers-on looking to take advantage of my good nature and generosity. Sadly, he passed away after a lengthy battle with cancer shortly after I had begun a new relationship with Bryce.

My relationship with Bryce is nearing the five-year mark now. We are incredibly happy together. That happiness is very hard won, though. We started our relationship together partying—he was fun, charming, and extremely good-looking. I fell in love with him soon after we started dating. The party turned into a nasty habit that didn't want to leave.

A year into it, we became homeless. We moved to my mother's property. It was summer, so we camped out in her 1,500-square-foot greenhouse, with all our belongings crammed onto shelves cleared of their plants for us. My two children stayed with other family and friends for the first two months of life without a home.

It was an extremely depressing time for my little family. Bryce and I constantly fought about every little thing—we were very abusive to each other. I can only imagine the pain I caused my kids. I cry now when I think about it. Drinking and drugs blinded me to what we were doing to ourselves, each other, and everyone around us.

Eventually, we found a small apartment, but continued with our abusive ways. Bryce once in a while would mention quitting and I would give it a weak attempt. No matter what path I chose, he would follow—always we were together.

After four years of chaos, neglect, and abuse, we managed to rise above the depressing life we had created for ourselves. After fighting so horribly that it became physical, we separated. A week later, Bryce came back a new man, determined to quit the lifestyle he had become a part of and take the woman he loved with him. He literally saved me.

Bryce is now working full time, I am a full time stay-at-home mom, and we are both clean, healthy, happy, and looking forward to our future.

When asked why I stayed in this horrible relationship when it looked as though one of us would surely kill the other, my answer is this: Hope.

About two years into our relationship, I had heartbreaking doubts about Bryce's love for me. I did not trust him. I did not believe he was true to me. I went to Glen's grave one day and poured out my heart to him. I told him everything that had been going on between me and Bryce and with the kids, and between sobs I said to him, "Glen, if ever I needed your good judgment of people, now is the time.

I need you to help me and tell me if Bryce is the person he says he is. Is he true to me? Does he truly love me? Can we ever get through all of this? I need you to send me a sign to let me know that he is the one. It has to be a big sign, something so big that I won't miss it, because I'm not so smart these days. Please, send me a sign I won't miss so that I know that Bryce is the one."

The next day, the old 1972 Dodge Demon that Glen built for me was parked in front of my mom's house.

~Betty Harrigan

Living Well with God and CF

In time of sickness the soul collects itself anew.
~Latin Proverb

The doctors told my parents devastating news when I was born. My mom and dad learned that I had cystic fibrosis. The doctors said that I wouldn't live past the age of thirteen. CF is an inherited lung disease. Having CF means that every day I have to do three to four hours of breathing treatments and take many medications. When I was twenty, I was diagnosed with CF-related diabetes, a common complication for adults with the disease. Having diabetes means I have to worry about insulin, exercising, and watching what I eat. If I don't take care of myself, I will have to deal with serious consequences from both diseases.

Now I am thirty-one, which is eighteen years of living beyond the doctor's expectations. At the age of twenty-three, I graduated from the University of North Texas. I am a preschool teacher of three-and four-year-old children. I love to exercise and live a very active life. I look healthy and strong. Beneath the surface, I am struggling with two diseases that can make my life very hard. I refuse to let my diseases interfere with my life.

CF sometimes is hard for me because I have coughing attacks that are unstoppable for a few minutes. Having these uncontrollable coughing fits tend to embarrass me in public because people think

I am sicker than I am and they think I have something contagious. Also, people stare at me until my coughing stops. I get frustrated when I have coughing attacks while I am talking or teaching because there is no way to stop them. I have to go to the hospital for a week at least once a year due to CF. I miss out on family birthdays, holidays, and work. Another frustration is that CF causes me to get sick and tire easily. If I stay up late one night or have a busy week, I need at least three days of going to bed early and rest on my days when I am off from teaching.

Having two diseases doesn't discourage me, because I choose to have hope in God. I look for the good in everything. I choose to be around positive people. I try not to dwell on the negative aspects of my life, and I turn to God to help me have peace of mind. James 1:2-4 talks about having joy in trials because trials develop a mature and complete faith.

Whenever I get discouraged with the medical responsibilities of CF and diabetes, I look to God's Word to give me hope. Besides having hope from God, I have received much encouragement and support from my family and friends. Having two diseases hasn't stopped me from living a fulfilled and happy life. In high school, I was a cheerleader on an award-winning team. I even received a national award from Christian Cheerleaders of America. I gave my testimony and received a standing ovation from more than 450 cheerleaders when I shared how God has helped me through tough times while dealing with CF.

I lived alone in an apartment during my college years due to many advances in CF care. I never thought I would be able to live by myself or travel freely, but I have enjoyed the excitement of traveling to New York, Hollywood, Disney World, and the Mall of America. I look forward to what God has in store for my future.

~Rebekah Phillips

The Source

Faith is building on what you know is here,
so you can reach what you know is there.
~Cullen Hightower

I was having a hard time getting the cold lump of fear out of my throat.

I deserved this hour of relaxation. I lay on the bed trying to read an inspirational magazine. But I couldn't stop worrying about the rent and bills due in only three days.

My husband, Wayne, and I were both good at sales. But lately it seemed everything we tried ranged from barely getting by to unsuccessful. The recession wasn't helping. Although we had worked hard and prayed hard, it had been a discouraging week. Sales already made were slow in paying, some had fallen through, and it seemed everyone else had conspired to "wait until after the first of the month to decide." Our little cash was disappearing with terrifying speed no matter how careful we were.

"Lord, help. I'm trying to trust you, but I know You don't usually rain down money from heaven. I know where money comes from. And if our hard work doesn't pay off, what are we going to do?" The lump in my throat tried to push its way out into full-blown panic.

Wayne headed for the garage to finish some repairs on our car, another unplanned expense. "I put a scoop of food in the dogs' dishes and closed the door," he informed me. "You can open the door when it's time for them to eat." He knew I was strict about their mealtime.

What Wayne hadn't counted on was that Tavis, our sheltie boy, turned frantic when he knew there was food he couldn't reach. Always food motivated, he pushed at the door with his nose, then his paw, but it was latched tightly. He stared at the door as though he could will it to open. "He's watching the supply instead of the source," I realized with a sudden flash of inspiration. "Why doesn't he come 'ask' me? I could easily open the door for him. I could feed him from the bucket of dog food in the garage, from the kitchen, or from McDonald's or some other place he doesn't even know about! I'm a never-ending source for him, and he's concentrating on one scoop of dog food he can't get to."

"Am I doing that, Lord? Am I looking at all the ways to make money, not at the Owner and Source of all things? I say I trust You, but then I count my resources as I see them and forget you have ways and means I can't even imagine."

I watched another few minutes quietly as Tavis continued to stare at the door, whined softly, and tried again to push it open with his paw. When would he realize he couldn't do it by himself? Would he come to me? How long would it take?

Finally I whispered softly, "Tav, tell me what you want." His ear twitched back in acknowledgment of my voice but he had important business to attend to. He lay down patiently but his eyes never left the door. "Tavis, come tell me." Another twitch but no attention.

God was whispering to my heart too. "Tavis is looking at the problem, not the solution." It all seemed so clear. I was doing the same thing. How long had God been whispering my name? "Look at Me, not the problem...."

Louder, I asked, "Tavis, what do you want?" He looked at me, then the door, ran halfway across the room toward me, but then returned to stare at his unattainable goal.

"That's my problem, too, God," I whispered. "I want to look to You. But I'm so consumed with my problems, I can't tear loose long enough to trust You."

"Tavis, come tell me." My firm tone finally broke through his concern. With a sudden look of doggy inspiration, he galloped to my side, wagging, whining, trying his best to "talk." He had remembered his source. And with his inspiration, I found my own.

Picking up my wiggly friend, I whispered to him, "I know how to open that door. Why didn't you come to me before?" As he showered my face with kisses, I added, "And you know how to open doors for us, Father. I don't know exactly how we'll pay all the bills next week or next month. But I know You're our Source, and You know the way."

The next morning, Wayne answered the phone. "The software we advertised last week? Yes, we have some left. Ten? Yes, we have them in stock. Yes, this afternoon would be fine. We'll see you then." We did a little victory dance around the kitchen, laughing and praising God. Why should we have been surprised? The money was exactly what we needed to cover the rent and bills.

Many times since then God has supplied our needs in surprising ways. We never know just what He will do, but we know now without a doubt where our Source is!

~Evie Mack

A Dandelion
Christmas Wish

Even the wishes of an ant reach heaven.
~Japanese Proverb

"Hurry mommy, make a wish!" my child said to me.
He held the dandelion puff so soft and tenderly.
"Maybe later," I replied, holding back a sob.
"Wishing won't pay past due bills or get me back my job."

"But mommy," piped his tiny voice.
　　"There's something you should know."
He plucked a white frond carefully, and then he let it go.
"I'm too busy," I replied, still angry at my fate.
"Wishing won't buy winter coats or put food on your plate."

"But, it's important," he declared and gave my hand a squeeze.
He looked up at the soft, white frond still floating in the breeze.
"Would you be still?" I pleaded. My mind began to roam.
"Wishing won't get our house back or bring your daddy home."

"Oh yes it will," he said at last. "You have to wait and see!"
He plucked another frond or two, and then he set them free.
His face grew very solemn and he gave a little nod.
"Half these seeds go off to Santa. Half go up to God."

"I wanna make a great big wish. God knows that I believe.
And if I'm a real good boy, he'll come on Christmas Eve.
God might slide down the chimney with answers that he's found.
He'll put my wish beneath the tree while reindeer dance around."

I stood in sad reflection, not sure of what to say.
I didn't want his heart to break once more on Christmas day.
He whispered something softly, then he blew upon the puff.
"*Whatever* God leaves by our tree... it's sure to be enough."

My lips began to tremble, and I dropped down to my knees.
I wrapped my arms around him and I gave him one long squeeze.
We cupped our hands together and we raised the puff up high.
Then we sent our hopeful wishes like seeds into the sky.

~Madeleine Kuderick

Tough Times, Tough People

Meet Our Contributors
Meet Our Authors
Acknowledgments
About Chicken Soup
Share with Us

Meet Our Contributors

Christopher Allen received his MA at Middle Tennessee State University where he was Graduate Student of the Year in 1994, and received awards for his essay "The Myth of Masculine Conscience" and for outstanding achievement in the study of literature. A corporate trainer in Germany, Allen writes fiction, literary humor and material for ESL training.

Diana M. Amadeo, award-winning author of books, short stories and essays, lives in New Hampshire with husband, Len, and children Angelique, Antony and Desiree and grandchildren Brody and Tavin nearby. Her father, Jerome Schmitt, is a published author and her mother, Josephine Schmitt is the most prolific writer of them all... mostly in letters to her family.

Ronda Armstrong lives with her husband and two cats in Iowa. Retired from school social work, she writes creative nonfiction, poetry, and fiction. Three nonfiction pieces were published recently in the *Des Moines Register*. She also enjoys ballroom dancing and connecting with family and friends. E-mail her at ronda.armstrong@gmail.com.

Brenda Barajas will graduate high school in 2011. She does well in all academic subjects and is proud of her 4.0 GPA. Brenda loves to play volleyball and spend time with family and friends. She hopes to get into a great college when she graduates.

Kerrie R. Barney lives with her border collie MacAiogdh and several dozen healthy houseplants in Powell Butte, Oregon. She is happy to say that the latest descendant of Brian, the Golden Pothos, is alive and well.

Glenda Barrett, a native of North Georgia, is an artist, poet and writer. Her chapbook, *When the Sap Rises*, is for sale on Amazon. com, and her artwork is on display at Yessy.com. Glenda's writing has appeared in *Woman's World*, *Nostalgia*, *Farm & Ranch Living*, *Rural Heritage*, *Living with Loss* and others.

M. Garrett Bauman and his wife live one mile from the nearest road in rural New York. He recently retired as a Professor of English at Monroe Community College in Rochester, NY. He is the author of *Ideas and Details* and essays in *Sierra*, *Yankee* and *The New York Times*.

Elizabeth Bogart writes about her domestic violence experience on behalf of battered women everywhere. She's written professionally in a corporate environment, and her poetry and nonfiction have received awards from The Greater Dallas Writers and Florida Writers Associations. A Texan at heart, she resides in Florida with her husband, Gary. E-mail: texasgirlb@gmail.com.

Juliet C. Bond is a Licensed Clinical Social worker and children's book author. She is the author of *Sam's Sister*, a picture book about open adoption and has been published in other collaborative works. Juliet is forever inspired by the transformative power of a great story. Please visit her at julietcbond.tripod.com.

Marcia E. Brown lives in Austin, TX. Marcia is a widow and freelance writer and has been sharing family stories in magazines, newspapers and anthologies including the *Chicken Soup for the Soul* series for fifteen years. She is a member of the National League of American Pen Women and Writers League of Texas. E-mail: Wordeze@yahoo.com.

Irene Budzynski, RN, is a surgical nurse at a city hospital in New England. Her work has been published in several *Chicken Soup for the Soul* books, Heartwarmers4u.com, *HeartTouchers*, and has been heard on Nightsounds Radio.

John P. Buentello is a writer who has published short stories, essays, and poems. Together with his brother Lawrence Buentello, he is the author of the novel *Reproduction Rights* and the short story collection *Binary Tales*. He can be contacted via e-mail at jakkhakk@yahoo.com.

Renie Burghardt, who was born in Hungary, is a freelance writer with numerous credits. She has been published in several *Chicken Soup for the Soul* books, and other anthologies and magazines. She lives in the country and loves animals, nature, and spending time with her family and friends. E-mail her at renieburghardt@semo.net.

Kathe Campbell lives on a Montana mountain with her mammoth donkeys, a Keeshond, and a few kitties. She is a prolific writer on Alzheimer's, and her stories are found on many e-zines. Kathe is a contributing author to the *Chicken Soup for the Soul* series, numerous anthologies, *Rx for Writers*, and medical journals. E-mail: kathe@wildblue.net.

Leah M. Cano has written for *Transitions Abroad*, *MAMM Magazine* and *Chicken Soup for the Breast Cancer Survivor's Soul*. She received her BA in Spanish at UC Irvine and Masters of Education at UC Santa Cruz. She teaches Spanish and French in Laguna Beach, CA. You can e-mail her at leahmc@hotmail.com.

Linda S. Clare is an award-winning writer and the author of several nonfiction books. Her debut novel, *The Fence My Father Built*, (Abingdon Press) releases in August 2009. Linda teaches writing at the college level in Eugene, Oregon, where she lives with her family and five wayward cats. Visit her blog at http://godsonggrace.blogspot.com.

Harriet Cooper is a freelance writer and instructor. She specializes in writing creative nonfiction and articles. Her work has appeared in several *Chicken Soup for the Soul* anthologies, as well as in newspapers, magazines, newsletters and websites. She often writes about health, nutrition, family, cats and the environment.

Billy Cuchens teaches music, pours coffee, and writes. He is living below his means in an apartment in the Dallas area along with his wife and two children. You can read more of his essays about being a husband and father in a multiracial family on his blog: goggycoffee. blogspot.com.

Leslie Cunningham has over seventeen years of professional experience in leading personal development workshops, developing educational programs and coaching individuals and businesses to achieve their extraordinary dreams. She is a sought after speaker, certified personal life coach and business consultant. Please e-mail her at leslie@ liveandloverichly.com.

Kay Day is a full time wife and mother. Her former career was in nursing, but now her sights are set on literary goals. She enjoys reading, blogging, attending Words for the Journey Writer's Guild, and gazing at her view of the Colorado Rocky Mountains. Kay is currently writing her first novel. E-mail: keep1hope@comcast.net.

Denise A. Dewald has been writing for the Christian market for over twenty years with her work appearing in many places, including radio. She enjoys her family, church, the outdoors, reading and her pets. She can be reached via e-mail at denise_a_dewald@ yahoo.com.

Sharon Donovan has been writing since the loss of her vision. Art was her passion. A new dream has resurrected. Today, instead of painting her pictures on canvas, she paints her pictures with words. Visit Sharon at: www.sharonadonovan.com.

Christina Dymock graduated from the University of Utah with a Bachelor's Degree in Public Relations. She is an avid reader and enjoys all genres. She has four children, a dog, two cats and seven chickens. It's a crazy life—but a good one.

Kristen Eberhard traveled the world as a model before returning to New York to earn her BA from Fordham University. She currently lives in the Catskill Mountains where she manages small businesses when she is not coaching her son's soccer team. Kristen's creative talents and spirit inspire her to help others turn obstacles into opportunities.

Although blind, **Janet Perez Eckles** thrives as a Spanish interpreter, international speaker, writer and author of *Trials of Today, Treasures for Tomorrow—Overcoming Adversities in Life*. From her home in Florida, she enjoys working on church ministries and taking Caribbean cruises with husband Gene. She imparts inspirations at www.janetperezeckles.com.

Jeannie Eggers is happily staying warm through the dark Alaskan winter with hubby Shawn. They'll welcome spring with salmon fishing and camping. Her forthcoming book, *The Prodigal Wife*, is taking form. A contrite wife seeks reconciliation with her family, but is met with a storm. Please e-mail her at hjs01234@aol.com.

Jill Eisnaugle has published the poetry books *Coastal Whispers*, *Under Amber Skies* and *Beside Still Waters*. Her work has been featured in magazines, newspapers and other collaborations, including more than one dozen radio airings. She lives in Texas City, TX with her family and pets. Please visit Jill's website, www.authorsden.com/jillaeisnaugle.

Annie Mannix Eitman resides in Southern California with her two sons. She has written for several regional publications. She enjoys music, horses and books that make you smile. Annie is currently writing a humorous book about her childhood. She can be reached via e-mail at eitman@mindspring.com.

Terri Elders, LCSW, lives near Colville, WA, with her husband, Ken Wilson, two dogs and three cats. A public member of the Washington Medical Quality Assurance Commission, she received the 2006 UCLA Alumni Association Award for Community Service for her work with Peace Corps. Contact her via e-mail at telders@hotmail.com.

Betsy Finn is a Certified Professional Photographer and Artist; she was named Michigan's Top 7 Photographer of 2008 & 2009. Her business, Betsy's Photography, is located in Southeast Michigan. Betsy enjoys all things artistic, reading, scuba diving, and spending time with family. Betsy can be contacted via her website http://betsyfinn.com.

Kathrin Fleming is the Corporate Relations Manager for a Fortune 100 company. She lives in New Mexico with her husband and five children and is very active on non-profit boards, assisting domestic abuse shelters, cancer organizations and health and human services. She can be contacted via e-mail at kathrinfleming@yahoo.com.

Sally Friedman, a frequent contributor to the *Chicken Soup for the Soul* series, lives—and sometimes vacations—in Moorestown, NJ. Her writing about family life frequently appears in national publications, including *The New York Times*. She is the mother of three daughters, and a grandmother of seven perfect grandkids! pinegander@aol.com.

Sherry Gaba, LCSW & Life Coach has helped hundreds with life-long addictions. She aired on VH1's *Celebrity Rehab 2 with Dr. Drew* using her trademark sensitivity to help cast members.

Amber Garza lives in Folsom, CA with her husband Andrew and her children Eli and Kayleen. She writes Christian fiction and hopes one day to fulfill her dreams of publication. She works as the Administrative Assistant to Outreach at Lakeside Church.

Monica Giglio is a published columnist, fine artist, interior designer, and contributor to *Chicken Soup for the Soul: Divorce and Recovery*.

Her local newspaper column, Monica's Corner, is humorous, reflective and inspirational with a positive take-away message for the reader. View her artwork at www.monicagiglio.com, or e-mail her at monicagiglio@optonline.net.

Tracy Gulliver writes for magazines and anthologies, including *Epilepsy USA* and *Chicken Soup for the Soul*. "A Minor Inconvenience" is from her memoir, *Unplanned: a mother's journey through her daughter's pregnancy*. Tracy has received grants from the McKnight Foundation and the Lilly Endowment. E-mail tgulliver@citlink.net, or visit tracygulliver.blogspot.com.

Linda Handiak teaches History in Montreal. She has also worked abroad as a language teacher and a volunteer for conservation projects. More information about these volunteer experiences can be found in her book, *101 Green Travel Tips*, and in articles she has written for *Transitions Abroad* magazine and for Matadortravel.com.

Betty Harrigan, born and raised in Port Alberni, BC, is a stay-at-home mother of two. She has always had a love of the written word, finding comfort and a place to hide in the magic that all stories, be they fact or fiction, can provide.

Laura Harris is an entrepreneur, author and professional speaker. Her passion is teaching business owners how to build businesses where employees think and act like owners. E-mail her at laura@lauraharris.com.

April Heide-Kracik has a BS degree in Art Education from Bemidji State University and an MA in English from Governor's State University. She is currently working on a Young Adult fantasy novel set in the Chippewa National Forest of Minnesota. Please e-mail her at tkcik@aol.com.

Ann Holbrook lives in Northwest Arkansas. She has been published in *The Storyteller*, *The Ozarks Mountaineer*, *Writing on Walls Anthology II*, *Echoes of the Ozarks Volumes III and IV*, and *Voices Anthology Volumes I and II*. She is currently working on an inspirational book for cancer patients and their families.

Patricia Hurtado attended BYU and received her bachelor's degree in Sociology in 1979. She recently transitioned into the education field as a teacher's aide. Patricia enjoys reading inspirational books, working with special needs children, writing short stories and spending time with her family.

Robbie Iobst, blessed wife of John and proud mom of Noah, is a freelance writer and speaker. She lives in Centennial, Colorado and is a member of Words for the Journey Christian Writer's Guild. E-mail Robbie at robbieiobst@hotmail.com or her blog www.robbieiobst. blogspot.com.

Bonnie Jarvis-Lowe is a retired RN. Her career spanned thirty years in Maritime Canada. She is the mother of two grown children and the grandmother of one little girl, all of whom live in the Canadian West while she and her husband now live in their home province of Newfoundland and Labrador, Canada.

Rebecca Jay writes from the heartland of Kansas where the buffalo no longer freely roam. She is the mother of one incredible son and the owner of one multi-colored cat. R.J. enjoys singing, gardening and raspberry chocolate anything.

Christy Johnson is a freelance writer and speaker who publishes *Tissues for Your Issues*, an inspiring column offering Biblical insight for life, love and the pursuit of decorating. She is working on two non-fiction books, *Finding Purpose Past the Pain* and *Breaking Up with Relationship Addiction*. Visit Christy at www.christyjohnson.org.

Jennifer Lee Johnson is a freelance writer and editor from Baltimore,

MD. You can read more of her finance writing on her blog, www. NextRichGirl.com.

Karen Kilby resides in Kingwood, TX with her husband, David. She is a Certified Personality Trainer with CLASServices, Inc. as well as a speaker for Stonecroft Ministries. Karen enjoys sharing her life experiences and has several stories in *Chicken Soup for the Soul* books as well as other publications. E-mail: krkilby@kingwoodcable.net.

Matthew Kinne received his BS from Wheaton College and his MA from Regent University in Communication. Matt was a writer/editor with *MOVIEGUIDE Magazine* and is now a freelance film producer. He published *Reflections for Movie Lovers* with AMG Publishers in 2004. Please e-mail him at matthew@matthewkinne.com.

Kathy Kitts received a BA in English from the College of Mt. St. Joseph. A former teacher and computer programmer, Kathy enjoys volunteering, gardening, and writing. She has written a children's non-fiction book called *The Minesweeper*, about a teenager who served with the 88th Infantry Division in Italy in WWII.

Karen Kosman is an inspirational speaker and author whose stories have appeared in several magazines and books. *Wounded by Words*, her book on verbal abuse, offers needed encouragement for victims. Karen enjoys her grandchildren, swimming, and gardening. Please e-mail her at ComKosman@aol.com.

Madeleine Kuderick lives in Florida with her husband and two children. She has a bachelor's degree from the University of South Florida and an MBA from Saint Leo University. She is a member of the SCBWI and a graduate of the Institute of Children's Literature. Learn more at www.madeleinekuderick.com.

Joe Lair is a writer and speaker who lives in Montana with his wife and three children. As a family they enjoy hiking, skiing and biking. Joe can be reached via e-mail at Josephtlair@aol.com.

Susan LaMaire currently lives in Parsippany, NJ with her husband Brian, three hermit crabs and many fish. She has worked as an English teacher, waitress, reporter and day camp counselor. She is currently working on a collection of humorous short stories. You may e-mail her at hunkoftin8@yahoo.com.

Jeannie Lancaster is a freelance writer from Loveland, CO. She is a lover of words — sharing them through her written work, weekly storytelling with a delightful group of preschoolers, and thirty-seven years of late night word games with her husband. She can be reached via e-mail at bjlancast@msn.com.

Sharon Landeen, a retired elementary school teacher, continues to work with youth by being a 4-H leader for over twenty years and by mentoring reading and teaching art in the local schools. If you have any information regarding her missing son, please contact her via e-mail at SLLandeen@theriver.com.

Marya Latson has a Juris Doctor degree from Florida State University. She lives in Central Florida with her husband, their twelve-year old son, and a menagerie of pets. Both Marya and her son are budding authors who keep each other intellectually stimulated through fervent debates and discussions.

Heather Pemberton Levy lives with her husband and two young children in Weston, CT. A graduate of Smith College, she had careers as a technology journalist, magazine editor and corporate vice president, before settling down to write MommyTruths.com, a blog of insights and ideas for raising young children.

Deanna Lowery is a published author who continues to write every day. Her best days are spent playing in the sand with her girls, relaxing in the sunset with her husband and finishing the day off with a few written words. Feel free to e-mail her at drlowery@hotmail.com.

Alexis Ludeman is a sophomore in high school. She loves writing and has been writing since she was six years old. Alexis also enjoys math, science and photography. She likes to inspire other people and cares about how they feel. She can be reached via e-mail at alexisludeman@ yahoo.com.

Natalia Lusinski created her first newspaper, *Nat's Neat News Notes*, at age ten. Since then, she has worked as a writers' assistant on several TV shows, and just associate produced a documentary for The History Channel. She also writes film and TV scripts, and short stories. E-mail her at writenataliainla@yahoo.com.

Evie Mack does lay counseling part-time. She enjoys walks with her dog, reading, and gardening. Evie loves to write short stories from real life, history and the Bible. She is currently working on a collection of inspirational parables called *Puppy Tales and Other Parables*. E-mail her at eviemack@solutions-95.com.

Karen Majoris-Garrison is an award-winning author, speaker, and teacher whose stories have appeared in *Woman's World, God's Way* books, Barbour Publishing, King Features' syndicated newspaper column and others. Karen credits God and her family as her sources of inspiration. Please visit her website: www.soothingsouls.us or e-mail her at innheaven@aol.com.

Tim Martin is the author of four books and seven screenplays. He has two children's novels, *Scout's Oaf* (Cedar Grove Books), and *Fast Pitch* (Blitz Publishing), scheduled for publication in 2009. His web page can be viewed at timothymartin.org. Please e-mail Tim at tmartin@ northcoast.com.

Michelle McCormick is currently attending seminary after completing a Bachelor's in Public Relations and a Master's in Journalism. She plans on writing Bible studies and non-fiction books geared toward high school age to the mid-thirties. Feel free to e-mail her at michellemccormick2@hotmail.com.

Mother of four and author of *Cancer Rhymes with Dancer*, **Linda McCowan** describes herself as an eclectic soul. She has a Bachelor of Arts degree and she loves to zumba, write, illustrate and travel. Feel free to e-mail her at: cancerwithdancer.com.

Daniel McGary's story was inspired by his experiences in the foster care system. He began writing to express himself at an early age, and enjoys working as a freelance writer to this day. He is also involved in efforts to reform the foster care system in Texas. Contact Daniel via e-mail at daniel.mcgary@gmail.com.

Sarah Clark Monagle is a Navy wife, mother of three daughters, guidance counselor, and brain tumor survivor. She has a bachelor's degree in Sociology and a master's degree in Counseling. Her personal goals include beating the brain tumor and having a book published. She can be contacted via e-mail at sarahmonagle@gmail.com.

Bill Mullis writes from the Upstate region of South Carolina, surrounded by his wife and family. His work has appeared in *The Christian Science Monitor*, *Common Ties*, and *The Ultimate Dog Lover*.

Karen Myers is a freelance writer who lives in San Francisco, CA. She is co-editor of the anthology *My Body of Knowledge: Stories of Chronic Illness, Disability, Healing, and Life*. Please visit her website at www.CrackedBellPublishing.com or e-mail her at CrackedBell@sbcglobal.net.

Author and motivational speaker, **Jennifer Oliver**, hails from Copperas Cove, TX, where she and househubby are raising four magnificent creative life forces. Her stories have appeared in several

Chicken Soup for the Soul books and other heartwarming publications. She dedicates this story to her wise and wonderful neighbor, Doris Morgan.

LaVerne Otis did not begin writing until her mid-fifties, has no formal writing education but hopes to take writing classes soon. She has had several stories published in *Country* and *Birds and Blooms Magazine*. Other hobbies include photography, reading, gardening and bird watching. You can e-mail her at lotiswrites@msn.com.

Saralee Perel is an award-winning nationally syndicated columnist and novelist. She is proud to be a multiple contributor to the *Chicken Soup for the Soul* series. Please visit her website at www.saraleeperel.com. Saralee welcomes e-mails at sperel@saraleeperel.com.

Diane Perrone, M.A., writes between babies—sixteen grandchildren so far. Her articles have appeared in several *Chicken Soup for the Soul* books and periodicals (*Redbook, Catholic Digest, Our Family* and aviation magazines). Diane speaks to seasoned citizens and companies that market to them. E-mail: Grandma1Di@aol.com.

Rebekah Phillips received her Bachelor's degree in Education from UNT in 2002. She has been teaching preschool children in a North Texas Christian school. Rebekah enjoys learning about God, sewing, reading, teaching, exercising, and being with friends and family. She would love to publish inspirational books and articles.

Jennifer Quasha is a published author of more than forty books. Her book *The Dog Lover's Book of Crafts* won the DWAA Best General Interest Book in 2002. Currently, she is a freelance writer and editor. Check out her website at www.jenniferquasha.com.

Jennifer Quist is an amateur general contractor and a freelance writer and researcher. She and her husband are currently raising five handyman sons in their home in western Canada.

Natalie June Reilly is a single mother of two handsome, teenage boys, Billy and Alec, and she is the author of the children's book, *My Stick Family, Helping Children Cope with Divorce*. She lives in Peoria, Arizona and can be reached via e-mail at girlwriter68@hotmail.com.

Samantha Richardson lives in Westerly, Rhode Island. She is currently in high school and plans on writing a book in the future.

Michelle Rocker is a woman who is passionate about her love for God, her husband, her four children, music and writing. She has been published in over 200 magazines throughout the United States over the past three years. She is currently seeking to publish an inspirational book and a novel. Please visit www.michellerocker.com.

Debbie Roppolo is a freelance writer residing in the Texas Hill Country with her husband and two children. In her spare time, she enjoys hiking, cooking competitions, and photography.

Sharon Rosenbaum-Earls holds a Bachelor of Science degree in Accounting. She had her first short story "The Best Gift" published in *Whispers from Heaven* in April 2003. Sharon is currently working on her second romance novel. Please e-mail her at SLREarls@aol.com.

Ashley Sanders is a published writer who lives in Kentucky with her husband and daughter, and a new arrival on the way. You can find more of her work on her personal blog, www.bosssanders.com.

Holly Sanford graduated with an accounting degree but her first love has always been writing. She currently lives in Louisville, KY with her two sons, Michael and Nicholas. Holly enjoys watching her boys play sports, traveling, and reading. She hopes to write a full-length novel in the future.

Eva Schlesinger is the author of the chapbooks, *Remembering the Walker and Wheelchair: poems of grief and healing* (Finishing Line Press,

2008) and *View From My Banilla Vanilla Villa* (slated for publication by Dancing Girl Press in December 2009). She lives in Berkeley, CA.

Elaine Ernst Schneider is the author of *52 Children's Moments*, found at amazon.com, and the senior editor of the curriculum web site www. lessontutor.com. She is also a practicing artist, painting on canvas, as well as antique wood and tin. She may be contacted via e-mail at julius@ionet.net.

Joyce Seabolt is a nurse and a writer. Upon retirement from the Genesis Corporation, she will be devoting all her time to writing and teaching. Joyce lives in Red Lion, PA with her husband, Hal. Please e-mail her at: joyceseabolt@hotmail.com.

Myla Seabrook is a student at Hofstra University, majoring in Creative Writing and Fine Art. In her spare time she enjoys traveling, reading, writing, and generally just going out and having fun. Myla aspires to write and illustrate books after graduation, particularly children's books. She seeks to inspire through her art.

Diane Shaw is an empty nester and is now staying at home after serving for eleven years as an Executive Secretary to a pastor of a large church in Colorado Springs. Diane enjoys writing, reading, playing with her grandchild and traveling with her husband. Please e-mail her at: needmorewordscs@gmail.com.

Deborah Shouse is a writer, speaker, editor and creativity catalyst. Her writing has appeared in various periodicals. Deborah is donating all proceeds from her book, *Love in the Land of Dementia: Finding Hope in the Caregiver's Journey* to Alzheimer's programs and research. For more information, visit Deborah's website www.TheCreativityConnection.com.

Candace Simar is a lifelong Minnesotan who writes poetry, inspirational writing, and historical fiction. Her debut novel, *Abercrombie Trail*, will be released by North Star Press in summer 2009. To see more of her writing or to sign up for her weekly devotional, check out www.candacesimar.com.

Johnna Stein received her BA from The College of William & Mary. She's studied in France and recently returned after ten years in The Netherlands. She's the proud mother of two spunky teenagers and wife to her devoted husband. Three of her stories will be published in inspirational magazines in 2009.

Jean Haynie Stewart lives a simpler life these days with her husband in Mission Viejo, CA, and feels sure these tough times won't last. She is an editor and also writes stories for *Chicken Soup for the Soul*, other anthologies, magazines and newspapers while enjoying her children and grandchildren.

Lois Greene Stone, writer and poet, has been syndicated worldwide. Poetry and personal essays have been included in hard and soft cover book anthologies. Collections of her personal items/photos/memorabilia are in major museums including twelve different divisions of The Smithsonian.

Carol Strazer was a recent winner in *Woman's Day* and the American Library Association's essay contest. Carol is writing a book about WWII German refugees, has a BS in Speech/English Education, Northwestern University and MA in Counseling Psychology, Lewis Clark College. Carol and Bob have three married daughters and three grandsons.

Janet Taylor is a registered nurse living in Franklin, TN with Robert, her biggest supporter. Her Mississippi family provides inspiration and is often the topic of her stories. Janet is a member of a wonderful writing group, "The Red Bandanas." Please e-mail her at: janet@4door.com.

Joyce Terrell is an avid reader who has been writing for leisure for twenty years, letting most of her writing come from personal experience. She enjoys cooking and gardening. Please e-mail her at yjterrell@yahoo.com.

Marla H. Thurman lives in Signal Mountain, Tennessee, with her dogs Oreo and Sleeper. She is currently working on draft four of her memoirs. Her dream is that one day her favorite author, Pat Conroy, will ask for her autograph.

In 2006, **Aimée L. Urban** was named a top 40 business professional under 40 and one of PA's Best 50 Women in Business in 2007. She serves on the Workforce Investment Board and is a past president of the American Business Women's Association. Aimée's greatest passions in life are her husband, two children and three dogs. E-mail: aimée.urban@adeccona.com.

Don Verkow is Assistant Principal at Paramount Charter School in Kalamazoo, MI. Don and wife, Katie, love to spend time with their three Labs, traveling, and spending time at their summer cottage in South Haven, MI. Don can be e-mailed at kadon@ameritech.net.

Beverly Walker enjoys writing, photography, scrapbooking, and being with her grandchildren. Her stories and poems appear in *Angel Cats: Divine Messengers of Comfort*, and in several editions of *Chicken Soup for the Soul* books.

Samantha Waltz is an award-winning freelance writer in Portland, OR. Her stories appear in the *Chicken Soup for the Soul* series, *Cup of Comfort* series, and a number of other anthologies. She has also published adult nonfiction and juvenile fiction under the names Samantha Ducloux and Samellyn Wood.

Lisa Wright-Dixon received her Bachelor of Arts degree in Sociology from Syracuse University. She currently resides in South Carolina with her husband Gregory and their six cats. Lisa is currently working on other short stories and plans to write a book of childhood memoirs.

Mary Jo Marcellus Wyse is a graduate of Vermont College's MFA in Writing Program. She is a former high school English teacher and currently a stay-at-home mom. Her essays and short fiction have appeared in various publications. She and her family live outside of Boston.

Meet Our Authors

Jack Canfield is the co-creator of the *Chicken Soup for the Soul* series, which *Time* magazine has called "the publishing phenomenon of the decade." Jack is also the co-author of eight other bestselling books including *The Success Principles™: How to Get from Where You Are to Where You Want to Be, Dare to Win, The Aladdin Factor, You've Got to Read This Book,* and *The Power of Focus: How to Hit Your Business and Personal and Financial Targets with Absolute Certainty.*

Jack is the CEO of the Canfield Training Group in Santa Barbara, California, and founder of the Foundation for Self-Esteem in Culver City, California. He has conducted intensive personal and professional development seminars on the principles of success for over a million people in twenty-three countries. Jack is a dynamic keynote speaker and he has spoken to hundreds of thousands of others at more than 1,000 corporations, universities, professional conferences and conventions, and has been seen by millions more on national television shows such as *The Today Show, Fox and Friends, Inside Edition, Hard Copy,* CNN's *Talk Back Live, 20/20, Eye to Eye,* and the NBC *Nightly News* and the *CBS Evening News.*

Jack has received many awards and honors, including three honorary doctorates and a Guinness World Records Certificate for having seven books from the *Chicken Soup for the Soul* series appearing on the New York Times bestseller list on May 24, 1998.

You can reach Jack at:
Jack Canfield
P.O. Box 30880 • Santa Barbara, CA 93130
phone: 805-563-2935 • fax: 805-563-2945
www.jackcanfield.com

Mark Victor Hansen is the co-founder of Chicken Soup for the Soul, along with Jack Canfield. He is a sought-after keynote speaker, best-selling author, and marketing maven. Mark's powerful messages of possibility, opportunity, and action have created powerful change in thousands of organizations and millions of individuals worldwide.

Mark is a prolific writer with many bestselling books, such as *The One Minute Millionaire, Cracking the Millionaire Code, How to Make the Rest of Your Life the Best of Your Life, The Power of Focus, The Aladdin Factor*, and *Dare to Win*, in addition to the *Chicken Soup for the Soul* series. Mark has had a profound influence in the field of human potential through his library of audios, videos, and articles in the areas of big thinking, sales achievement, wealth building, publishing success, and personal and professional development. He is also the founder of the MEGA Seminar Series.

He has appeared on *Oprah*, CNN, and *The Today Show*. He has been quoted in *Time, U. S. News & World Report, USA Today, The New York Times*, and *Entrepreneur* and has given countless radio interviews, assuring our planet's people that "You can easily create the life you deserve."

Mark has received numerous awards that honor his entrepreneurial spirit, philanthropic heart, and business acumen. He is a lifetime member of the Horatio Alger Association of Distinguished Americans.

You can reach Mark at:
Mark Victor Hansen & Associates, Inc.
P.O. Box 7665 • Newport Beach, CA 92658
phone: 949-764-2640 • fax: 949-722-6912
www.markvictorhansen.com

Amy Newmark is the publisher of Chicken Soup for the Soul, after a thirty-year career as a writer, speaker, financial analyst, and business executive in the worlds of finance and telecommunications. Amy is a *magna cum laude* graduate of Harvard College, where she majored in Portuguese, minored in French, and traveled extensively. She is also the mother of two children in college and two grown stepchildren who are recent college graduates.

After a long career writing books on telecommunications, voluminous financial reports, business plans, and corporate press releases, Chicken Soup for the Soul is a breath of fresh air for Amy. She has fallen in love with Chicken Soup for the Soul and its life-changing books, and really enjoys putting these books together for Chicken Soup's wonderful readers.

You can reach Amy and the rest of the Chicken Soup for the Soul team via e-mail through webmaster@chickensoupforthesoul.com.

Thank You!

We owe huge thanks to all of our contributors. We know that you pour your hearts and souls into the thousands of stories and poems that you share with us, and ultimately with each other. We appreciate your willingness to open up your lives to other Chicken Soup for the Soul readers.

We can only publish a small percentage of the stories that are submitted, but we read every single one and even the ones that do not appear in the book have an influence on us and on the final manuscript.

We want to thank Chicken Soup for the Soul editor Kristiana Glavin for reading every story and poem that was submitted for this book and for her assistance with the final manuscript and proofreading. We also want to thank our assistant publisher, D'ette Corona, and our editor and webmaster Barbara LoMonaco for their expert editorial, proofreading, and organizational assistance, as well as Leigh Holmes, who keeps our office running smoothly.

We owe a very special thanks to our creative director and book producer, Brian Taylor at Pneuma Books, for his brilliant vision for our covers and interiors. Finally, none of this would be possible without the business and creative leadership of our CEO, Bill Rouhana, and our president, Bob Jacobs.

Chicken Soup for the Soul
Improving Your Life
Every Day

Real people sharing real stories—for fifteen years. Now, Chicken Soup for the Soul has gone beyond the bookstore to become a world leader in life improvement. Through books, movies, DVDs, online resources and other partnerships, we bring hope, courage, inspiration and love to hundreds of millions of people around the world. Chicken Soup for the Soul's writers and readers belong to a one-of-a-kind global community, sharing advice, support, guidance, comfort, and knowledge.

Chicken Soup for the Soul stories have been translated into more than forty languages and can be found in more than one hundred countries. Every day, millions of people experience a Chicken Soup for the Soul story in a book, magazine, newspaper or online. As we share our life experiences through these stories, we offer hope, comfort and inspiration to one another. The stories travel from person to person, and from country to country, helping to improve lives everywhere.

Share with Us

We all have had Chicken Soup for the Soul moments in our lives. If you would like to share your story or poem with millions of people around the world, go to chickensoup.com and click on "Submit Your Story." You may be able to help another reader, and become a published author at the same time. Some of our past contributors have launched writing and speaking careers from the publication of their stories in our books!

Your stories have the best chance of being used if you submit them through our website at

www.chickensoup.com

If you do not have access to the Internet, you may submit your stories by mail or by facsimile. Starting in 2010, submissions will only be accepted via the website.

Please do not send us any book manuscripts, unless through a literary agent, as these will be automatically discarded.

Chicken Soup for the Soul
P.O. Box 700
Cos Cob, CT 06807-0700
Fax: 203-861-7194

This follow-on book to *Tough Times, Tough People* continues Chicken Soup for the Soul's focus on inspiration and hope in these difficult times. These inspirational stories remind us that each day holds something to be thankful for—whether it is having the sun shine or having food on the table. Power outages and storms, health scares and illnesses, job woes and financial insecurities, housing challenges and family worries test us all. But there is always a silver lining. The simple pleasures of family, home, health, and inexpensive good times are described. These stories of optimism, faith, and strength will make a great start to 2010.

978-1-935096-42-9

More Hope and Inspiration for Difficult Times...

Chicken Soup for the Soul

www.chickensoup.com